Inventing Intelligence

HOW AMERICA CAME TO WORSHIP IQ

Elaine E. Castles

PRAEGER

AN IMPRINT OF ABC-CLIO, LLC
Santa Barbara, California • Denver, Colorado • Oxford, England

Copyright 2012 by Elaine E. Castles

Library of Congress Cataloging-in-Publication Data

Castles, Elaine E.
  Inventing intelligence : how America came to worship IQ / Elaine E. Castles.
    p. cm.
  Includes bibliographical references and index.
  ISBN 978-1-4408-0337-6 (hardcopy : alk. paper) — ISBN 978-1-4408-0338-3 (ebook)
1. Intelligence levels—United States—History. 2. Intelligence tests—United States—History. I. Title.
  BF431.C343 2012
  153.90973—dc23   2012005006

ISBN: 978-1-4408-0337-6
EISBN: 978-1-4408-0338-3

16 15 14 13 12   1 2 3 4 5

This book is also available on the World Wide Web as an eBook.
Visit www.abc-clio.com for details.

Praeger
An Imprint of ABC-CLIO, LLC

ABC-CLIO, LLC
130 Cremona Drive, P.O. Box 1911
Santa Barbara, California 93116-1911

This book is printed on acid-free paper ∞

Manufactured in the United States of America

To my father,
William E. Ehrensperger
And in memory of my mother,
Norma Peterson Ehrensperger
Their gifts to me are beyond measure.

Contents

Preface

Why, you might well be asking, would anyone want to write (or read) yet another book on the subject of intelligence? After all, our bookstores and libraries are awash in books cataloging the evils of IQ testing, on the one hand, or advising us on how to achieve higher scores on the other. Magazines and op-ed pages are regularly peppered with competing opinions about the role of testing in our public schools, colleges, and universities, and hiring decisions—all issues that evoke disturbing and controversial questions about genetics, race, and class in America. And then there are the battles over affirmative action, sometimes civil but more commonly virulent, that rage over talk radio and the Internet. What could there possibly be left to say?

Well, perhaps what is needed is a fresh perspective—something that I will offer in the following pages. I am a practicing clinical psychologist with more than 30 years of experience administering, interpreting, and teaching about IQ tests. In the course of my work, I have learned that much good can come from this practice. But I have also seen considerable potential for harm. Some of these negative effects I have observed firsthand; others have become clear to me as I have followed with great interest the public debate over race, class, and IQ.

What strikes me most about these debates is the fact that they are never resolved. For more than a century, advocates on both sides have been making exactly the same arguments, predictable almost entirely from their political leanings. But despite the quantity of ink spilled and the volume of the rhetoric, no one seems to have addressed the most basic questions. Where did this notion of intelligence come from in the first place? Why does it seem so compelling to us? And how in the world did scores on IQ tests (or their equivalents) come to be considered the legal equivalent of merit in modern America?

It is to answer these questions that I have written *Inventing Intelligence*. The story of how Americans became infatuated with the idea of intelligence is a fascinating saga in and of itself. It is also a near-perfect example of how supposedly objective scientific concepts are in fact subject to social and cultural influences. In addition to being intrinsically interesting, the story of IQ in America helps to put into perspective some of our most daunting social problems. In the last three chapters of the book, I use the historical perspective developed in the first nine to step back and offer my own informed assessment of how we might more productively view the intertwined issues of intelligence, heredity, and merit. It is my hope that understanding how Americans came to worship at the altar of IQ might be a first step in resolving our vitriolic, unproductive, and interminable wars about intelligence and its measurement.

Acknowledgments

I owe a debt of gratitude to the many scholars whose work has helped shape my thinking about intelligence and its measurement. Foremost among them is John Carson, whose 1994 doctoral dissertation (later expanded into his book *The Measure of Merit: Talents, Intelligence, and Inequality in the French and American Republics, 1750–1940*) provided initial guidance on how one might approach the concept of intelligence from a historical perspective. Robert Sternberg's impressive body of research on adaptive intelligence demonstrated for me how much more there is to intelligent behavior than one's score on an IQ test. Richard Nisbett's *The Geography of Thought: How Asians and Westerners Think Differently . . . and Why* provided a fascinating glimpse into cross-cultural concepts of intelligence. I would also particularly like to acknowledge the influence of *The Mismeasure of Man* by Stephen Jay Gould, *Constructing the Subject* by Kurt Danziger, *Keeping Track* by Jeannie Oakes, and *The Big Test* by Nicholas Lemann.

My editor at Praeger, Debbie Carvalko, has provided enthusiastic and informative guidance throughout the publication process. Somewhat closer to home, lively discussions with the many skilled, experienced, and dedicated teachers in my extended family have helped me to articulate my ideas and sharpen my reasoning. Katherine Castles has been involved with the book from the beginning, prodding me to refine my focus, offering insightful critiques of the work in progress, and providing valuable editorial assistance. A special thanks to the many clients who have granted me entry into their lives during my 30 years in the practice of clinical psychology. Their experiences have powerfully illustrated for me the effects of IQ testing on real-life people.

Finally, I would have never gotten through the 10-year process of writing this book without the love, support, and encouragement of my husband Steve. Thanks from the bottom of my heart.

Chapter 1

Worshipping at the Altar of IQ

The image is iconic—the wild halo of white hair, the rumpled suit, the enigmatic smile, the piercing eyes. It adorns tee shirts, coffee mugs, posters, and advertisements for everything from eyeglasses to SUVs.[1] Seven times it has graced the cover of *Time* magazine, most recently under the banner "Person of the Century." The image, of course, is instantly recognizable as that of Albert Einstein, widely known, in the words of *Time*, "as both the greatest mind and paramount icon of our age."[2] Some readers undoubtedly wondered why a newsmagazine chose to honor a theoretical physicist as the most influential person of the twentieth century. There were, after all, so many more obvious choices—statesmen like Winston Churchill or Franklin Delano Roosevelt, great moral leaders such as Mahatma Gandhi or Nelson Mandela, even tyrants like Hitler and Stalin. In my view, however, *Time*'s selection of Einstein as "Person of the Century" reflects one of the most significant cultural trends of our era. Albert Einstein is the perfect symbol of America's century-old love affair with intelligence.

Most Americans recall vaguely that Einstein proposed something called the "theory of relativity." When pressed, some of us may even be able to dig around in our memories and unearth the formula $e = mc^2$. Few, however, could explain what these symbols actually mean or why they are considered so important. (Indeed, the *New York Times* claimed in 1919 that there were no more than 12 people in the world who could truly understand Einstein's ideas.)[3] No, it was not the brilliance of his theories that made Einstein such a cultural icon. What he was really famous for was being smart. In the words of the *Time* cover story, Einstein's "face [is] a symbol and his name a synonym for genius."[4] Genius. Much more than his actual scientific work, it is Einstein's reputedly outsized intellect that has galvanized the popular imagination.

Few outside the scientific community had even heard of this obscure Swiss patent examiner until 1919, when astronomer Arthur Eddington presented to London's Royal Society the first experimental confirmation of the theory of general relativity. "REVOLUTION IN SCIENCE: NEW THEORY OF THE UNIVERSE," blared the headline in the London *Times*.[5] And suddenly Einstein's name was on everyone's lips, his reputation for genius circling the globe. On his first tour of the United States in 1921, adoring crowds thronged to greet him. His name was featured in popular songs and movies, and on one occasion he was even invited to perform at Variety at the London Palladium.[6] (One has to wonder what sort of entertainment the theory of relativity would have provided!) Einstein, it appears, had become a genuine international rock star.

But, as I have noted, it was not the content of Einstein's theories that most people found so compelling; it was the magnificence of his mind. Even today, more than 50 years after his death, the name "Einstein" remains a synonym for genius. And I believe it is no accident that the popular frenzy over Einstein's brilliance coincided with another development, the introduction into the United States of an exciting new psychological tool: the IQ test. The idea that experts might actually be able to measure the mind sparked a national obsession with the idea of intelligence that has persisted to this day. And so the iconic image of Albert Einstein, the greatest genius of the century, seems an appropriate picture to keep in mind as we begin to explore the origins of American's enduring fascination with IQ.[7]

AMERICA'S LOVE AFFAIR WITH IQ

In the eyes of most modern Americans, intelligence *is* IQ. Psychologists, we have been told, can use their mysterious tests to peer deep into our minds, magically uncovering the secret of how smart we *really* are. Character, talents, achievements—all pale in comparison with the all-powerful IQ score. Take, for example, Marilyn vos Savant, familiar to the 79 million readers who regularly receive *Parade* magazine with their Sunday newspapers. Since 1986, vos Savant has written a weekly column for *Parade*, offering advice on every conceivable topic. "I work at a restaurant in a large city," wrote one reader. "You'd be amazed at the attitudes and actions I encounter every day. . . . Can you suggest how diners should behave in a restaurant?" "Why are humans so drawn to diamonds?" asked another. "I say that romantic love isn't rational, and it can cause all sorts of senseless behavior. Am I wrong?" queried a third.[8]

And what is it that makes Marilyn vos Savant so uniquely qualified to answer such questions? There is only one reason: she is listed in the *Guinness Book of World Records* as having the highest IQ score ever recorded. Never mind that this record is based on a nonstandardized test put out by an obscure group known as Mega, supposedly the world's most selective organization of geniuses. Ignore the fact that test scores at the extreme ends of any distribution are notoriously unreliable. Forget that vos Savant graduated 178th out of her class of 613 in high school, married young, failed to finish college, and by her own report reads very little. None of this is meant to downplay her very real accomplishments; by all accounts, vos Savant is a sensible and grounded woman, and she has won several awards for her work in the fields of education and communications. But her fame came, in the words of journalist Julie Baumgold, "only because of the glory of that number." If vos Savant has "the highest IQ ever recorded," surely she must be an expert on everything under the sun.[9]

It is perhaps not surprising that we regard people with high IQ scores as smarter and more knowledgeable than the rest of us. There seems to be little harm in this assumption; such abilities are, after all, what these tests purport to measure. But our national love affair with intelligence actually goes far deeper, and its implications are arguably less benign. Many Americans regard IQ as the primary indicator of basic personal worth. Individuals with high IQs are perceived as somehow *better* than other people. As early as 1922, testing pioneer Lewis Terman proclaimed that "there is nothing about an individual as important as his IQ, except possibly his morals."[10] The passage of time has done little to moderate this assumption. In his fascinating history of the SAT, for example, journalist Nicholas Lemann observed that SAT performance has come to be "a scientific, numeric assignment of worth which . . . lodge[s] itself firmly in the mind, never to be forgotten."[11] (Indeed, I can still remember my SAT scores from nearly 50 years ago. I would venture to guess that many of my readers can do the same.) So firmly ingrained is our cultural identification of intelligence with personal value that eminent psychologist Jerome Kagan has ruefully termed IQ "our modern substitute for saintliness, religiosity, [and] courage."[12] A big burden to put on one little number.

Few of America's opinion makers find reason to challenge this cultural assumption that IQ reflects innate individual worth. Most of them, after all, take it for granted that they dwell among the cognitive aristocracy.

A 1995 London *Times* article by psychologist Richard Lynn perfectly expresses this smug belief. "Virtually all the readers of this article will belong to this intellectual elite," Lynn wrote. "Don't imagine the rest of the population are like you. They aren't." Victor Serebriakoff, former president of the high IQ society Mensa, once proclaimed that "there is no more fascinating discussion to most people than a discussion of 'the smarts' and who has them and who doesn't." Easy for Serebriakoff to say, of course; he could be confident that he and his fellow Mensa members would most likely come out on the top of any such comparisons.[13]

But even confident and outspoken high achievers can become strangely uncomfortable when asked to provide concrete evidence of their own presumed cognitive superiority. *Esquire* magazine once asked a group of notable individuals to take the SAT and then attend a party at which their scores would be publicized. The reaction was horrified. "Oh, the humiliation would be just too intense," demurred Midge Decter. "Could I send my son instead?" "That is too humiliating. No! I won't! God forbid, no! It would be a trauma!" stammered Irving Kristol. "NO!!!" Susan Brownmiller gasped. "I'm coasting on my high school IQ."[14] Even IQ testing enthusiast Daniel Seligman refused to provide information about his own test scores. Writing about his experience in taking an individually administered IQ test, Seligman admitted rather sheepishly, "I decline to state the number on the bottom line. I do insist on mentioning, however, that the scores were adversely affected by my age. . . . I may go back for a retest."[15]

If even the movers and the shakers find themselves anxious about what their IQ scores might reveal about their real abilities, what about the rest of us? Well, it seems that almost everyone worries from time to time about how smart they are. For example, an astounding 95 percent of the respondents to a 1969 survey admitted that they sometimes compared their intelligence with that of others.[16] And you don't need to be a rocket scientist to understand that not being smart is a pretty bad thing. Earlier in my career, I worked extensively with people who had been diagnosed with mental retardation. My clients made it very clear to me that this label was devastating to their self-esteem. "The retarded, they ain't good for nothing," one young man told me. He might have been "retarded," but he was certainly smart enough to understand that he had been tried by our intelligence-obsessed world and found lacking.[17]

PUSHING THE COGNITIVE LIMITS

In modern-day America, we assume that high intelligence is the primary prerequisite for leading a happy, productive, and prosperous life.

And so it is not surprising that parents feel compelled to do everything possible to give their children that all-important cognitive edge. The common (mis)conception that IQ is determined largely by heredity has done little to stop this obsessive quest for higher test scores. Programs claiming to make children smarter have been around for years. Take, for example, Dr. Glenn Doman's Better Baby Institute in Philadelphia. "Not only is Doman convinced that every child *should* be a genius," enthused one 1983 magazine article. "He's certain each one *can* be."[18] And so for several decades, anxious parents have been forking over hundreds of dollars to Doman's program, introducing children as young as eight months of age to reading, math, physical development, Japanese, and Suzuki violin. A well-publicized 1994 Carnegie Corporation report advocating appropriate environmental stimulation for young children provided even more impetus for such programs.[19] These days, failure to provide one's offspring with every possible educational advantage is viewed as evidence of parental malpractice, placing innocent children at risk for a lifetime of stunted intellectual development.[20]

Education can now begin in utero. One California obstetrician advertises courses to stimulate the fetal brain, available through his Prenatal University; the BabyPlus Prenatal Education System makes similar claims for its set of special CDs. Several years ago, after hearing of research (later debunked) suggesting that listening to Mozart raised IQ, Governor Zell Miller of Georgia launched a program to provide every newborn baby in the state with a classical music CD. Florida soon jumped on the bandwagon, mandating one-half hour of classical music per day in all day care centers. Modern parents eagerly peruse online advertisements for flash cards, CDs, and videos that purport to teach newborns the rudiments of counting, reading, and bits of factual information. The "Language Nursery DVDE Gift Set," intended for children as young as one year, claims to provide instruction in *seven* languages (English, Spanish, French, German, Hebrew, Russian, and Japanese). And of course no modern nursery is complete without stimulating educational toys from companies such as Baby Genius, IQ Baby, Brainy Baby, and Zany Brainy.[21]

Naturally, the pressure to produce the brightest possible kids seems most intense in hypercompetitive New York City, where getting one's child into the right nursery school is viewed as the necessary first step on the road to Harvard. In a recent article in the *City Journal*, Kay Hymowitz reflected on this frenzied competition among upper-middle class New York parents. "Their children's school reflects their most revered quality, their own intelligence," she wrote. "Your child's brain power says a lot about who you are in New York City." A preschooler's score on an individually administered IQ test is the single largest factor governing admission to the most elite nursery schools. Acknowledging that "applying to nursery schools can be overwhelming for first time parents," one organization offers workshops for children aged one to four to help prepare them for the admission tests. Indeed, parents are now paying more than $1,000 for coaching that promises to give their preschoolers an edge in the nursery school admission sweepstakes.[22]

But giving our children the best possible start in life—educational toys, Suzuki violin lessons, elite nursery schools—is only the first step in the quest to produce the perfect, high-IQ son or daughter. Concerned parents pore over rankings of schools' test scores so they can buy homes in the best districts. They lobby to have their children tested for entry into Talented and Gifted programs, sometimes even seeking out a psychologist who is willing to tweak the results for their child's benefit. Some pressure school personnel to diagnose their children with subtle learning disabilities or attentional problems that might entitle them to modifications (such as extra time) on standardized tests. Interestingly, private school students are four times as likely to be granted such accommodations as those from public schools.[23]

And then come the dreaded SATs. In *The Big Test,* Nicholas Lemann has described how the desperate quest for the highest possible SAT scores has become a central focus in the lives of upper-middle class teenagers and their parents. Intensive coaching programs can begin as early as eighth grade, when many students take their first practice tests. There is in fact considerable controversy about the effectiveness of these coaching programs; most studies suggest that they improve scores no more than 10 or 20 points. But anxious parents don't feel that they can afford to take any chances. In a revealing 2001 article in the *Washington Post,* public high school student Samantha Henig described her experience during a year spent in an exclusive private school in New York. At this school, she reported, "it's not only common for students to spend thousands of dollars on SAT tutoring, it's expected." She then went on to describe a 40-hour SAT tutoring basic package that cost more than $10,000; private sessions were available at a price of up to $480 per hour. Pity the poor students whose parents cannot afford such largesse.[24]

WHAT'S WRONG WITH THIS PICTURE?

The foregoing examples suggest, at least to me, that Jerome Kagan was right in suggesting that intelligence has indeed become our secular national religion, with Albert Einstein as its patron saint and IQ scores the Holy Grail after which we quest.[25] I suspect that many of my readers see nothing wrong with this state of affairs. Given the option, after all, few of us would choose to have dull children rather than bright ones. And pundits and politicians from both the right and the left constantly remind us that our economic well-being and competitiveness in the global marketplace depend on America's children winning the IQ race. Why should we not do everything in our power to help them do so?

Certainly, all of our children deserve the opportunity to develop their potential to its fullest. And clearly, their minds, bodies, and spirits cannot grow if they are reared in unstimulating, neglectful, or abusive homes, educated by teachers who do not believe they can learn, or immersed in cultures permeated with a sense of helplessness, hopelessness, anger, and despair. There is a big difference, however, between providing children with the conditions required for healthy growth and chasing frantically after ever-higher test scores. Researchers agree that the Mozart tapes, the educational videos, the flash cards, and the coaching programs are almost totally ineffective. In fact, young children who watch educational TV shows and videos actually have *smaller* vocabularies than those who do not. Nor, as noted earlier, do SAT coaching programs generally result in more than modest increases in test scores. The evidence suggests that our cultural obsession with IQ has caused us to waste a great deal of time, energy, and money on useless enrichment programs.[26]

But the issues at stake go beyond a simple waste of resources. In 1969, researcher Orville Brim surveyed a cross section of Americans about their views on intelligence. He found their responses to be rather disturbing. There was no personal quality, Brim's data indicated, that Americans valued more highly than IQ—not creativity, or altruism, or leadership, or even basic honesty. What, he asked with some concern, might be the long-term consequences of such a single-minded national focus on intelligence?[27] Well, the intervening years have provided a few answers to this question, and the results are sobering. Our cultural veneration of IQ has taken a personal toll on children, parents, and families. It has narrowed and distorted the focus of our educational system. It has led us to turn a blind eye to some fundamental moral and ethical values. And, perhaps most disturbingly, it has served to perpetuate America's daunting social, economic, and racial inequities. Let us turn now to a more detailed exploration of these effects.

Eminent developmental psychologist Edward Zigler has vividly described a child of his acquaintance.

He has two educated, professional parents who have delayed childbearing until their early thirties. He has all the best baby equipment that money can buy—the

right furniture, the right stroller, and a genuine shearling cover for his car seat.
Eric has swimming lessons, looks at flash cards of famous paintings and simple
words, plays with the best "developmentally engineered" toys and will begin
the study of the violin in a year or two. He also has enough stimulation in the
course of a day to make even a college student want to take a nap and shut it all
out—which is just what Eric does.[28]

Eric's parents, like most of their peers, feel compelled to give their child
every possible intellectual advantage. But all too often, this frantic quest
leaves both parents and children feeling stressed, overwhelmed, and
exhausted.

Zigler worries that "the relentless and sometimes joyless pursuit of
high intensity learning experiences" robs young children like Eric of crucial opportunities for spontaneous play. Or, as a 2001 *Time* magazine
cover story put it, "Kids who once had childhoods now have curricu-
lums."[29] Unfortunately, days filled with educational videos, flash cards,
and foreign language lessons leave little time for making trains out of
cardboard boxes or playing dress up with mommy's old clothes. And
research suggests that such unstructured play activities are crucial to a
child's physical, emotional, and intellectual development. Furthermore,
this single-minded focus on cognitive achievement can leach much of the
natural joy out of learning. Consider, for example, a newsletter put out
by the Suzuki School of Violin. This article gives five reasons for teaching children to play a musical instrument. First on the list is "Playing a
Musical Instrument Makes You Smarter." Only at the very end does the
article acknowledge that "Playing a Musical Instrument is Fun."[30]

As children become older, this stress only intensifies. By the time they
reach high school, many of our most highly achieving teenagers are
already on the verge of burnout. Fifty-six percent of the respondents
to a recent survey of Washington, DC, area high school girls, for example, reported that they frequently felt stressed. Somewhat to the surprise
of the interviewer, the source of most of this stress was not, as one might
expect, family or peer problems. It was school. Some of these students
had started taking SAT prep courses at the age of twelve. "I've put so
much time into those stupid tests," one young woman lamented. "This
is how sick I am! Think of all that I could have been doing instead."
Added the mother of another, "We're just mired in a system that takes
this position that huge amounts of stress are somehow beneficial."[31]
The relentless quest for ever-higher test scores leaves these students with
precious little time or energy to engage in the self-discovery and exploration so crucial to healthy adolescent development. And by the time these
hard-working young people finally achieve their lifelong goal of making

it into the elite college of their dreams, they are at risk of having lost much of their innate intellectual curiosity, their love of learning, and their sense of adventure.

But it is not just individual families and children who are affected by our overzealous focus on intelligence. It is becoming increasingly clear that our national obsession with tests has distorted the priorities of our entire educational system. IQ tests—and their close relatives, such as the SAT—tap only a narrow segment of the wide array of skills and abilities required for success in the modern world. These tests are generally administered under strict time limits, thus penalizing individuals who prefer to think deeply and carefully. Most require respondents to select one answer from a limited range of choices. Their content focuses narrowly on verbal facility, conventional thinking, and familiarity with the dominant culture; rarely do test-takers have an opportunity to demonstrate such crucial qualities as critical thinking skills, ability to complete long-term projects, persistence, or creativity. And if the tests do not measure it, the schools are not likely to teach it. As a consequence, we are at risk of turning out a generation of cookie cutter children who lack the creativity, flexibility, and initiative they will need to compete in a global economy.

Our test-driven educational culture may be stultifying for typical learners, but it can be sheer torture for children who learn differently. Much of my clinical practice has focused on children who have unique cognitive styles—or, in the current parlance, learning disabilities. In my experience, many of these students are impressively curious, independent minded, and creative. Curiosity and creativity, however, are of little interest to the developers of our multiple-choice, time-driven, one-size-fits-all standardized tests. As a result, most unconventional learners struggle to fit into the traditional public school classroom; by the time they come to me, many are convinced that they are stupid. Paradoxically, however, it is often people with quirky brains who end up making the most profound contributions to society. Consider, for example, Albert Einstein, whose delayed language skills led many of his teachers to dismiss him as hopelessly backward. Or think of those two famous college dropouts Bill Gates and Steve Jobs. I doubt that their scores on conventional IQ tests would have given a hint of their remarkable creativity, initiative, or sheer entrepreneurial spirit.

But our cultural love affair with IQ does not threaten only the potential Einsteins and Steve Jobses among us. There is growing evidence that excessive focus on innate intelligence can actually depress the academic achievement of many ordinary students. Much of this fascinating research has been conducted by psychologist Carol Dweck. In one series of studies, Dweck questioned a group of students just entering middle school about their views on intelligence. Some of these students were convinced that IQ was a fixed characteristic, something they were simply born with and helpless to change; others, however, believed that they could cultivate intelligence through their own hard work. At the beginning of middle school, the math achievement levels of these two groups were approximately equal. By eighth grade, however, students who regarded IQ as malleable had begun to outpace their hereditarian peers, and during high school this advantage grew even more marked. Researchers studying college students have documented a similar relationship between belief in fixed, innate IQ and lower class grades. Furthermore, they have discovered that explicitly teaching students that they can develop intelligence through their own efforts measurably improves their classroom performance. Clearly, grades depend on many factors other than native intelligence. In fact, recent research indicates that it is actually self-discipline, not IQ, that appears to be the most powerful determinant of academic achievement—a fact that any good tiger mom could have told you.[32]

Self-discipline is one of those old-fashioned virtues to which we all pay lip service. Yet all too often, in our frantic quest for high test scores, we have allowed such qualities of character to fall by the wayside. Take, for example, our concept of individual merit. We Americans pride ourselves on being a meritocratic society, believing that individuals should rise or fall solely on the basis of their own personal qualities. But in fact, as recent Supreme Court decisions on affirmative action illustrate, these days merit is little more than a synonym for one's score on a standardized test. And so many achievement-oriented parents, striving desperately to prepare their children for success in the American meritocracy, have come to value intellectual accomplishment more highly than such traditional virtues as interpersonal sensitivity, or kindness, or integrity, or a commitment to social justice. Increasingly, even participation in charitable activities has become just another strategy for burnishing the all-important college applications.

In my experience, one of the most disturbing casualties of parental anxiety about IQ scores has been simple, basic honesty. Some desperate parents bring their children to unscrupulous psychologists who promise to document extraordinary IQ scores, or conversely, to diagnose a learning disability or attentional disorder that will grant them special testing accommodations. Even more common are parents who unapologetically write their children's college essays or who encourage them to cheat rather than get poor grades. In the words of author Alexandra Robbins, "Instead of learning how to develop into independent, self-aware adults, many children are being taught by their parents how to game the system."[33] And unsurprisingly, these children have indeed learned from their parents' example. In one recent survey of high-achieving high school students, more than half of the respondents reported that they saw nothing wrong with cheating. Is it any wonder, then, that so many of our business and government leaders seem to see basic honesty as a quaint relic of a bygone age?[34]

Another apparent casualty of our obsession with IQ has been the venerable concept of wisdom. Think about it—when is the last time you heard a political candidate described as wise? Most of us stand in awe of Ivy League credentials. (At last count, for example, all nine justices of the Supreme Court were graduates of one of the Ivies.) But rarely do we question whether being smart necessarily leads to wise decision making. And the evidence suggests that it often does not. The propensity of many so-called intelligent people to behave unwisely is illustrated perhaps most vividly in David Halberstam's best-selling 1973 book *The Best and the Brightest,* in which he documents in detail the actions of the brainy group of men brought into government by John F. Kennedy. According to Halberstam, these men—the epitome of the American meritocracy—never doubted for a moment "the validity of their right to serve." "If there was anything that bound the men, their followers, and their subordinates together," Halberstam reported, "it was the belief that sheer intelligence and rationality could answer and solve anything."[35] In retrospect, of course, we are all too painfully aware of the results of the disastrous Vietnam War policy promulgated by this self-assured cadre of our nation's best and brightest. As this example so clearly illustrates, sheer intelligence alone is not sufficient to solve the world's problems. We ignore other virtues at our peril.

IQ AND SOCIETY

So yes, America's cultural obsession with IQ creates stress in families and distorts child-rearing practices. It narrows our focus, leading us to undervalue diverse styles of thinking and to lose sight of virtues like honesty and wisdom. But perhaps most corrosive to our social fabric is the way in which our overvaluation of intelligence has perpetuated racial and economic inequalities. Judging on the basis of cognitive potential, we grant some people access to privilege while shunting others into dead-end positions.

We like to think of America as the land of equal opportunity for all. But the fact is that using objective test data to control access to desirable schools, jobs, and professional programs advantages some groups while discriminating against others. Scores on tests of intelligence (and their cousins such as the SAT) are strongly correlated with socioeconomic status and racial and ethnic group membership. The higher the parental income, the better the children's test performance; in fact, in many cases scores can be predicted simply by looking at the test-taker's zip code.[36] Furthermore, taken as a whole, most racial and ethnic minority groups perform significantly less well than white Americans on these tests. (The exception to this rule is Asian Americans, who tend to have the highest scores of all.) The inevitable result, of course, is that the use of arbitrary cutoff scores on tests like the SAT reduces minority enrollment in our colleges, universities, and professional schools.[37]

The debate about the root causes of these racial and socioeconomic discrepancies has been shrill, angry, and singularly unenlightening. Some argue that genetic racial differences account for much of the gap in black and white scores, while others insist just as adamantly that the educational, economic, and psychological effects of centuries of discrimination provide all the explanation that is needed. Many (most notably the authors of the best-selling 1994 tome *The Bell Curve*) are convinced that poor people have been unable to make it in America precisely because they have lower IQs—the intellectual cream rises naturally to the top, while the dregs sink to the bottom, so to speak. The counterargument, of course, is that it is precisely the opportunities and privileges available to the wealthy that account for their higher IQ scores. As we will see in later chapters, political ideology all too often trumps objective scientific data in these debates. But whatever their merits, these arguments have been highly corrosive and damaging to our national unity.

Nowhere has this divisiveness been more evident than in our acrimonious, intemperate, and often downright nasty national debate over affirmative action. This debate focuses almost entirely on the appropriate use of tests. In essence, the practice of affirmative action allows employers or college admission officers to give less weight to test scores when considering applicants from groups that have suffered historically from discrimination. When this idea was first introduced in the 1960s, it met with wide popular support, from whites as well as blacks, Republicans as well as Democrats. Most Americans agreed that such a practice was a fair and reasonable strategy for evening out a traditionally bumpy playing field.[38]

But in recent years, as the country has turned more socially conservative, affirmative action has become one of our most contentious wedge issues. Members of historically privileged groups now claim reverse discrimination when minority individuals with lower test scores take the places to which they believe that they are entitled.[39] Voters and courts have both weighed in, generally in the direction of limiting or even banning these compensatory practices. Huge gaps in perception now exist; the majority of whites believe that racial discrimination has largely dissipated, while most blacks still experience it as being very much alive.[40] This stark racial polarization was clear in the 2006 vote on the constitutional amendment to ban affirmative action in Michigan. The amendment was supported by almost two-thirds of white voters but only by one in seven blacks.[41] Similar disparities have been found in other states.

These gaps in perception have been exploited by politicians anxious to capitalize on their capacity to drive wedges between voters. Many of us remember, for example, the famous 1990 television ad aired by North Carolina Senator Jesse Helms, who was locked in a tight race with the African American former mayor of Charlotte, Harvey Gantt. The ad showed a pair of white hands crumpling a rejection letter, while the announcer intoned, "You needed that job, and you were the best qualified. But they had to give it to a minority because of a racial quota." Less qualified, of course, simply because he had lower test scores. Helms went on to win the race.[42]

So here we have what is perhaps the deepest indictment of our cultural obsession with IQ. We like to view ourselves as a just and egalitarian society. We believe that rewards should be allocated solely on the basis of personal merit and that no one should be granted an unfair advantage because of such irrelevant factors as ethnicity, culture, or family wealth. But our unexamined identification of merit with intelligence has had precisely the opposite effect. For many complex reasons—which I will examine in more detail in Chapter 11—IQ scores are inextricably intertwined with race and class. So while pretending to ourselves that we are promoting democratic ideals, our use of IQ as a marker for merit actually serves to perpetuate an inequitable status quo. In the words of writer James Fallows, we have deluded ourselves into thinking "we have found a scientific basis for the order of lords, vassals, and serfs." Or, to quote critic Brigitte Berger, "If there is one thing more disturbing than a ruling class based on privilege, it is a ruling class that believes it deserves its position by virtue of its intelligence."[43]

Well, the reader may or may not have found the foregoing critique convincing. But most would admit that at the very least it raises some interesting questions. How and when, for example, did we Americans come to value intelligence so highly? What are those mysterious IQ tests all about, and why do we find them so fascinating? Through what process did IQ scores become a legal proxy for merit? And finally, are there any alternative perspectives on the issue of intelligence that might better serve us and our society?

The following chapters are my attempt to answer these questions. This quest will take us on a wide-ranging historical tour, touching on topics as diverse as Puritan theology, Enlightenment political philosophy, evolutionary biology, the quirky discipline of phrenology, fervent debates over unchecked immigration, and a national obsession with "the menace of the feebleminded." We will consider industrialization, progressivism, democratic ideology, the rise of the modern science of man, and the birth of the infant discipline of psychology. Along the way, we will encounter a cast of interesting characters, including Thomas Jefferson and John Adams, Charles Darwin and his younger cousin Francis Galton, and a previously obscure French psychologist named Alfred Binet. My hope is that, by the end of our journey, the reader will have developed a fresh and more balanced perspective on America's ongoing love affair with IQ.

Chapter 2

Intelligence in Historical Context: The Colonial Experience

The [idea of] intelligence is . . . as universal and ancient as any understanding about the state of being human. . . . Gossip about who in the tribe is cleverest has probably been a topic of conversation around the fire since fires, and conversation, were invented.[1]

Along with Richard Herrnstein and Charles Murray, authors of *The Bell Curve* (that massive and controversial 1994 tome about class and intelligence in America quoted above), most of us assume that we know what intelligence is. We believe that we are all born more or less smart. Through some mysterious process, practitioners wielding special tests have the power to delve deep into our psyches, uncovering that magic number known as IQ. We take it for granted that individuals possess different amounts of intelligence and that those with the highest IQs achieve—and in general deserve—the most success in life. And, we assume, people have always thought this way.

But have people at all times and in all places actually valued intelligence in the same way that we do today? The answer is a resounding no. The concept of intelligence, in the sense that we now understand the term, is actually what historian Lorraine Dashton has termed a "brashing modern notion."[2] In fact, our modern conception of intelligence as a largely inborn trait along which people can be rank-ordered did not begin to emerge until the latter half of the nineteenth century, a product of dramatic changes in science and society that were occurring during that period. And it was not until the dawn of the twentieth century that a reliable technology for measuring this new construct appeared on the scene.

So, in reality, there is nothing at all "universal and ancient" about the idea of intelligence. IQ is, in fact, a peculiarly American construct. True, the scientific foundations for this concept can be traced back to Europe, and it was a Frenchman, Alfred Binet, who developed the first practical test of intelligence. It was in the United States, however, that this idea fell on most fertile ground. In the space of one short decade, the Binet Scales, originally created with the rather modest goal of diagnosing mental retardation in Paris school children, had taken American culture by storm. This virtual explosion of interest in the new technology of IQ testing provides a textbook illustration of the complex ways in which science and society interact.

As I argued in the last chapter, the effects of America's love affair with IQ have been far from benign. Our national infatuation with intelligence has created stress for individuals and families, led to imbalances within our educational system, and distorted our national priorities. Our unthinking equation of IQ with merit has hardened existing social inequities and contributed to class and racial tensions. Psychologists, educators, politicians, and pundits have argued endlessly about the nature of intelligence, its hereditability and malleability, and the proper use of IQ tests. But these supposedly scientific questions are no closer to resolution than they were a hundred years ago. America's century-long cultural war over IQ is at a stalemate, with both sides dug into their trenches, throwing out the occasional grenade and in the process exhausting themselves, their ammunition, and their credibility.

But what if they are all arguing about the wrong thing? What all participants in this battle share is an unquestioning acceptance of the objective *existence* of intelligence. But perhaps it is this very concept of intelligence as a measurable quality along which people can be rank-ordered that is the problem. As I hope to demonstrate in the following chapters, intelligence is in fact a cultural construct, specific to a certain time and place. Understanding how the intertwined concepts of intelligence and merit have developed in the United States over the past 200 years sheds new light on both of these ideas. And this broader perspective in turn suggests fresh and potentially more productive ways of framing the ongoing debate about IQ.

Our modern concept of intelligence has its roots in the transformations in science and society that rocked nineteenth-century America. In Chapters 3 and 4, I will explore in some detail these revolutionary new ideas about the nature of the human mind, the organization of society, and the relationship of both to emerging concepts of merit and intelligence. But the precursors of these changes can be discerned even earlier, in colonial Puritan theology and in the Enlightenment philosophy of our founding fathers. The Puritans of Massachusetts Bay Colony were not the earliest European settlers in British North America, nor were they the most numerous. However, with their uncompromising Calvinist theology, their intellectual rigor, and—it must be added—their impressive economic acumen, they exerted a disproportionate influence on the social and intellectual life of the infant colonies. Calvinist theology remained the dominant influence in colonial American intellectual life for many decades. By the early part of the eighteenth century, however, radical new ideas were beginning to make their way across the Atlantic. The Enlightenment philosophy of thinkers such as Locke and Rousseau profoundly affected the framers of our Constitution, laying the intellectual foundation for many of the upheavals of the following century. And so, before proceeding to a fuller discussion of the nineteenth-century transformations in science and society that constitute the heart of our story, it would be useful to explore briefly how Puritan theologians and Enlightenment thinkers approached the related concepts of reason and individual merit.

CHANGING CONCEPTS OF THE HUMAN MIND

In many ways the social and intellectual views of the early American colonists were surprisingly traditional, reflecting those of a Europe only recently emerged from the medieval age. Intellectual life was firmly grounded in religious concepts. From the time of the ancient Greeks, ideas about the human mind had been inseparable from theology. The modern word "intelligence" comes from the Latin root *intellectus,* which is in turn a translation of the Greek *nous,* or reason, referring to the ability of humans to apprehend first principles. *Nous* was thus the quality that made it possible for humans to relate to the spiritual realm. Unlike our modern concept of IQ, in which people are rank-ordered in terms of quantity of intelligence, reason was viewed not as a continuum, but as a fundamental attribute common to all human beings, differentiating them from the animal world and linking them with the divine. The early Christian fathers incorporated the Greek perspective on reason into their own theology. Human reason, they believed, was a divine gift, bestowed by a benevolent God so that men might better understand Him and His will.[3]

As had the early Greeks, the Puritans of colonial New England placed the concept of reason at the heart of their theology. They assumed that God's governance of His world was rational; only through the divine gift of reason, they believed, could human beings understand His truth, His law, and His will for their lives. Consistent with this belief, almost immediately after landing in the New World, these early Puritan settlers turned their minds to education. Amazingly, a mere six years after the founding of the Massachusetts Bay Colony, its leaders had established a college in the wilds of Cambridge, named after clergyman John Harvard, whose bequest of his library of 400 books provided the foundation for the new institution. Virtually all Puritan clergymen were college graduates, and ministerial writings (mainly sermons, but also histories, works of science, and political speculations) dominated the meager output of the early colonial presses. These educated ministers were not content to require complex reasoning of themselves and their peers; they expected it from their parishioners as well. Visitors to New England often marveled at the ability of ordinary farm hands to follow the intricacies of sophisticated sermons and to debate complex issues of free will and predestination.[4]

Given the culture wars that have raged during the past 150 years between the teachings of modern science and the tenets of fundamentalist religious denominations, it may surprise many readers to learn that these early Calvinists experienced no conflict between science and their religion. Like the ancient Greek philosophers and earlier Christian theologians (most notably St. Thomas Aquinas), Puritan thinkers assumed that all knowledge was part of one overarching and unified whole. Because every discipline harmonized with every other, it was inconceivable that the findings of science might conflict with theology, the "queen of the sciences."[5] Believing that God revealed His will in part through events in the natural world, Puritan ministers were very quick to accept new ideas emerging from the physical sciences, most notably the work of Sir Isaac Newton. They taught that men had a positive moral duty to use their God-given reason to glorify the Creator by learning more about the marvels of His world and putting this knowledge to use for the benefit of their fellow man. It is no accident that most of the scientists in colonial America were in fact ministers.[6]

Despite their veneration of reason and their respect for science, Calvinist theologians, like virtually all of their contemporaries, continued to regard divine revelation as the ultimate source of authority. But even as refugees from England began trickling into the New World, radically new ideas were starting to circulate among the European intellectual elite. Members of the movement that has come to be known as the Enlightenment rejected the idea of supernatural revelation, placing their faith instead in man's capacity for knowledge and his ability to use the natural faculties of his mind and the techniques of science to unravel the mysteries of nature. Calvinists had viewed people as helpless and hopeless sinners. Enlightenment thinkers, in contrast, emphasized the human capacity for knowledge and social improvement. Instead of relying on divine guidance, they believed, men (and presumably at least some women) could use their own reasoning abilities to discern the rules of appropriate moral behavior.[7]

Any examination of the Enlightenment understanding of reason must begin with the ideas of Englishman John Locke. In his *Essay Concerning Human Understanding,* published in 1690, Locke made the first serious attempt to explain the functioning of the mind in purely naturalistic terms. Although he was himself a highly religious man, Locke did not posit the need for any divine intervention in the development of reason. Every human being, he suggested, comes into the world with his mind a blank slate, or *tabula rasa.* Over time, the child absorbs experiences through the senses and then organizes these experiences through a process of association. As the resulting mental structures become ever more complex, reason naturally develops. Locke's theories found a ready welcome in the rationalist intellectual milieu of the Enlightenment era, and his *Essay* was soon familiar to every educated person—including, significantly, virtually all of America's founding fathers.[8]

Some European intellectuals, most notably philosopher David Hume, carried Locke's ideas to their logical extreme; if reason developed through a totally natural process, then why invoke the existence of an all-powerful and all-knowing God at all? Few Americans, however, were willing to go this far. They found a much more comfortable home in common sense philosophy, a system of thought that emerged during the eighteenth century in the Scottish universities of Edinburgh and Aberdeen. Although thinkers such as Thomas Reid and his disciple Dugald Steward accepted most of Locke's ideas about the naturalistic development of reason, they asserted that it was only common sense to admit that people are born pre-wired to accept certain self-evident principles, such as a belief in God and a sense of morality. And unlike Locke, they believed that the human mind also comes equipped at birth with a number of active powers or faculties, each of which can be improved through exercise or discipline.[9]

The ideas of Reid and his followers spread rapidly through American colleges, and by the 1790s common sense philosophy had come to dominate higher education in this country—an influence that lasted well into the 1870s. Common sense philosophy was in fact a perfect match for a vigorous and devout young nation. It was practical, optimistic, and forward looking, emphasizing the development of each individual's faculties and a faith in human possibilities. Agreeing that the mind was a

gift from God and the moral sense an innate human quality, this school
of thought was fully consistent with the dominant Protestant theology.
Its primary emphasis, however, was on reason and science. Following
Locke's lead, common sense philosophers taught that the human mind
developed according to natural laws that could be studied and understood logically. Although its basic approach was philosophical rather
than scientific, this system helped pave the way for a more purely naturalistic conception of the human mind, an approach that culminated a
century later in our modern notion of intelligence.

THE DEVELOPING CONCEPT OF MERITOCRACY

The Puritans of colonial New England brought with them to the New
World a concept of society not far removed from that of medieval Europe. In common with almost all of their contemporaries, these early
settlers envisioned their universe as an orderly and hierarchical structure, a pyramid with an all-powerful God seated at the head of a Great
Chain of Being. Below God, ranked in order of grade of perfection,
could be found the angels, then men, and finally, at the base, all of the
other living creatures and inanimate objects in Creation. Although un-
familiar to most of us today, this concept, which originated with ancient
Greeks and was brought into Christian theology by the early church
fathers, remained fundamental to Western thought at least through the
end of the eighteenth century.

Consistent with this vision of the Great Chain of Being was the Calvinist doctrine of predestination—the belief that all human beings are
born totally depraved but that God, in His inscrutable wisdom, has
preordained some of them for salvation. No one could know for sure
whether he or she was among this elect group (although the "saints" of
early New England seemed quite certain that *they* were surely destined
for glory in the hereafter!). But though virtuous behavior was no guarantee of salvation, it was at least one possible *sign* that one was among
the elect. Believing as they did in a God who sat atop a rational universe,
the Puritans were convinced that the just would be rewarded and the
unjust punished, in this life as well as the next.

Such a theology led quite easily to an assumption that people generally got what they deserved in life. Worldly success flowed naturally
from virtues such as initiative, sobriety, and thrift; just as naturally, sin-
ful living led to the affliction of poverty. Puritan ministers often advised
their parishioners that they could achieve economic prosperity by leading a godly life, and the saints of early New England in fact became the
forebears of a thriving merchant class. As historian Max Weber has so

colorfully described it, "a religion with roots in the idea that all men are brothers proved uniquely suited to the creation of an economic system that takes Cain and Abel as its model of brotherhood."[10]

Paradoxically, although Puritan New England had been founded in an act of rebellion against the established church, its leaders placed great value on the virtues of order, harmony, and obedience to authority. The doctrine of predestination and the belief that God rewarded His own in this life as well as the next were fully consistent with the vision of an orderly, hierarchical society that had come down from the ancient Greeks. God in His wisdom had provided some individuals with the qualities needed for leadership; others were better fitted for more lowly pursuits. It was the duty of human beings to do their best in whatever position God had seen fit to place them. Alexander Pope captured the essence of this concept in these famous lines from his 1733 *Essay on Man*, familiar to every educated person of the time:

> Order is Heav'n's first law; and this confessed,
> Some are, and must be, greater than the rest . . .
> Honour and shame from no Condition rise;
> Act well your part, there all the honour lies.[11]

Mainstream American religious thought has long since moved beyond the discomfiting doctrine of predestination, and probably few modern Americans accept the Puritan assumption that the existing social structure reflects divine will. Our definition of merit has also changed considerably, shifting from a preoccupation with godly behavior to a focus on intellectual prowess and test scores. However, our cherished ideal of meritocracy—that people should achieve success solely through their own personal qualities—can be traced directly to Puritan theology. Indeed, writer Nicholas Lemann has argued that we now anoint our elect by admitting them to our best schools, viewing high SAT scores as a modern sign of salvation. No wonder that critic David Layzer has referred to our modern version of meritocracy as "intellectual Calvinism."[12]

This traditional vision of a divinely ordained social structure in which individuals remained content in their allotted positions, bound together by a web of mutual responsibility, had held sway in the Western world for centuries. But the emergence of Enlightenment thought, with its emphasis on individualism, natural law, and progress, inevitably called these assumptions into question. Nor was such a hierarchical, status-based social organization well fitted to the realities of the new capitalist economic order. Self-interest, profit motive, individual initiative—these fundamental characteristics of capitalism required a more fluid social structure. With the traditional rationale for social distinctions becoming increasingly unworkable, Enlightenment thinkers had to posit a more rational basis for maintaining an orderly society while at the same time leaving the door open for movement between classes. Their solution was the notion that individual ability rather than inherited status should serve as the organizing principle for society.[13]

The idea that social position should be based on personal ability was not a new one; it can be traced back at least as far as Plato and his philosopher kings. According to Plato, each individual, regardless of parentage, should be given "the position in society his nature deserves." Following Plato's dictum, America's founding fathers believed that republican government must be based on a foundation of individual merit rather than inherited social status. James Madison summarized this view succinctly in the *Federalist Papers*. "The aim of every political constitution," he wrote, "is, or ought to be, first to obtain for rulers men who possess most wisdom to discern, and most virtue to pursue, the common good of the society." Thomas Jefferson concurred. "There is a natural aristocracy among men," he famously proclaimed. "The grounds of this are virtue and talents." Jefferson's idealized natural aristocrats were public-spirited and self-sacrificing citizens, accepting the responsibilities of leadership more as an obligation than as a right and freely offering their talents for the benefit of the larger society.[14]

Although this idealized vision of society might have sounded quite democratic, in reality there was little chance that it would lead to the dreaded leveling of society. Most people assumed that the autonomy required for such virtuous, public-spirited behavior was possible only for those blessed with the independence of property ownership. True, a few liberal souls suggested that lower classes might produce the occasional exceptional individual. Jefferson, for example, asserted that "nature has sown [her talents] as liberally among the poor as the rich"; natural aristocrats, therefore, could be found among all classes of society. By and large, however, most eighteenth-century American leaders assumed that the ranks of the meritorious would most naturally be filled by members of the propertied classes. And even liberals like Jefferson agreed that inequality of innate gifts would quite naturally and properly lead to inequality of status.[15]

And so, despite the natural rights rhetoric of the founding fathers, class distinctions in American society on the eve of the Revolution remained substantial. Few publicly questioned the appropriateness of differences in wealth and status based on individual ability; most people viewed the resulting uneven distribution of property as both proper and inevitable. As in Europe, a fundamental distinction existed between commoners, or working people, and gentlemen—those who had the wealth and the leisure to work with their minds rather than their hands. And of course no one even imagined that an individual who was not white and male could possibly merit a position of leadership. Women, children, slaves, servants, apprentices, the very poor, and the mentally deficient were all assumed to lack full reasoning ability; naturally, then, they would remain subordinate to their betters. The natural rights so cherished by Enlightenment political theorists were actually deemed relevant only to a small minority of individuals, primarily white, property-owning men.

But though it may have applied to only a limited segment of society, by the end of the eighteenth century, the Enlightenment ideal of meritocracy had become well established in American thought. The Puritans believed that the existing order of society reflected personal merit, with an all-powerful God bestowing on those who followed His commands earthly as well as eternal rewards. By the time of the American Revolution, the focus of merit had shifted from personal godliness to a combination of individual talents and virtues, and leadership had come to be viewed more as a responsibility than as a privilege. But despite the changing focus of merit—from godliness to talents and virtue to, in more recent years, intelligence—one belief has remained central: those atop the social hierarchy are there because they deserve to be. Journalist Daniel Seligman expressed this assumption very clearly in a 1992 article. "People at the top in American life are probably there because they are more intelligent than others," he wrote, "which is doubtless the way most of us think it should be."[16] Well, one may agree or disagree with Seligman's statement, but the evidence suggests that his viewpoint is a natural outgrowth of the meritocratic ideals we have inherited from our forebears.

THE FIRST STIRRINGS OF DEMOCRACY

Those of the better sort, initially Puritan ministers and theologians and later public-spirited Enlightenment thinkers, clearly dominated intellectual life in America during the colonial period, and it is to their influence that we can trace much of our modern understanding of the interrelated concepts of intelligence and merit. However, as we shall see in later chapters, our story is not confined to these intellectual elites. As the eighteenth century drew to a close, the traditional patterns of deference and subordination, accepted for so long, were beginning to weaken. Beneath the hierarchical social structure, a new spirit of democracy was simmering. The factors involved in the emergence of this democratic impulse are far too complex to discuss in detail here. However, two merit at least a brief discussion: the mass religious movement known as the Great Awakening and the impact of the American Revolution on the common men who served as its foot soldiers.[17]

Unlike the rationalist strain of Protestantism predominant among the descendants of the New England Puritans, the religion of the Great Awakening appealed primarily to ordinary people. Under the leadership of English evangelist George Whitefield, who conducted several wildly popular revival tours in the American colonies during the 1730s and 1740s, this religious movement swept across the country like wildfire. Whitefield and his followers focused their teachings on the necessity for an intense emotional experience of salvation; intellectual understanding, they insisted, was meaningless in the absence of such an experience. The primary requirement for the ministry was thus personal conversion rather than impressive educational credentials. In contrast to the highly intellectual New England Calvinism, this emotional approach to religion appealed strongly to those who perceived themselves to be disenfranchised, dispossessed, and disrespected.

The implications of the evangelical religion of the Great Awakening were in fact radically democratic. A direct, personal relationship with God was available to all who chose to open themselves to the experience of conversion, regardless of social class or educational background. Congregations could choose their own ministers; in many denominations, the call to preach was all that was required for the ministry. Ordinary uneducated people felt comfortable with the informal style of worship. Their rejection of the religious style and liturgy of the upper-class church suggested a revolt against aristocratic manners and morals in general. Charles Chauncey, an influential leader of the Boston clergy, seemed fully aware of the dangerously democratic implications of Great Awakening religion when he fulminated against the "*insolence* of the upstarts from miscellaneous occupations who had come to challenge the ministry."[18] Common people who felt empowered in their religious lives might eventually come to feel empowered politically as well.

The second major force promoting democratization in the infant United States was the experience of the American Revolution itself. The founding fathers may have believed that the natural aristocrats (meaning, of course, individuals like themselves) would by right lead the new republic. However, it had of course been ordinary men, not the intellectual elite, who served as the actual foot soldiers in the Revolution, and many of these common people had been far more motivated by evangelical religion than by abstract Enlightenment political theory. Their active participation in the war empowered these former soldiers, unleashing a groundswell of democratic fervor among many who had formerly been excluded from political debate. After winning the Revolution, they were not inclined to return to the old ways. This conflict between the forces of tradition and those of democracy played out in the surprisingly virulent debate over the adoption of the new Constitution. The pro-Constitution Federalists, supported by the most powerful men in the country, eventually prevailed, but it would not be many decades before the forces of democracy had their say. Together, the Great Awakening and the American Revolution helped form the battle lines for a debate between meritocracy and democracy, or equality of opportunity versus equality of results, that remains fundamental to our seemingly insoluble modern controversies over issues related to merit and intelligence.

And thus, by the end of the eighteenth century, the traditional society of colonial America, with religion as its bulwark and social status determined by birth, was crumbling. The Enlightenment; the rise of an industrialized, free market economy; the Great Awakening; the experience and ideology of the American Revolution—all challenged established beliefs, moving them in a recognizably modern direction. A developing view of the intellect based solely on natural laws undermined the traditional concept of reason as man's link with the divine. The vision of an organic society in which status was determined by birth was slowly giving way to a more merit-based social system. As we will see in the next several chapters, these new ideas did not blossom fully until the nineteenth century. However, the intellectual, social, and economic changes of the colonial period helped prepare the ground for our modern biologically based understanding of intelligence and the test-based conception of merit that developed alongside it.

Chapter 3

Science in Nineteenth-Century America: Intellect, Intelligence, and the Science of Man

Americans have always been fascinated by science. Even as they were struggling to plant their version of the gospel on the shores of the New World, Puritan clergymen were conducting scientific explorations and natural history expeditions. Many of our Enlightenment-influenced founding fathers, men like Benjamin Franklin, Thomas Jefferson, and Benjamin Rush, were noted amateur scientists as well. And so it is not surprising that the story of intelligence in the United States is closely intertwined with the history of its science. During the course of the nineteenth century, the nature of American science changed in fundamental ways, leading to a radically new concept of the human mind. As we saw in the last chapter, prior to the 1800s, virtually all of those who thought about the matter had conceptualized the mind in terms of reason, a gift bestowed by God on all men and best studied through the techniques of moral philosophy. But by the dawn of the twentieth century, the focus had shifted from reason, or intellect, to intelligence—biologically based, the product of a soulless, impersonal evolution, and the province of secular, scientific psychology.

In America, as in Europe, the Enlightenment approach to science had been empirical, mechanistic, and atheoretical. Its giant was Newton and its model a physical universe governed by unchanging natural laws. The newly established American colleges had been quick to incorporate Newton's *Principia* into their curricula, and Newton himself was regarded with a reverence that verged on worship. Alexander Pope reflected this popular veneration of Newton in his famous couplet:

Nature and Nature's Laws lay hid in Night.
God said, Let Newton be! and all was Light.[1]

If Newton was the theoretician of Enlightenment science, its method-
ologist was Francis Bacon. Following Bacon's dictates, America's early
amateur scientists focused on collecting concrete, observable facts—
facts that could then be successively classified into higher and higher
orders of abstraction, in hopes that eventually the ultimate order or
final truth might be revealed. Indeed, as Michel Foucault has pointed
out, Enlightenment science *was* classification. Practitioners of natural
history sought to understand their world by collecting, identifying, and
classifying living things; a similar approach characterized such fields as
geology, astronomy, and chemistry.[2]

As we have seen, even the strictest of New England Puritans perceived
no conflict between religion and Newtonian science. This long-standing
vision of religion and science as part of the same magnificent, divinely
ordained system remained pervasive in the United States during the
years leading up to the Civil War.[3] Science, morality, and religious belief
all came together in the discipline of moral philosophy. Grounded in
the common sense philosophy then dominant in American higher education, moral philosophy (or mental philosophy, as it was sometimes
termed) was the predecessor of what we now call psychology. In virtually all American colleges, from colonial times until well after the Civil
War, the course in moral philosophy was the capstone of the curriculum. It was usually taught by the college president, a fact that served to
emphasize its importance.[4]

Moral or mental philosophy (it is revealing that the two terms were
often used interchangeably) was defined as the naturalistic, scientific
study of man and his relationships. Its practitioners conceived of the
mind as a natural phenomenon, subject to empirical study through the
use of biological or mechanical models. Since all of nature, including
mankind, was a part of the same divinely ordained system, such study
would, of necessity, lead to a better knowledge of God and His world.
As psychologist John O'Donnell has explained, moral philosophy was
both the precursor to the social sciences and the successor to theology.
It sought to "provide a rational basis for religious and social precept
independent of revealed theology. Assuming that Truth is one, academic
moralists argued from analogy that the natural and moral worlds were
in perfect accord."[5]

It is instructive to peruse some of the old textbooks used in these
moral or mental philosophy courses. The gulf between their methods
and those of modern psychology is striking. The approach of their

authors was systematic and logical. However, from the modern perspective that equates science with rigorous, objective experimentation, the discipline of moral philosophy would be labeled as theological and philosophical rather than scientific. The authors of these texts uncritically accepted Locke's associationist view of the human mind. In true Baconian tradition, they sought lawful relationships between facts—facts that could come from sense perceptions, conscious introspection, anecdotal observations of human and animal behavior, literature, and even the Bible. The explicit intent of mental philosophy courses was to provide a scientific foundation for moral behavior.[6] Mark Hopkins's widely used text, *An Outline Study of Man,* even ends with a hymn of praise to the Creator of the magnificent system to which the author has devoted his book.[7]

This, then, was American science on the eve of the Civil War. In most ways, it was still the science of the Enlightenment. Its purpose was utilitarian. Its model was Newtonian physics, and its primary method was the collection, organization, and classification of empirically observed facts. Science, philosophy, and religion were viewed as mutually supportive elements in one grand, divinely inspired system. But this formerly seamless web was soon to be torn to shreds. New ideas about biology, evolution, and the science of man were beginning to emerge from Europe, ideas that paved the way for our modern concept of intelligence and shattered the long-time unity of science and religion.

THE RISE OF EVOLUTIONARY THINKING

If the Enlightenment period could be called the age of physics, the nineteenth century was the age of biology. The natural philosophers of the Enlightenment era had approached the study of living things through natural history, the practice of collecting, identifying, and classifying specimens. Natural history's crowning achievement was the work of Carl Linnaeus, who developed a framework within which all plants and animals could be classified (essentially the system that we still use today). But, as Michel Foucault has argued, during the course of the 1800s the focus of science changed gradually from the "table" to "history," from classification to causality. Natural history was evolving into biology.[8] And these new biologists were not satisfied with simply ordering and classifying their observations. They wanted to understand how living systems, including the human brain itself, actually worked and to explore the processes through which these systems had developed. This focus on the development of living systems led almost inevitably to the idea of evolution.

Contrary to popular opinion, the concept of evolution did not originate with Darwin. The idea of human history as movement toward some ultimate goal had long been integral to Western thought. During the eighteenth century, naturalists such as Erasmus Darwin (grandfather of Charles) had observed how the physical structures of plants and animals seemed to develop into other, more complex structures. Such developmental changes appeared to these thinkers to be a progressive realization of God's natural plan for His creation. The first comprehensive theory of evolution (although this specific term was not yet in general use) was proposed by French naturalist Jean-Baptiste Lamarck during the early years of the nineteenth century. Lamarck suggested that organisms change their structures over time in response to the demands of their environments. For example, short-legged wading birds might gradually stretch their legs in the effort to find food in deeper water. These incremental changes in leg length would be passed on to their offspring, the eventual result being the long-legged heron.[9]

Lamarck's theory of "the inheritance of acquired characteristics" was well known and widely accepted among professionals in the field of biology. The event that first brought evolutionary ideas to widespread public attention, however, was the anonymous publication of a book called *Vestiges of the Natural History of Creation* in England in 1844. This account started with the beginning of the universe and proceeded through the formation of the earth (using the evidence of geology), the development of the different animal forms, and finally the emergence of human beings. Although criticized by scientists because of its amateur quality and by the church because of its potential threat to religion, *Vestiges* excited a lively interest among the public at large. The tome was read by at least 100,000 people in England, a literary phenomenon that rivaled that of Dickens's early novels, and it garnered considerable attention in America as well.[10]

Clearly, then, the publication of Charles Darwin's *The Origin of Species* in 1859 did not arrive as a bolt out of the blue. Earlier concepts of evolution, however, had been largely speculative. What Darwin did was to present in support of his theories a mass of data so extensive and so convincing that it virtually compelled acceptance. Even more significantly, he suggested natural selection as a credible explanation for the actual mechanism of evolution. Natural selection presented a much more difficult challenge to conventional thought than did evolution itself. After all, it had been fairly easy to explain evolution as the gradual unfolding of God's plan for His world. But natural selection was different—an impersonal and mechanical process, governed by blind chance rather than divine intelligence and directed toward no overarching goal. With the publication of *The Descent of Man* in 1871, Darwin extended his theory of natural selection to include humans as well as the lower animals. Instead of being the culminating glory of God's special creation, human beings now appeared as nothing more than the random product of blind natural forces.[11]

Although Darwin's work focused primarily on the evolution of the physical characteristics of various organisms, he believed that his theories applied to mental traits as well.[12] In *Expression of the Emotions in Man and Animals*, written in 1872, he presented evidence that the human mind has developed according to the same evolutionary principles that govern animal development. Evolution, he suggested, might therefore help explain at least some of the cultural and behavioral differences between the various races of mankind.[13] Even more significant for modern ideas about intelligence was Darwin's focus on individual variation. Natural selection, of course, seizes on such random variations as its basic raw material. Previous biologists had been most interested in the commonalities among groups of organisms. Darwin shifted the spotlight to the individual differences between them, a change that proved to be fundamental to the development of our modern conception of intelligence.

Darwin's impact on American thought was immediate and immense. *The Origin of Species* was widely reviewed in the press upon its publication in the United States in 1860, and Darwin's theories received extensive coverage in daily newspapers and in magazines such as *Popular Science Monthly, Atlantic Monthly,* and *Nation.*[14] Within a decade, most American scientists had fully accepted the Darwinian account of evolution. Understandably, the religious establishment lagged behind the scientific world in coming to terms with Darwin's ideas. Initially, virtually all religious groups registered strong opposition to the theory of evolution. By 1885, however, most liberal Protestant clergymen (most notably, the prominent Henry Ward Beecher) had found ways to reconcile their religious beliefs with the tenets of evolution and natural selection.[15] Conservative clergymen, of course, saw things very differently. Their relentless attacks on Darwin and his theories reflected a cultural divide between liberal and conservative religious groups that continues as wide and deep today as it was 150 years ago.

Second in influence only to *The Origin of Species,* especially in America, was the work of English philosopher and sociologist Herbert Spencer. Spencer had begun thinking and writing about the topic of evolution as early as the 1840s. Indeed, it was he, not Darwin, who had first used the now-familiar terms "survival of the fittest" (in an 1852 article) and "evolution" (in 1857). When Darwin published his seminal work in 1859, Spencer enthusiastically accepted his findings, lamenting only that he himself had failed to recognize the mechanism of natural selection. Darwin, in turn, often cited Spencer as an important influence. Spencer's goal was even grander than Darwin's: he wished to explain all natural processes—biological, psychological, and sociological—in terms of one comprehensive theory of evolution.[16]

It was Spencer, in the later versions of his immensely influential *Principles of Psychology,* who popularized the use of the word "intelligence" in its modern evolutionary and biological sense. In this book, Spencer defined intelligence as the adaptation of the organism to the environment, or, as he expressed it, "an adjustment of inner to outer relations."[17] As environmental demands become more complex, the organisms able to respond most intelligently would have a competitive advantage. Thus defined, intelligence became the primary mechanism of evolution. Spencer's view of intelligence was thoroughly biological; he believed that the same natural laws governed the mental processes of all organisms, from the lowest to the highest. He dismissed the conventional concepts of reason, memory, imagination, and will, so dear to centuries of philosophers, as nothing more than particular mechanisms of adjustment. Several generations of moral philosophy textbooks had explained reason, or intellect, as a universal attribute; it would not have occurred to these authors to compare the reasoning abilities of different people, much less those of people and the lower animals. Spencer, on the other hand, explained intelligence as an impersonal and individually variable process of biology, common to all living beings.[18]

Spencer's work was immensely influential in America throughout the latter half of the nineteenth century. His books, which sold hundreds of thousands of copies, were familiar to virtually all educated people. Spencer's 1882 visit to America has been described as a triumphal procession, and individuals as different as writers Jack London and Theodore Dreiser, sociologist William Graham Sumner, and industrialist Andrew Carnegie acknowledged their debt to him. His enormous popularity in America was due largely to Spencer's application of evolutionary principles to social development.[19] (It has been noted that the theory now known as "Social Darwinism" would more accurately be labeled "Social Spencerism.") But his scientific impact was also enormous. Before Spencer, the concept of intelligence had belonged to the realm of philosophy; now it was firmly seated in biology. The importance of this shift can hardly be overestimated.

THE SCIENCE OF MAN

The emergence of the discipline of biology during the nineteenth century led to great advances in the scientific understanding of the brain

and the nervous system. Flourens conducted seminal studies of the localization of brain functions; Ball and Magendie discovered the differences
between motor and sensory nerves; Muller measured the velocity of
nerve impulses; Volta discovered the electrical nature of nerve conduc-
tion. Prior to the 1800s, the human mind had been viewed as man's link
with the divine. Now it was firmly identified with the physical structures
of the brain.[20]

Michel Foucault has described this shift from philosophy and natural
history to biology as part of a larger revolutionary change that was occurring in Western intellectual life. Humans had traditionally viewed
themselves as special creatures of God, standing apart from the rest of
the natural world. But the theory of evolution placed human beings
squarely in the midst of that creation, potentially objects as well as subjects of scientific study. And if human society operated by laws just as
scientific as those governing the natural world, one should be able to
study human thought and behavior using the methods of science. As
Edward Youmans, the founder of *Popular Science* magazine and one
of the foremost proponents of modern science in the United States, remarked in 1867, in the past "not man, but mind" had been the object of
inquiry. But now, he wrote, by using the techniques of modern science
"the study of man is entered upon in the same temper, and by the same
methods" that had so successfully advanced the natural sciences.[21]

The pioneers in the scientific study of human behavior were anthropologists. Beginning in the years before the Civil War, Paul Broca in France
and Samuel Morton and Louis Agassiz in the United States began performing painstaking measurements on a wide variety of human skulls.
Among their primary goals was to demonstrate differences in the skull
characteristics of different races and then scientifically to link these variations to supposed racial disparities in intellectual ability. These early
anthropologists were among the first to use the word "intelligence" to
refer to a cognitive characteristic that could be manifested in degrees
and used to distinguish one human group from another. Not surprisingly, their measurements purported to demonstrate the intellectual superiority of the European races and the innate inferiority of Indians and
Negroes. In recent years, author Stephen Jay Gould has demonstrated
how both Morton and Broca (most likely unconsciously) manipulated
their data to fit their predetermined conclusions. At the time, however,
their work enjoyed great scientific respectability and significant popular
appeal. So influential was Morton's work in the United States, in fact,
that during the Civil War the Sanitary Corps measured the heads of all
military recruits. As one might expect, they reported that these measurements demonstrated the superiority of native-born whites to immigrants, Negroes, and mulattoes.[22]

Another of the early social sciences was sociology. Our old friend Herbert Spencer is generally credited with the establishment of this discipline. As we have seen, Spencer's grand goal was to use the tools of science and the perspective of evolution to explain all of human behavior. His *Study of Sociology,* written in 1873, was very well received in the United States, where prominent Yale professor William Graham Sumner took up the Spencerian banner, enthusiastically promoting his theories in both professional and popular venues. Sumner confessed that "sociology is yet in a tentative and inchoate state," but he affirmed with great certainty "that social phenomena are subject to law, and that the natural laws of the social order are in their entire character like the laws of physics."[23] Sumner, who went on to become one of America's foremost advocates of Social Darwinism, emphasized the competitive aspects of evolution—the struggle for dominance and the survival of the fittest. Other American sociologists, most notably Lester Ward, chose to focus instead on evolution's more optimistic aspects, emphasizing mankind's potential to use education and cooperation to control the course of its own evolution. Whether politically liberal or conservative, however, these early sociologists were united in their conviction that their fledgling science could provide the answers to many social problems.

Both anthropology and sociology contributed significantly to our modern concept of intelligence. Most relevant to our story, however, is the new science of psychology. The term "psychology" had been in use since the mid-eighteenth century, and several textbooks had been published on the subject, including Alexander Bain's *The Senses and the Intellect* (1855), Herbert Spencer's first edition of his *Principles of Psychology* (1855), and Hippolyte Taine's massive *On Intelligence* (1870).[24] However, this early version of psychology, which was grounded in common sense philosophy and based on Locke's long-accepted associationist theories of the mind, actually had more in common with moral or mental philosophy than with the modern discipline of psychology. Wilhelm Wundt, who established the first experimental laboratory in Leipzig in 1879, is generally credited with being the founder of modern scientific psychology. Wundt's approach was to investigate the fundamental functions of the normal adult human mind by breaking down conscious processes into their individual elements, primarily through the techniques of introspection and focus on simple sensations. In contrast to the moral philosophers, he approached his subject empirically, basing his conclusions on concrete data rather than logical, abstract reasoning and theological concepts.[25]

Virtually all of the first generation of American psychologists traveled to Germany to study with Wundt. Many of them, however, were actually more strongly influenced by two other European social scientists. The first of these, as we have already seen, was Herbert Spencer, whose introduction of evolutionary theory into the field of psychology was fundamental to the development of the modern concept of intelligence. The second was the British polymath Sir Francis Galton (a cousin of Charles Darwin). Galton was fascinated by the biological variation that provides the basis for natural selection among individuals. He collected voluminous data on people's performance of various simple mental tasks and used statistical techniques, many of his own invention, to try to relate differences in test performance to more complex cognitive functions (although, it must be said, without notable success). It was Galton who influenced many American psychologists to study individual differences between people rather than focusing on Wundt's "mind in general."

During the 1870s and 1880s, young European-trained American psychologists gradually began displacing the entrenched mental philosophers in American colleges, especially in the new research-oriented universities. Unlike their philosophical predecessors, these young researchers approached their discipline as scientists. They viewed the human mind as the natural product of the blind forces of evolution, not as a special creation of God. And increasingly, they focused on how people differed rather than on what they had in common. G. Stanley Hall was probably the most energetic early practitioner of this new approach to psychology. Strongly influenced by evolutionary theory, Hall studied both animal and human development in order to learn more about the evolution of the human mind. Another influential first-generation American psychologist was James McKeen Cattell. While visiting in England, Cattell had fallen under the spell of Sir Francis Galton, and he returned to the United States determined to devise practical techniques for measuring individual differences in mental functioning. As we shall see in later chapters, Cattell was to play a key role in the development of the discipline of mental testing.

By the dawn of the twentieth century, this distinctively American version of psychology had become well established in its colleges and universities. This new discipline was firmly evolutionary in its focus and more concerned with individual differences than with the generalized mind. It was also strongly pragmatic. From the beginning, American psychologists had emphasized the practical application of their findings, touting their potential usefulness to fields as diverse as education, criminology, industry, business, and advertising. Claiming the authority of modern scientific knowledge, they worked to position themselves as the professionals most qualified to be consulted on a variety of issues of social concern.[26]

And so, by the time the nineteenth century drew to a close, the foundations for our modern concept of intelligence were firmly in place. The physical brain, not divine intervention, was now understood as the seat of reason. Intelligence was defined as a biologically based property shared by all living organisms; as one climbed the evolutionary ladder, its processes simply became more adaptive and more complex. And the infant discipline of psychology stood by, ready and eager to apply this new understanding of intelligence to the problems of the day. However, one remaining issue merits discussion. Anthropologists, sociologists, and psychologists engaged in the measurement of human characteristics were collecting enormous masses of data. But how were they to make sense of this virtual embarrassment of riches? What they needed was an objective method to help them organize and interpret the information they were gathering, allowing them to detect the large-scale order that they assumed existed beneath seemingly random variations.

They found this tool in a newly developed mathematical technique called statistics. The discipline of statistics is based on the so-called Gaussian distribution or bell curve. This mathematical distribution describes the pattern in which many natural phenomena occur; most cases cluster near the middle, or average, value, while fewer and fewer are found as one approaches either extreme. The graphical representation of this distribution is shaped like a bell: hence its name. Mathematicians had originally developed this model to predict the probability of various outcomes in games of chance, and early-nineteenth-century astronomers then appropriated it to describe the pattern of their errors of observation. A Belgian named Adolphe Quetelet is credited with the idea of applying this new technique to the description of social problems. Quetelet also originated the concept of the "normal man" (or average person) around which such variation occurs.[27]

It was the ubiquitous Sir Francis Galton, however, who first thought of using the so-called normal curve to describe biological characteristics. As we have seen, Galton was fascinated by the notion of individual differences, and he had recruited large numbers of volunteers to take a variety of simple tests of perception, sensation, and memory. But he was then faced with the daunting problem of somehow making sense of all of his data. He found his answer in Quetelet's concept of the norm. Extending Quetelet's work, Galton developed a new statistical technique known as correlation, which was then extended and further developed by his protégé Karl Pearson. The correlation coefficient, now a staple of modern psychology, is a single number that describes how closely two variables are related to one another. This statistical tool gave Galton and his successors a totally new way of classifying individuals. The traditional method of analysis had been to sort people into separate, discrete classes; when describing intellectual abilities, for example, an individual could be placed into one of three categories: genius, normal, or defective. Galton's new statistical techniques, however, allowed him to rank the members of these three separate groups along one single scale of mental ability. For the first time, it was possible to speak meaningfully about an individual's "amount" of intelligence.[28]

Statistical reasoning led to an entirely different way of conceptualizing the human mind. The job of philosophers had been to study the *nature* of reasoning. But statistical techniques encouraged practitioners of the new discipline of psychology to ask a different question—how *much* intellectual ability does one person (or organism) have as compared to another? Writer George Boas commented on the effects of this radically new way of thinking in a 1927 article in *Harper's Magazine*. Throughout most of Western history, he noted, people have reasoned in what he called classical or Aristotelian terms, placing individuals into classes or categories on the basis of what they have in common. In Boas's words, "The typical was important, the individual was trivial."[29] But statistical thinking is different; its focus is on individual variations rather than commonalities. The effect of statistical thinking was to change the focus of inquiry from understanding the nature of human reasoning to measuring who had the most of it. And measuring individual variations in mental ability was, of course, what the soon-to-be-developed IQ test was all about.

SCIENCE AND THE AMERICAN PUBLIC

It was primarily members of the intellectual elite—biologists, anthropologists, psychologists, and the occasional well-educated amateur like Galton—who laid the theoretical and practical foundations for our modern concept of intelligence. But interest in these new ideas was not confined to the intellectual classes. In newly democratic nineteenth-century America, ordinary citizens enthusiastically set out to learn about the latest scientific discoveries. As faith in the old verities began to crumble, they turned increasingly to a new class of scientific experts for answers to life's questions. Near-universal literacy (at least among the native-born, white population) and the production of inexpensive books, magazines, and newspapers allowed information about science to reach into the working classes. The popular penny newspapers provided extensive coverage of scientific topics, with articles providing exciting accounts of expeditions of discovery and relating the latest findings in astronomy, geology, meteorology, and botany. Probably the most important written vehicle for the spread of scientific information was *Popular Science Monthly,* founded in 1872 by E. L. Youmans; by 1886, its circulation had reached 18,000, a figure that was very impressive for that era.[30]

Ordinary Americans also flocked to a wide variety of lectures, presentations, and demonstrations on topics related to science. The Lyceum circuit, founded in the late 1820s, brought such lectures and debates into the smallest of American villages and farming communities. Even more influential was Chautauqua, whose program of lectures, discussion groups, and self-study courses reached more than 9,000 communities; indeed, it was estimated that 1 of 11 Americans attended at least one of these lectures each year. Their subject matter varied from social issues to travel to reform, but scientific topics were always among the most popular. In this day of watered-down mass entertainment, modern Americans would be amazed by the extent to which these lengthy scientific lectures represented genuine popular entertainment. Somewhat less intellectually challenging were the numerous traveling fairs, circuses, curiosity shows, and dime museums, which, in addition to dioramas of historical events and foreign countries, generally included exhibits on natural history (including strange creatures claimed to be the missing evolutionary link). Although modern critics may scoff at such vulgar enterprises, in their time they reflected a genuine popular desire to share in the fruits of scientific knowledge.[31]

True to the country's long-standing Baconian tradition, most Americans were far more interested in the practical applications of science than in its theoretical underpinnings. They believed with an almost religious fervor that the exciting new scientific discoveries about which they were hearing so much could lead to concrete improvements in their own lives. But material progress was not their only goal. For many centuries, religion and the social traditions associated with it had provided people with all of the answers they needed about the world and their place in it. Science, however, was beginning to replace religion as the primary source of authority. And so in the pervasive search for self-improvement that characterized nineteenth-century culture, science naturally became a key tool for people hoping to enhance their lot in life. Claiming to provide the self-knowledge essential for personal advancement, "sciences" such as mesmerism and phrenology (about which more will be said in Chapter 5) had enjoyed brief periods of wild popularity. But who better to provide the latest scientific expertise about how the mind *really* worked than the newly minted psychologists, cloaked in the mantle of legitimate scientific authority? As the century drew to a close, psychologists began publicly to tout their claim that the qualities of the mind could be measured and that people could potentially use this new knowledge about their own abilities for personal, economic, and even moral advancement. It is therefore not surprising that when the first IQ test appeared on the scene in 1905, it was greeted by an American public primed to embrace its benefits.

Chapter 4

Merit and Social Status in Nineteenth-Century America

A hypothetical time traveler transported from the days of the founding fathers to the dawn of the twentieth century would most likely have been puzzled by the significant changes he observed in the world of science. But if he (yes, the time traveler would have almost certainly been a man) was confused by its science, he would have been utterly dumbfounded by the social milieu that characterized this modern America. At the end of the Revolutionary War, the infant United States had been primarily a nation of farmers and villagers, with political control held firmly in the hands of an intellectual and economic elite. The relatively homogeneous white population was of primarily northern European heritage, and the rate of immigration was low. Under the new Constitution, enslaved blacks were not even recognized as full human beings. Contrast this relatively stable and homogeneous society to the bustling urbanized and industrialized United States of the year 1900. Wealthy capitalists now sat firmly at the top of the economic heap. A strong and upwardly mobile middle class increasingly asserted its influence, while a restive working class simmered beneath. The economic system was fiercely competitive. The relative ethnic homogeneity of 1800 was a thing of the past, swept away by a tidal wave of immigration from southern and eastern Europe. Former slaves and workers imported from Asia added to the polyglot mix.

In this confusing new world, traditional methods of determining social status were swept away. As political democratization, social mobility, and ethnic diversity increased and the newly empowered masses struggled to climb the social ladder, established groups worked fiercely to maintain control. The Puritans had believed that God would reward the virtuous with worldly success, but now science, not religion, seemed to be the ultimate authority. Jefferson had counted on a public-spirited natural aristocracy to guide the new republic. However, in the no-holds-barred capitalist system that dominated the country by the end of the century, self-interest had trumped a commitment to the public good. The old verities were seemingly in shreds. Although Americans were still strongly attached to the idea of merit, the old definitions were no longer working.

As I will demonstrate in the following pages, many found the answer to this dilemma in the emerging concept of intelligence. Speaking at Yale University in 1908, banker Henry Clews gave clear voice to this new definition. "Birth," he proclaimed, "is nothing. . . . Merit is the supreme and only qualification essential to success." He then went on to add, "Intelligence rules worlds and systems of worlds. Here only a natural order of nobility is recognized."[1] Clews's identification of merit with intelligence seemed to offer something to everyone. The concept of intelligence was modern, scientific, and consistent with the latest Darwinian theories. Ordinary people welcomed the idea that their own personal qualities, not accidents of birth, should determine their chances for advancement in the world. The ruling elites, comfortable in the assumption that people similar to themselves would dominate the ranks of the most intelligent, could pay lip service to democratic ideals while keeping the reins of power firmly within their own hands. And so, as we shall see, the social upheavals of nineteenth-century America left the country ripe for the introduction of a tool that purported to objectify judgments of merit by quantifying individual differences in amount of intelligence.[2]

AMERICAN SOCIETY IN TRANSITION

The social history of nineteenth-century America was characterized by ongoing tension between two powerful forces—a rising tide of democratic egalitarianism, on the one hand, and the struggles of elite groups to maintain their position of privilege on the other. In the period before the Civil War, these two competing poles were represented by the Jacksonian Democrats and the Whig establishment. The popular war hero Andrew Jackson (the first American president who was not a member of the gentry) personified the spirit of democracy. As the industrial revolution made its way across the Atlantic, Americans eager for economic advancement began moving from farms and villages into the rapidly growing cities. Others streamed across the Appalachians into the frontier of the newly opened West, forming rough-and-ready societies in which inherited wealth and aristocratic parentage counted for little. And after a long period of relatively low immigration, refugees from German social unrest and the Irish potato famine (many of them desperately poor) began to pour into the United States. These restless movements of people across the ocean, over the mountains, and into the cities disrupted traditional status hierarchies. Now even the humblest schoolchildren learned from their *McGuffey Readers* that "in this free community, there are no privileged orders. Every man finds his level. If he has talents, he will be known and estimated, and rise in the respect and confidence of society."[3]

This new democratic spirit was evident everywhere. Most striking perhaps was the radical extension of the suffrage. In 1790, only Vermont had offered the vote to all white males; by 1840, Rhode Island was the only state still requiring men to own property in order to vote. (At the same time, it is important to note, specific exclusions for women, free blacks, Native Americans, and paupers—all of whom had previously been able to vote in some places—were enshrined into law.) Reformers insisted that education was necessary to help equalize the conditions of all citizens and prepare them for participation in a democracy. And so by 1860, almost 95 percent of the adults in the nonslave states were literate, and nearly all children received at least a few years of schooling.[4]

The new spirit of democracy also led to a different perspective on work. In pre–Revolutionary War America, those viewed as gentlemen had generally been individuals of independent wealth, allowing them the leisure for intellectual pursuits and political service. But Jacksonians regarded such idleness as immoral; virtue was associated instead with the actual, immediate production of goods. Jackson himself did not question the generally accepted belief that different natural endowments would lead to different economic outcomes. But, he asserted, those who were willing to work should be able to rise as far as their own personal talents and energy could take them. The role of government was to level the playing field, to "shower its favors alike on the high and the low, the rich and the poor."[5] Individual merit, not birth, wealth, or social status, should determine a person's position in life.[6]

Just as Andrew Jackson and his Democrats exemplified America's emerging democratic impulse, the Whigs embodied the conservative reaction against democracy's perceived excesses. The Whig party itself was in existence for only about 20 years, from 1834 to 1854; its principles, however, have played an ongoing role in American thought. The Whigs sought a stable social order based on economic expansion and a traditional class structure, with the reins of government held firmly in the hands of the men best endowed socially, economically, and intellectually for positions of leadership. In contrast with their social conservatism, most were economic liberals (as the word was understood at that time). The Whigs believed fervently in the market economy and economic expansion and preached the rhetoric of individual initiative. Because they were convinced that all Americans had been blessed with equal opportunities, they believed that success was due solely to talent, character, and hard work. Failure and poverty, on the other hand, were the inevitable result of laziness and immorality.[7]

The Whigs were at the forefront of an active social reform movement that was very influential in America during the 1820s, 1830s, and 1840s. Consistent with their belief in individual initiative, these reformers regarded personal morality, not the structure of society, as the primary focus of their efforts. Their self-proclaimed mission was to alleviate the misery of society's unfortunates by teaching them the virtues of industry, frugality, self-control, and self-denial. Like their Puritan forbears, however, they assumed that social and economic inequality would remain an intrinsic part of God's order for mankind. This outlook is exemplified in these words from a popular hymn:

> All things bright and beautiful,
> All creatures great and small,
> All things wise and wonderful,
> The Lord God made them all.
> The rich man in his castle,
> The poor man at his gate,
> He made them high and lowly
> And ordered their estate.[8]

The Democrats and the Whigs agreed, then, that personal virtue and hard work—in other words, merit—should govern economic advancement. They differed radically, however, about what the results of such a merit-based society would be. Believing as they did that the playing field was already reasonably level, the Whigs assumed that a merit-based society would leave things just about the way they were. The Democrats, on the other hand, were convinced that the existing social system offered unearned advantages to those in positions of privilege. In the absence of such advantages, they believed, true merit would operate to reduce economic inequality. As we shall see in later chapters, the difference between these two perspectives fuels arguments about the relationship between merit and intelligence to this day.

The rapid pace of social change that characterized the Jacksonian era threatened to career completely out of control in post–Civil War

America. By the end of the nineteenth century, the United States no longer bore any resemblance to Jefferson's agrarian ideal. The country was now fully in the grip of an industrialized, urbanized, fast-paced, and impersonal modern economy, with all of its attendant problems. Factories multiplied in both number and size, and cities filled with what historian Arthur Schlesinger has termed a "rootless, bewildered, unstable population," many "living a scanty and desperate life at day labor."[9] Pictures of these urban slums were disseminated in the popular press (most famously in Jacob Riis's book *How the Other Half Lives*), leading many Americans to fear that the very fabric of their society was under attack.[10]

A dramatic increase in immigration acted like bellows to fan the flames of these fears. Many native-born Americans had felt threatened by the Irish and German immigrants who streamed into the United States in the years before the Civil War. But this earlier alarm was a mere foretaste of the panic created by the massive flood of immigrants, primarily from southern and eastern Europe, who began pouring into America's cities after 1870. During the period between 1880 and 1920, more than 27 million immigrants entered the country; for the sake of comparison, the entire population of the United States in 1900 was only 76 million. In New York, Boston, Chicago, and Milwaukee, more than 70 percent of the residents were immigrants or their children.[11] Not surprisingly, this huge influx of foreigners (many of them poor, uneducated, and Catholic—or, even worse, Jewish) threatened the accustomed power of established groups.

The late nineteenth century was also a time of labor unrest and economic instability. A series of violent labor battles during the late 1870s and 1880s culminated in the bloody Pullman strike of 1894. Indeed, many Americans believed that 1894 was the most difficult year that they had experienced since the Civil War. In addition to labor unrest, Americans also suffered through two major economic panics and their ensuing depressions. The Panic of 1893 and the four-year depression that followed were the worst to date in American history. It is little wonder that, feeling at the mercy of forces beyond their control, even ordinary Americans started to question the adequacy of their traditional democratic institutions.[12]

In this turbulent new world, the Jacksonian argument that America should be a classless society (and the pretension of the Whigs that it already was) began to seem almost quaint. The gulf between the rich and the poor widened dramatically during the closing decades of the nineteenth century. When we think of the Gilded Age, the images that come to mind are those of unfettered capitalism, powerful robber barons, the violent suppression of labor unrest, and virulent racism. Many thinkers of the day justified the blatant inequities of this system with the convenient philosophy of Social Darwinism, which appealed to the scientific spirit of the era by giving to the competitive struggle the force of natural law. Progressive reformers, somewhat more socially conscious, sought to temper the most egregious inequalities of raw capitalism. But, as we shall see, neither the Social Darwinists nor the Progressives had any intention of relinquishing their own positions of power. And for both groups, the concept of intelligence was to become a useful tool for justifying and maintaining their privileges.

THE PROTECTION OF PRIVILEGE

Darwin's theory of evolution sent shock waves through Western culture from which it has still not recovered. And the impact of this shock extended far beyond the field of biology. The ink had hardly dried on *The Origin of Species* before social theorists, Herbert Spencer foremost among them, began reexamining the entire structure of society through the lens of evolutionary theory. The principles of natural selection and survival of the fittest, these theorists asserted, were not confined to the development of biological structures; they also explained the origin of social problems and determined their solutions. The resulting sociological theory became known as Social Darwinism (though, as I have previously noted, it might better have been termed Social Spencerism). According to this theory, individuals who were best adapted to their environments were destined to succeed. The progress of the human race required that the weaker simply be allowed to fall by the wayside. This process was viewed as natural, rational, and inevitable, putting the imprimatur of natural law on the competitive modern capitalist economy.

Social Darwinism's most vigorous and influential American proponent was Yale sociologist William Graham Sumner. In Sumner's view, the competitive struggle was ordained by nature; if left unfettered, this struggle would eventually draw all of society upward. Attempts to interfere with this process out of some misguided sense of social justice would be not only unproductive but actually immoral. Indeed, asserted Sumner, "it would be hard to find a single instance of a direct assault by positive effort upon poverty, vice, and misery which has not either failed or . . . has not entailed other evils greater than the one which it removed."[13] Individuals must be left entirely free to rise or fall on the basis of their own merit. And merit, in the worldview of Social Darwinism, was adaptive fitness—or, as Spencer had defined it, intelligence.

Jefferson had assumed that his natural aristocrats, those talented and virtuous exemplars of merit, would be socially responsible and civic-minded, unselfishly using their talents for the greater good of society. But in this new, highly competitive and individualistic society, the word "merit" was coming to take on a very different meaning. As historian David Hogan has ably demonstrated, by the middle of the nineteenth century, the primary focus of merit had shifted from the political realm to the entrepreneurial. Rather than obligating one to contribute to the broader social good, extraordinary merit was now equated with personal financial success. Jefferson's natural aristocracy of talents and virtues had been reduced to a meritocracy based solely on ability and aimed single-mindedly toward financial advancement.[14]

After an initial period of resistance, many socially conservative, mainstream Protestant churches seized eagerly on Social Darwinist ideology. Calvinists had long assumed that God would reward His own with worldly success. Modern clergymen repackaged this Puritan belief in more objective, scientific language designed to appeal to modern sensibilities. One of the most vociferous of these religious promoters of the doctrine of Social Darwinism was Congregationalist clergyman Josiah Strong. So influential were his writings that the librarian of Congress once compared their impact with that of *Uncle Tom's Cabin*. Strong was contemptuous of those who argued for a more equalitarian society. "So long as the individual members of classes easily rise or fall from one to the other, by virtue of their own acts," he proclaimed, "such classes are neither unrepublican nor unsafe."[15] He also believed strongly in the innate superiority of the Anglo-Saxon race and used Darwin's theory of natural selection to support his views. Darwin would have to agree, he said, that the northern European races represented the epitome of evolutionary advancement, characterized by physical fitness, vigor, and—most important of all—intelligence.

The ideology of Social Darwinism probably sounds harsh and strident to most modern ears (although it still finds a happy home in much of conservative talk radio). In contrast, the reformers of the Progressive movement couched their beliefs in the language of social concern. This reform movement, which developed as a reaction against the unbridled capitalism of the Gilded Age, got its start during the last few decades of the nineteenth century and maintained its influence and vitality into the early decades of the twentieth. Unlike the Social Darwinists, Progressives believed that values other than self-interest were required in public life. Many were proponents of the Social Gospel, which emphasized the brotherhood of *all* men under the love of Christ. But whether religious or secular in their motivations, most Progressive reformers interpreted evolution very differently than did the Social Darwinists. Noting that Darwin's theory was based on the adaptation of organisms to their environment, they reasoned that changes in the environment should lead eventually to significant improvement in the human race itself. Rather than focusing on its competitive aspects, they stressed evolution's potential to increase cooperation between people.[16]

Unlike the heartless Social Darwinists, the Progressives considered themselves to be humanitarians. But they were also elitists. Progressive reformers came primarily from the same comfortable social strata as had the reformers of the pre–Civil War era. Most lived in the northeast, most were middle class (many of them rising professionals), and they were overwhelmingly white and Protestant. As befit their social status, these reformers were secure in their positions and supremely confident of the correctness of their views. More than one historian has observed that they were worthy successors to the old New England Calvinist elect, and, as Nicholas Lemann has suggested, they displayed "a Puritan attraction to improvement of the human state through system and order."[17]

Progressive reformers believed that it was possible to improve the lot of everyone by using principles of efficiency and scientific management to increase the size of the total economic pie. Increased order and control—under the guidance of experts such as themselves, of course—would provide the necessary corrective to a society buffeted by rapid industrialization, massive immigration, and grinding urban poverty. The Progressives had an absolute mania for efficiency; for many, in fact, efficient and good were virtually synonymous. And they believed fervently in the power of science to improve society. Advocating the application of scientific principles to social problems and industrial management, these reformers had an almost touching belief in the power of numbers, measurement, and statistics. Scientific techniques could efficiently sort people into the jobs for which they were best suited. Schools could be standardized. Unsurprisingly, it was Progressive reformers who were responsible for such now-familiar practices as age grading, the measurement of student performance, and mechanisms for educational accountability.

Although sympathetic to the plight of the poor, Progressive reformers rarely raised questions about the basic structure of their society. In fact, the reforms that they advocated actually consolidated rather than threatened the power of middle-class, respectable, and well-educated experts such as themselves. Distrustful of the excesses of democracy and concerned about good government, they sought to limit voting rights to those whom they considered worthy. Poll taxes, literacy tests, and complex voter registration procedures were all typical Progressive reforms. But perhaps the quintessential Progressive program was civil service reform. Marrying their desire for a competent government with their belief in scientific efficiency, these reformers mounted a successful campaign to enact legislation mandating that government positions be awarded on the basis of merit (meaning generally scores on a test) rather than patronage.

It is clear that many of these middle-class reformers actually feared the very masses whose lives their reforms were intended to improve. Among more than a few, this distrust of democracy merged into sentiments that were frankly racist and xenophobic. It is no accident that Progressives played a key role in the drastic restrictions in immigration legislated in the early 1920s. Many were also ardent eugenicists, convinced that the improvement of the race required the sterilization of individuals thought to be feebleminded, defective, or criminal. With our sensibilities formed by the horrors of Nazism, it is difficult for modern Americans to believe that eugenic principles were once considered eminently respectable. But, as we shall see in later chapters, it was these thoroughly respectable Progressives who during the 1910s and 1920s were to use the new technology of IQ testing to promote policies that excluded, segregated, or even sterilized the "undesirables" among us.

THE DEMOCRATIC SENSE OF SELF

Established groups responded to the social turmoil of late nineteenth-century America by striving to protect their own privileges and lobbying to restrict the perceived excesses of democracy. But the democratic impulse that had been unleashed by the Great Awakening, the American Revolution, and Jacksonian politics was not easily squelched. During the course of the century, this stubborn democratic spirit merged with an increasing fascination with the idea of the self to create a peculiarly American mix that might be termed "democratic selfhood." This democratic self (usually a man, of course) was a unique individual—self-determining, self-aware, free from the expectations of the past, and eager to use his own particular talents to forge his way in life. Interestingly, many ardent democrats came to see IQ testing as a tool that might assist them in this quest.

In his biography of Western writer Wallace Stegner (who wrote in the twentieth century but whose work reflected the continuing influence of the frontier spirit), Jackson Benson observed that Americans, especially Westerners, have long been preoccupied with two primary questions: "Who am I?" and "Where do I belong?" "As banal as they may sound," he goes on to say, "these have been the key questions for Americans, who are not assigned roles as they may be in other, more settled societies, but must find them for themselves."[18] In other words, Americans need to create their own selves. And certainly a virtual obsession with the self is one of the most salient characteristics of our modern culture. This is well illustrated by the fact that my edition of the *Webster's New World Dictionary* lists nearly 150 entries containing the word "self," ranging from "self-abasement" to "self-winding."[19]

Readers may therefore be surprised to learn that the concept of the self barely even existed prior to the Enlightenment. Traditionally, human beings had perceived themselves as links in the Great Chain of Being, interlocking components in an orderly, hierarchical universe in which each person remained content in his or her own preordained position. People identified themselves primarily as members of communities, not as individuals.[20] (Indeed, this communitarian view still prevails in many non-Western cultures.) It was John Locke who first articulated the Western idea of the self in its modern form. Locke equated the self with rationality and consciousness (including self-consciousness), qualities that made possible memory of one's past experiences and thus a sense of unique personal identity.[21] His emphasis on the personal self strongly influenced the thinkers of the Enlightenment, including our own founding fathers, with their famous proclamation of the natural rights of each individual human being and their focus on conscious self-development and self-improvement.

But it was in the Romantic movement of the nineteenth century that the celebration of the individual self flowered most fully. The core of romanticism was an appreciation of the qualities of each individual person and an encouragement—indeed, one could even say a moral duty—to develop one's own unique identity to its fullest. The American prophet of the Romantic movement was Ralph Waldo Emerson, who famously wrote in his journal in 1827, "It is the age of the first person singular."[22] In his well-known 1837 address "The American Scholar," he went on to proclaim, "Another sign of our times . . . is the new importance given to the single person. . . . The world is nothing, the man is all."[23] If Emerson was the prophet of romantic individualism, then Walt Whitman was its poet. "I celebrate myself, and sing myself," he wrote in *Leaves of Grass*. "I exist as I am, that is enough."[24]

This glorification of individual potential contributed to the uniquely American preoccupation with self-knowledge and self-improvement. The quest to understand one's own interior self has a long tradition in American culture. The early Puritans taught that believers must engage in constant self-reflection in order to supervise their own state of grace. Similarly, evangelist John Wesley's "method" (from which Methodism received its name) involved continual self-examination, with converts being required methodically to monitor their own conduct and their relationship with God. Self-reflection and self-knowledge had more worldly applications as well. As we shall see in the next chapter, for example, the promise that it would lead to improved self-understanding helped drive the wildly popular phrenological movement of the mid-nineteenth century. George Combe, one of the movement's most influential advocates, wrote that phrenology's goal was to provide "knowledge of our own constitution . . . with a view of regulating our conduct according to rules drawn from such information."[25] Phrenology eventually faded from the scene, but the desire for fuller self-understanding did not.

Whether religious or secular in their motivation, few of these apostles of self-reflection advocated self-understanding purely for its own sake. The goal of self-knowledge was self-improvement. Benjamin Franklin was of course the first popular American prophet of self-improvement. Virtually all of us are familiar with the aphorisms of *Poor Richard's Almanack,* in which Franklin advised his readers "'Tis a laudable ambition that aims at being better than his neighbors" and "God helps them that help themselves."[26] Franklin even formed a self-improvement society in Philadelphia called the Junto.[27] Self-culture and self-improvement were also trademarks of the Transcendentalists. Through self-culture, they proclaimed, even ordinary Americans could develop their unique identities and thus achieve their own personal destinies. In his famous 1838 lecture on "Self-Culture," Unitarian minister and Emerson friend William Ellery Channing wrote that "in this country the mass of people are distinguished by possessing means of improvement, of self-culture, possessed nowhere else." Even common laborers, he added, had the means to "make the best and most of the powers which God has given us."[28]

This national obsession with self-knowledge, self-culture, and self-improvement reached its natural culmination in the cult of the self-made man. What idea could be more quintessentially American? By the dint of hard work and good character, a boy (yes, it was always a boy) from even the most humble of circumstances could hope to scale the pinnacles of wealth and influence. Our national mythology abounds with such examples. Think of "Honest Abe" Lincoln, studying by candlelight in his log cabin, or plucky Scottish immigrant Andrew Carnegie, arriving penniless in New York at the age of twelve and going on to achieve unfathomable wealth. The developing competitive market economy required individual initiative and a relentless focus on personal achievement. The mythology of the self-made man extolled these traits in a way that fed the imaginations and nurtured the hopes of young men throughout the country.[29]

It was Henry Clay who first used the term "self-made man," in a speech to the Senate in February 1832. But Clay had simply coined a term for a concept that was already in wide currency. *Poor Richard's Almanack,* for example, is a virtual Bible for a poor boy hoping to achieve success. ("Early to bed, early to rise, makes a man healthy, wealthy, and wise."[30]) Generations of young Americans were raised on the *McGuffey Readers,* honing their reading skills on such sentiments as, "The road to wealth, to honor, to usefulness, and happiness, is open to all, and all who will, may enter upon it with the almost certain prospect of success."[31] But it was in the years following the Civil War that the cult of the self-made man achieved its firmest grip on the American imagination. In the competitive frenzy of the Gilded Age, business leaders and industrial tycoons became the new national heroes. Most men in positions of wealth and influence had in fact started life in relatively comfortable circumstances; enough poor immigrants or farm boys managed to pull themselves up by their bootstraps, however, to keep the myth alive. This mythology found its quintessential expression in the series of 107 books written by Unitarian clergyman Horatio Alger. Alger's books (which sold a total of more than 17 million copies) famously told the stories of poor boys (many of them penniless orphans) who achieved astounding success through the exercise of perseverance, courage, frugality, and hard work.[32]

The evolving concept of intelligence seemed to have much to offer to a society focused so intensely on self-knowledge, self-improvement, and self-advancement. Most of us will admit to an uneasy fascination with the workings of our own minds, but self-knowledge potentially offers benefits beyond the satisfaction of simple curiosity. The upheavals of the nineteenth century had overturned traditional assumptions about how an individual's choices of work, marriage partner, and social behavior should be determined. The ideology of the self-made man assured young Americans that they could rise in the world as high as their own personal talents might take them. But how could they best take advantage of these new choices and opportunities for mobility? How might they establish a sense of personal identity in such an open society, with few traditional guideposts to follow? Many came to believe that a better understanding of their own mental abilities might assist them with these crucial choices.

The Progressive quest for social control and the democratic search for self-determination seem in many ways to be in direct opposition to one another. One group, after all, was determined to open up opportunities for all citizens, while the other focused on strategies for rationalizing and controlling social advancement. But these two movements in fact had at least one very important principle in common: the ideal of meritocracy. Progressives, Social Darwinists, and democrats alike insisted that individual merit, not family history, inherited position, or connections in high places, should determine a person's chances in life. And increasingly, all of these groups came to associate the idea of merit with the concept of intelligence. I believe it is no accident that the democratic understanding of the self as a unique entity and the scientific understanding of intelligence as a unitary, biologically based trait developed in parallel with one another. The modern concept of intelligence focuses not on individuals' commonalities but on their differences—differences that have come to be central to our sense of personal identity, or selfhood.

In 1887, Edward Bellamy published a utopian novel called *Looking Backward, 2000–1887*. It quickly became one of the most popular books of the late nineteenth century, selling more than a half million copies in the first decade after its release. Interested readers flocked to the 162 Nationalist Clubs that arose spontaneously to explore and discuss Bellamy's ideas. *Looking Backward* provides an almost perfect example of how the ideals of democratic self-determination and scientific social control came together during this era. At first glance, Bellamy's utopian society would seem to have been admirably democratic. Opportunities for desirable jobs were equally available to all qualified individuals. All workers received the same pay, theoretically eliminating class conflict and economic hierarchies. But this supposedly free and egalitarian society was in fact tightly controlled. The national government regulated all industry and apportioned jobs on the basis of demonstrated abilities. Women were encouraged to seek out the best and noblest men as reproductive partners, ensuring the eugenic progress of the race. To modern eyes, the utopia of *Looking Backward* was a Progressive's dream turned nightmare.[33]

In 1887, when Bellamy's book was published, Alfred Binet's scales of intelligence were still nearly 20 years in the future. But if Bellamy had written *Looking Backward* two decades later, I have little doubt that this newly developed IQ test would have played a central role in his utopian system. This visionary writer would have immediately recognized that IQ scores could provide an inarguably scientific basis for assigning individuals to the jobs best suited to their particular abilities and guiding them in making healthy eugenic choices. *Looking Backward* described the perfect merit-based society. Intelligence tests would have been the ideal technology for ensuring that this soulless utopia remained pure.

Chapter 5

Phrenology: A Precursor to IQ Testing

By the middle of the nineteenth century, the social and scientific changes that paved the way for our modern concept of intelligence were already well under way. Biologists were investigating the physical properties of the human brain and bandying about interesting new ideas about evolution. Jacksonian Democrats had taken charge of the government, and the popular imagination was afire with the belief that ordinary men could create their own futures. Respectable middle-class reformers were beginning to look critically at education and at the treatment of the insane and the defective, working to improve social conditions while at the same time assuming that they themselves would remain firmly in control of the system. It was into this potent mix that the phenomenon of phrenology exploded.

Today, those few Americans who have even heard of phrenology—the practice of reading mental traits from bumps on the skull—regard it as one of those unaccountable nineteenth-century enthusiasms, foisted on a gullible public by traveling snake oil salesmen and completely divorced from the spirit of proper science. The real story of phrenology, however, is much more complex and far more interesting. Far from being viewed as antiscientific, phrenology was avidly embraced by some of the finest minds of the day, its powers extolled by both prominent reformers and the upwardly striving citizens of a newly democratic America. The basic tenets of phrenology were ultimately proved to be wrong. But its insistence that the human mind could be objectively measured, and that measured individual differences in mental functioning could guide important life choices, passed into the larger culture, finding a natural home in the early twentieth century with the introduction of the IQ test. Rather than being a mere curiosity from a credulous past, the phrenology movement was actually the first step in America's love affair with intelligence testing. Its history provides a cautionary preview of the power of social context to determine perceptions of supposedly objective reality—a caution that it would be wise to keep in mind as we proceed with our story of intelligence.

THE SCIENTIFIC BASIS OF PHRENOLOGY

As far back as the days of Plato and Aristotle, Western thinkers have speculated about the connections between physical appearance and psychological characteristics. Medieval theologians taught that God had purposely provided special exterior marks or signs to reveal the inner nature of things (a belief that makes more understandable many medieval superstitions). These attempts to connect internal qualities with external appearances assumed a more recognizably modern form in the work of an eighteenth-century Swiss scientist, Johann Caspar Lavater. Basing his conclusions on empirical observations, Lavater asserted that there were lawful regularities between certain physical structures (mainly in the face) and mental qualities of temperament and character. His system, which he labeled physiognomy, elicited a great deal of interest among the educated classes in both Europe and America. Although his claims did not long hold up to objective scrutiny, Lavater's physiognomic theories prefigured the modern conception of intelligence in two important ways: he explicitly connected mental qualities with physical structures, and he focused on differences between individuals rather than on their commonalities.[1]

Phrenology was a somewhat more systematized and sophisticated version of physiognomy. The founder of scientific phrenology was German anatomist Franz Joseph Gall, who lived from 1758 until 1828. Gall was a respected scientist, well known for his anatomical skills. A specialist in the structures of the head and the brain, he carefully studied and compared the brains of different animals and those of various groups of humans, including children, old people, and individuals who had suffered neurological damage. Gall was particularly interested in the relationship between the physical characteristics of the skull and various mental traits, a fascination that reportedly stemmed from observations he had made on his classmates while still a schoolboy. Although he ridiculed Lavater's popularized physiognomy, there is little doubt that he was influenced by the physiognomic views then current in his society.[2]

Gall's system, which he labeled phrenology, was based on four fundamental assumptions. First, he was convinced that the brain was the organ of the mind. Although today we take this understanding for granted, the connection between mind and brain was far from self-evident at the end of the eighteenth century. Second, Gall asserted that each faculty (or mental ability) had its own organ in the brain (an idea that in much more sophisticated and nuanced form is accepted today as localization of brain function). Third, he believed that the size of each brain organ reflected the strength of its associated faculty, and finally, he assumed that the size of the underlying organ could be determined by measuring subtle bumps on the skull. Gall's list of mental faculties was drawn from the work of Thomas Reid, one of the foremost thinkers of his day and, as we have seen, the founder of common sense philosophy. A representative sample of these faculties includes such qualities as abstraction, activity, attention, consciousness, deliberation, gratitude, imitation, judgment, memory, reasoning, moral faculty, reflection, and thirst.

Although Gall took his list of mental faculties from Reid, he insisted that his work was empirical rather than philosophical. He conducted his investigations by collecting skull measurements from people of all types and then seeking to uncover the relationships between these phrenological measures and behaviors reflecting the assumed underlying traits. It is clear to us now, of course, that the unavailability of appropriate statistical tools to quantify these supposed correlations (tools that were not developed until the 1870s) left Gall's conclusions vulnerable to selective interpretation, overreliance on anecdotes, and inadequate attention to contrary data. However, the unsophisticated—and ultimately erroneous—nature of his data analysis does not change the fact that Gall's intent was to bring the tools of science to the study of the human mind.

Gall introduced his phrenological theories to the public in a series of lectures in various European cities between 1800 and 1810. These lectures attracted widespread interest and were in general quite well received. However, Gall was not particularly interested in the practical application of his theories. He considered himself first and foremost to be a scientist—and his legacy here is in fact substantial. Gall was among the first to bring the methods of science to the study of the human mind and to engage in objective and systematic attempts to measure mental traits. And rather than focusing on the mind in general, he emphasized the identification of individual differences between people. These ideas, quite radical for their time, are absolutely fundamental to our modern concepts of intelligence and its measurement.[3]

THE POPULARIZATION OF PHRENOLOGY

Gall's intention had been to develop phrenology as a science, and he looked askance at attempts to popularize his new discipline. This task was thus left to two of his followers, Joseph Gaspar Spurzheim and George Combe. Spurzheim had begun studying with Gall in 1800, and for the next 10 years the two had lectured together throughout Europe. Unlike Gall, however, Spurzheim was interested mainly in the social implications of phrenology; he viewed the discipline primarily as a tool for human betterment. Although he acknowledged that an individual's complement of faculties was given at birth, Spurzheim was convinced that through education and effort people could strengthen these innate qualities and bring them into better balance. Not surprisingly, he was active in a number of social reform movements, including penology, education, and the care of the insane. Spurzheim's enthusiastic and highly successful promotion of phrenology came to an untimely end in 1832, when he died suddenly while on a lecture tour in Boston.[4]

George Combe was a young lawyer who had first heard Spurzheim's lectures in Edinburgh during 1814 and 1815. Although initially skeptical of Spurzheim's claims, he was soon persuaded to engage in his own three-year study of phrenology; by the time he completed these studies, he had become an enthusiastic convert to the movement. Combe then began to write and lecture about phrenology on his own, and after the death of Spurzheim he became the movement's foremost proponent. Combe's most famous book, *The Constitution of Man,* was originally published in Edinburgh in 1828 and released in an inexpensive popular edition in 1836. The book was known, at least by reputation, to virtually every literate person in America and Britain; some claim that its sales during this period were exceeded only by those of the Bible, *Pilgrim's Progress,* and *Robinson Crusoe.*[5] No lesser personages than Queen Victoria and Prince Albert were impressed by his work. They had two of their sons phrenologized and even employed a phrenologist as tutor to several of the royal children.[6]

Like Spurzheim, Combe had a basically optimistic view of human nature. Progress was mankind's natural state and human history a gradual ascent through eras of savagery, barbarism, and chivalry to the current age of science. Mankind, he proclaimed, now stood on the brink of a new era, in which the self-understanding made possible by phrenology promised to advance the human race to heights previously unimagined. This optimistic belief in human potential led Combe, like Spurzheim, to support efforts at social reform. And unlike many of his contemporaries, Combe believed that potential could be found in the working class and non-European races. "If mankind at large . . . had been intended for mere hewers of wood and drawers of water," he wrote, "I do not believe that the moral and intellectual faculties which they unquestionably possess, would have been bestowed on them. . . . I cannot subscribe to the doctrine of their permanent incapacity."[7]

Although Combe continually emphasized the scientific foundation of phrenology, *The Constitution of Man* actually reads more like a treatise on natural religion than a scientific exposition. Combe explained that God had created a world in which a natural harmony exists between the mental faculties of individual human beings and the demands of the external world. One need only apply the wonders of phrenological science to discover the pursuits for which he or she was best suited by nature. Living in harmony with God's plan would inevitably lead to material success for individuals and a more just society for all. *The Constitution of Man* was a powerful confluence of science, religion, and self-improvement, a combination that would prove irresistible to our practical-minded, democratic, and devout young nation.

PHRENOLOGY IN AMERICA

By 1820, information about the wonders of phrenology was beginning to filter across the Atlantic. Physicians were among the first Americans to respond positively to the claims of this new science. Two of the most prominent of these, Charles Caldwell and John Bell (both former students of the illustrious physician Benjamin Rush), went on to establish the nation's first phrenological society in Philadelphia in 1822. It was not until the early 1830s, however, that American interest in phrenology really took off, fueled by the excitement of Spurzheim's 1832 lecture tour. This tour was a genuine popular sensation. Spurzheim's every word was breathlessly reported in the press, and his lectures at Yale and Harvard attracted enormous crowds. Possibly as a result of the strain of his nightly lectures in Cambridge, Spurzheim contracted a fever and died suddenly. On the day he was buried, the bells of the city tolled in his memory, and more than 3,000 people attended his funeral in Boston. Combe's 1838 lecture tour created an almost equal sensation. His enthusiastic audiences included physicians, ministers, writers, educators, and reformers, and these contacts led to friendships with many of the most important intellectuals of the day.[8]

At first phrenology appealed mainly to the educated classes. Although many intellectuals remained skeptical of its claims, others were convinced that this new discipline offered an objective, scientific tool for attacking vexing social problems. Psychologists Alexander Bain and Herbert Spencer, both very influential in America, were early advocates of phrenology in Europe. Prominent American adherents of the movement included psychologist William James, reformers Horace Mann and Samuel Gridley Howe, ministers Henry Ward Beecher and William Ellery Channing, historian George Bancroft, writers Walt Whitman, Edgar Allan Poe, and Herman Melville, and public figures Daniel Webster and Nicholas Biddle. Most American presidents during this period submitted their heads to the calipers for measurement, and popular magazines reported the results. Both Clara Barton and Bernard Baruch credited phrenologists with providing the advice that helped them embark on their illustrious lifelong careers.[9]

Not surprisingly, given the examples set by Spurzheim and Combe, many of America's earliest and most enthusiastic advocates of phrenology were social reformers, the most notable of whom were probably Samuel Gridley Howe and Horace Mann. Mann is still famous for his pioneering work in the reform of American education; what is less well known is that he based many of his instructional theories on the principles of phrenology. Howe was an early advocate for the rights of people with disabilities. Among other accomplishments, he established innovative schools in Massachusetts for the education of the deaf, the blind, and individuals with mental deficiencies. (Howe, in fact, trained Anne Sullivan, the famous teacher of Helen Keller, and Sullivan used his principles, many of them grounded in phrenology, in devising treatment strategies for her young pupil.) Howe believed that mental deficiency was due to an underdevelopment of the appropriate mental faculties. With proper phrenological guidance, he was convinced, such deficiencies could be virtually eliminated.

Phrenology's appeal for these reformers is easy to understand. The discipline claimed to be scientific and objective, providing what appeared to be a solid empirical grounding for social reform. And, at least as articulated by Spurzheim and Combe, it took a very optimistic view of the possibilities for human progress. Reformers were hopeful that the techniques of phrenology would give them effective tools for strengthening undeveloped faculties and helping people to develop their full, untapped potential. But although reformist, phrenology was safely nonradical. Certainly people from all walks of life had the potential to benefit from its guidance, but few advocates suggested that individual talents would ever be equally distributed. Indeed, one could even argue that phrenological practices could make the poor and the defective more functional and therefore less threatening to the established order. Phrenology therefore appeared to offer a safe, effective, and scientific method for maintaining benevolent control over the accustomed social order.

Social reformers may have been interested in phrenology primarily because it promised moral and mental uplift to the disadvantaged. But the discipline appealed strongly to ordinary Americans as well. Much of this popular excitement can be traced to the firm of Fowler and Wells. Orson Fowler was introduced to phrenology as a young divinity student in the early 1830s. Impressed with the potential of this new science to improve the lives of everyday people, he and his brother Lorenzo soon began spreading the gospel of phrenology throughout the northeast. From these rather modest beginnings sprang the enormously influential phrenological firm of Fowler and Wells, with offices in New York, Boston, and Philadelphia. The firm performed thousands of phrenological readings of leading citizens. It published the *American Phrenological Journal,* which by 1847 boasted one of the largest circulations of any periodical in America. The Fowlers and their colleagues wrote numerous books, including guides to health and child-rearing and charts to help readers select an appropriate vocation—or a compatible spouse. The firm sold phrenological paraphernalia. It trained phrenologists, booked lectures, and provided guidance on how to establish local phrenological societies. Although competing phrenological businesses soon appeared, it was the firm of Fowler and Wells that made phrenology a national industry.[10]

Most of the larger cities in the United States soon had practicing phrenologists who maintained offices in which they administered phrenological examinations, dispensed practical advice, conducted lectures and demonstrations, and sold books and supplies. The city of Charleston alone supported four such phrenologists during the 1830s and 1840s. Bookshops carried publications about phrenology, and local literary and scientific societies discussed its latest claims and findings. Many cities also had museums displaying collections of skulls and phrenological equipment; later in the century, the popular dime museums brought these exhibits into smaller cities and towns as well. But access to phrenology was by no means confined to cities. During the middle years of the nineteenth century, a network of itinerant phrenologists roamed the United States, their travels bringing them into virtually every crossroads town and village in America. Many of these traveling phrenologists were completely uneducated, inflating their credentials simply to con money from a gullible public. Others, however, had been trained by such respectable firms as Fowler and Wells and regarded themselves as serious professionals.

In essence, phrenologists were the family or vocational counselors of their era. Many people sought out these practical phrenologists for vocational guidance. Practitioners matched individuals to the most appropriate careers on the basis of specific aptitudes revealed by phrenological examination. Prominent phrenologists also produced a number of self-help books outlining the phrenological characteristics required in various occupations; among the most popular of these were Fowler and Wells's *New Illustrated Self-Instructor in Phrenology and Physiology* (written in 1859) and their colleague Nelson Sizer's 1877 *Choice of Pursuits, or What to Do and Why.*[11] Fowler and Wells also marketed phrenology to businessmen, promoting their discipline as a valuable tool in employee selection. In fact, some want ads of the period specified that applicants must submit phrenological charts along with their application forms.

But phrenologists did not confine their advice to vocational counseling. A proper match of phrenological charts could help one to choose the most compatible marriage partner. Phrenologists provided advice to parents about child-rearing and offered prescriptions for maintaining good health. The Fowlers themselves shunned alcohol and were avid followers of Sylvester Graham's famous diet of whole grains and vegetables. Over time, phrenology allied itself with such popular health movements as temperance, vegetarianism, and mesmerism. Phrenologists even made pronouncements about etiquette; Samuel Roberts Wells of the firm Fowler and Wells was the author of the popular etiquette manual *How to Behave* (written in 1857).[12]

Phrenology seemingly had much to offer to upwardly striving Americans. It was entertaining, easy to learn, and could be understood by almost everyone. It purported to be scientific during a period in which popular interest in science was exploding. Most important, it promised to help ambitious Americans make the most of the new opportunities available to them. What vocation should I follow? Who should I marry? How should I raise my children? How should I behave in public? Tradition might no longer provide satisfactory answers to these questions, but phrenologists claimed that they could. In the words of an advertisement from Fowler and Wells, "A correct Phrenological examination will teach, with SCIENTIFIC CERTAINTY, that most useful of all knowledge—YOURSELF; YOUR DEFECTS, and how to obviate them; your EXCELLENCES, and how to make the most of them; your NATURAL TALENTS, and thereby in what spheres and pursuits you can best succeed."[13] And the evidence suggests that many of its most skilled practitioners used their well-developed powers of observation and deep knowledge of human psychology to provide advice that was genuinely helpful to its recipients.

THE LEGACY OF PHRENOLOGY

Phrenology's hold on the intellectual classes lasted little more than a generation. The work of biologist Pierre Flourens, whose surgical ablations of animal brains failed to yield the results that Gall had predicted, seriously eroded its purported scientific foundations. Although Gall tried to counter these new discoveries, by the 1840s Flourens's findings had become widely accepted in the scientific community. Religious leaders, horrified by Combe's apparently naturalistic religion, added their own challenges to phrenology's respectability. But perhaps most damaging, in the eyes of the sophisticated, was the movement's increasing popularization and perceived vulgarization. Itinerant lecturers, many of them poorly trained, roamed the countryside dispensing their nickel pamphlets and dime charts, their special hats and lotions purporting to develop parts of the brain. As historian J. D. Davies has observed, over time what had been a mainstream, respectable movement was left with only its eccentricities.[14] By the time of the Civil War, few educated people any longer placed credence in phrenology.

But the disenchantment of the intellectuals did little to dampen the enthusiasm of ordinary Americans. Phrenology's popular appeal remained potent at least into the 1880s. One phrenological journal continued publication well into the twentieth century, and the firm of Fowler and Wells (and its associated American Institute of Phrenology) remained in existence, though in a much reduced form, into the 1930s. A phrenological vocational guidance clinic was operating in Minneapolis as late as the 1930s. And in 1931, an inventor named Henry Laverty developed a psychograph machine designed to be used for phrenological measurements and vocational guidance. Laverty actually sold 45 of these machines to various businesses and even exhibited his invention at the 1933 World's Fair.[15] The continuing popularity of phrenology, even in the face of its complete loss of intellectual and scientific respectability, is a testament to the strength of the human needs that it claimed to fill.

Several historians, most notably Roger Cooter and John O'Donnell, have observed that the science of IQ took up where phrenology left off at the end of the nineteenth century. The continuities between the two concepts are in fact striking. Most important is the basic idea, first clearly articulated by Gall and now fundamental to modern psychology, that human behavior can be explained by the properties of the brain. If this is true, then measuring aspects of the mind, or brain, should provide an objective basis for the prediction and control of behavior. No idea could be more fundamental to the enterprise of IQ testing. Second, unlike the philosophers of their day, phrenologists focused on individual differences rather than on human commonalities. As we have seen, it is precisely this focus on human variability that distinguishes the modern concept of intelligence from the older idea of the intellect. Finally, like the IQ testers who succeeded them, phrenologists were utterly practical.

By collecting small amounts of very specific information, they believed that they could rapidly make accurate predictions of great personal significance—predictions that satisfied natural human curiosity about psychological functioning, suggested avenues for self-improvement, and provided a scientific basis for social engineering. A few decades later, these same claims would fuel the enthusiastic popular reception of IQ testing in America.[16]

There are of course some crucial differences between phrenology and IQ testing. The most obvious is that the scientific foundation of phrenology has been utterly discredited. The two disciplines also differ in their outlook on human nature and human potential. Phrenology came to prominence during a time when the prevailing scientific theories were informed by the optimistic, environmentally informed work of Lamarck; the IQ testing enterprise, on the other hand, arose during a much more deterministic and pessimistic era. But the parallels between the two disciplines remain striking. Both phrenology and IQ testing perfectly fit the spirit of their times by providing a scientific explanation for human behavior and by offering an attractive and purportedly effective tool for reformers concerned with social control and for ordinary people bent on self-improvement. The story of phrenology provides a cautionary reminder about the power of social context to affect our perceptions of objective reality. And it raises the question of whether our current love affair with IQ testing is due more to its scientific validity or to the fact that it conforms so neatly to the social and cultural characteristics of our era.

Chapter 6

Intelligence and Its Measurement

It should be clear by this point in our discussion that, far from being as "universal and ancient as any understanding about the state of being human," as the authors of *The Bell Curve* so confidently asserted, the concept of intelligence is indeed a "brashing modern notion."[1] Of course, people have always pondered the workings of their own minds. But throughout most of human history, speculation about the functioning of the mind and the nature of reason, or intellect, had been the province of theologians and philosophers. Reason—a gift bestowed by God on all normal human beings—was mankind's link with the divine and the foundation of all moral understanding. As such, the intellect was an exclusively human *quality*, not a *quantity* shared by all living beings. By the closing decades of the nineteenth century, however, the venerable construct of the intellect had been largely supplanted by the modern notion of intelligence. Human beings and their behavior were now objects of legitimate *scientific* inquiry, and intelligence was conceived as an evolutionary-based, biologically determined property of the brain. Animals, groups of people, and individuals could be arrayed along a single continuum of intellectual ability, with higher levels of intelligence indicating a greater degree of adaptive fitness.

But there was one major problem with this developing concept of intelligence. Although its proponents all agreed that intelligence was a concrete, brain-based characteristic that varied between individuals, no one had yet found a way to measure it. In his 1859 text *The Emotions and the Will,* for example, psychologist Alexander Bain lamented that "to come now to Mental Qualities, there is an almost total absence of numerical or measured estimates."[2] A man ahead of his time, Bain went on to discuss the possibility of developing tests of ability and aptitude and foresaw their application in training, industry, and the military. But in the absence of any such practical measures, the concept of intelligence as an evolutionary, biologically based, and individually variable quality remained a purely theoretical construct.

THE MENTAL TESTING MOVEMENT

The failure to develop practical measures of intelligence during the nineteenth century was not for lack of trying. Mental tests and examinations of various sorts had been around for centuries. In fact, records of examinations for "idiocy" exist in England as far back as the thirteenth century. These examinations continued in similar form into the Victorian era, although responsibility for their administration gradually shifted from the courts to the medical profession. These tests generally consisted of brief assessments of speech, self-care abilities, simple counting and money skills, and basic level of judgment. During the nineteenth century, physicians developed more formal methods for assessing psychiatric and neurological disorders. For example, Joseph Guislain (1797–1860) constructed a standardized set of questions to test memory, reasoning, and judgment in the mentally ill, and Hubert von Grashey (1839–1914) developed a battery of tests to diagnose neurological dysfunction.[3]

These early mental tests were designed to detect pathology—to distinguish deviants from the normal population. It had apparently not yet occurred to anyone to try to identify different levels of ability within the normal range. Toward the end of the nineteenth century, however, psychologists began to imagine new possibilities for mental tests, possibilities that reflected emerging ideas about the nature of intelligence. These newer tests shared with their predecessors the assumption that one can objectively infer information about mental functioning from a small sample of information collected in a short period of time. (This, in fact, is one of the basic characteristics of any test.) However, these new mental tests went a step further. Rather than simply determining whether or not pathology was present, they were designed to compare normal individuals along a continuum of ability. Such comparisons required that the test administration be standardized, with the exact same items presented to each subject in precisely the same way. Consistent rules for scoring and interpretation could then yield numerical scores, allowing the examiner objectively to compare the performance of individual subjects.[4]

The disciplines of physiognomy and phrenology might be regarded as early versions of mental testing, in that both used supposedly objective measures (in this case, physical characteristics of the face and head) to assess individual variations in mental functioning. By the middle of the nineteenth century, these disciplines had lost their scientific respectability (although not necessarily their popular appeal). However, interest in finding an objective, scientific method for exploring individual differences in mental ability continued unabated. The focus of this search now shifted from phrenology to the infant science of psychology. In Germany, Wilhelm Wundt and his disciples led the way, developing tests of sensory discrimination, attention, memory, motor dexterity, and association that became the cornerstone of the new psychology. However, Wundt and his European colleagues had little interest in using these tests to compare the abilities of different individuals; their focus was on the mind in general—characteristics of intellect common to all human beings.

Although Wundt's contributions were significant, the real father of modern mental testing was Charles Darwin's younger cousin Sir Francis Galton. Galton initially became interested in mental testing as a result of experiments with word associations and mental imagery that he performed on himself. In 1884, he began offering similar tests to the general public in his Anthropometric Laboratory at the International Health Exposition in London. When the exposition closed, he transferred his laboratory to the South Kensington Museum, where he maintained it for another six years. Members of the public could pay a fee of three pence to have their mental abilities measured; over the course of time, more than 9,000 people took advantage of this opportunity. Galton's tests were typical of his era, including measures of reaction time, grip strength, keenness of vision, auditory discrimination, and a variety of physical measurements. However, he also blazed entirely new ground by using statistical techniques, many of his own invention, to objectively compare the test performance of different individuals. Like most of his contemporaries, Galton accepted the traditional Lockean assumption that these elementary sensations constituted the basis of all higher mental powers. Perhaps for this reason, he never managed to develop a functional test of general intelligence. His efforts in that direction, however, laid the foundation for all subsequent IQ testing.[5]

It was psychologist James McKeen Cattell who imported the idea of mental ability testing into the United States. Cattell, who studied at Johns Hopkins under G. Stanley Hall and then at Leipzig under Wundt, had become an enthusiastic convert to Galton's views during a trip to London. On his return to America in 1889, he immediately established a testing program among students at the University of Pennsylvania, and in 1890 he published an influential article in the journal *Mind* in which he coined the term "mental test." Cattell then moved to Columbia, where in 1894 he obtained permission to administer his battery of tests to all entering students. Following Galton's lead, Cattell focused primarily on tests of basic mental processes. His battery included, for example, measures of dynamometer pressure, reaction time, sensory acuity, short-term memory, pitch perception, rate of movement, and various head measurements. He was also curious about the more general intelligence of his subjects. In the absence of any objective measures of global intelligence, he had to rely on course grades and teacher ratings of mental ability as rough estimates of this quality. Cattell publicized his work both in professional journals and in popular publications such as *Science,* where he touted the potential practical applications of his mental tests.[6]

Cattell's work quickly caught the imagination of the infant American psychological community. Soon, many of his colleagues were conducting their own experiments with mental tests. For example, in 1890, Joseph Jastrow set up a testing program at the University of Wisconsin, where he administered various tests of sensory acuity and bilateral movement to college students. Hugo Munsterberg and E. W. Scripture both chose to work with schoolchildren, using measures similar to but somewhat more complex than Cattell's. Following up on his earlier work with puzzle boxes for animals, E. L. Thorndike developed a series of tests for specific mental functions and associations, and in 1904 he published the first text on measurement theory, *Introduction to the Theory of Mental and Social Measurements.*[7]

There was only one problem with this two-decade-long flurry of mental testing activity: the tests did not work. With a few exceptions (such as assessments of musical talent and a few tests of learning disabilities), these measures of basic sensory and motor abilities did not in fact relate to actual educational or vocational performance. The failure of these tests to predict any real-world outcomes became very clear in 1901, when Cattell's graduate student Clark Wissler (at Cattell's own request) applied Galton's new statistical techniques to Cattell's masses of accumulated data. To his surprise, Wissler found virtually no significant relationships among the various tests and none at all between any of the tests and college grades. Wissler's study sounded the death knell for this particular form of mental testing. Commenting on the state of the discipline at the turn of the century, Charles Spearman remarked that "at that time, the 'mental tests,' initiated by the genius of Galton and taken up with characteristic energy in the United States, had so lamentably disappointed expectations as to have sunk into a general by-word of scorn."[8]

The mental testing movement—like phrenology before it—may have been discredited. However, the social and scientific factors that had contributed to the almost giddy professional and popular enthusiasm for these new tests remained potent. Psychologists were now firmly wedded to a concept of intelligence that was evolutionary, developmental, comparative, and quantifiable. New statistical tools made it possible objectively to compare the abilities of groups and individuals. Despite the failure of their mental tests, psychologists continued to experience significant professional, scientific (and in some cases eugenic) motivations for finding techniques to measure mental abilities. And members of the general public had had their appetites whetted for scientifically supported instruments that promised to promote self-knowledge, self-improvement, and social advancement. All that was lacking was a practical, reliable, and meaningful way to measure general intelligence. It was into this fertile environment that Frenchman Alfred Binet introduced his new scale of intelligence in 1905.

THE DEVELOPMENT OF THE BINET SCALES

Alfred Binet was a French psychologist who achieved recognition as both an experimental scientist and an acute clinical observer. In his early years he, like most of his colleagues, had fully accepted the tenets of associationist psychology. He was familiar with the conventional mental tests of his day and had himself conducted investigations using craniometric measurements. However, Binet was also fascinated by developmental processes. Early in his career, he had made careful and systematic observations of the intellectual development of his three young daughters. This experience sparked his interest in finding more objective techniques for studying the complicated processes of mental development. So during the 1890s, combining his clinical and experimental interests, he and his colleague Victor Henri began studying normal elementary-school children. They started by giving students a variety of then-popular mental tests and tried to correlate test performance with age and level of development. But the results of these studies were disappointing, convincing Binet that the study of individual faculties in isolation was of minimal value (a conclusion that would have come as no surprise to Clark Wissler). The tests of sensory discrimination, simple memory, and attention then in vogue, he came to believe, could not adequately capture the complexities of real-world intellectual functioning. Something more was needed.[9]

In 1905, the Paris public school authorities asked Binet to create a practical test that could identify feebleminded schoolchildren in need of special educational services. He and his colleague Theodore Simon set about this task with enthusiasm. The instrument that they developed turned out to have little in common with the usual disconnected series of simple sensory, memory, and attentional tasks. The new Binet–Simon Scale consisted of 30 items, ranked in order from the easiest to the most difficult. These items, which Binet had collected from a variety of sources (including traditional mental tests, the work of German psychologist Hermann Ebbinghaus, and his own research), tapped such complex mental abilities as comprehension, vocabulary, imagination, and aesthetic judgment, in addition to usual memory and motor tasks. The items selected for inclusion were those that in the judgment of teachers distinguished bright from dull students. Based on his previous research, Binet ordered these items according to what the typical child at each age level could be expected to know.

The Binet Scales were a radical departure from the increasingly discredited mental testing tradition. Unlike his predecessors, Binet started from practice rather than theory. Instead of focusing on the simple sensory, motor, attentional, and memory tasks that Galton, Cattell, and their colleagues assumed formed the building blocks of complex intellectual functioning, Binet listened to teachers. He focused on the skills that in their experience differentiated students who learned easily from those who did not. As a result, he ended up with a rather ad hoc variety of test items. For example, students at the lowest level were expected to perform such tasks as follow a lighted match with their eyes, distinguish food from nonfood items, and follow simple commands. Older children were asked to repeat a series of digits, distinguish the heavier of two weights, identify objects and pictures, define words, and copy geometric designs. The most difficult items involved more abstract reasoning skills. For example, respondents had to synthesize three words into one sentence, reply to abstract questions (e.g., "When anyone has offended you and asks you to excuse him—what ought you to do?"), and define abstract terms (e.g., "What is the difference between esteem and affection?").[10] It is interesting to note that similar items are still found on most modern intelligence tests.

But it was not their content alone that distinguished the Binet Scales from the more traditional mental tests. First, rather than calculating separate scores for each item type, he combined these scores to create a single global index of ability—a truly revolutionary leap. Second, in his 1908 revision of the test, Binet incorporated norms describing the average performance of typical children of each age. The examiner could compare each individual subject's scores with these norms and use them to determine what was termed a "mental age" (MA). For example, a ten-year-old child who could correctly answer only the number of items passed by the typical eight-year-old would be said to have an MA of eight. Students whose MA scores were significantly below chronological age (CA) expectations could then objectively be diagnosed as feeble-minded. The greater the degree of discrepancy, the more severe the level of retardation. Although originally developed for the diagnosis of mental retardation, the mental age concept was equally applicable to intellectually normal and gifted children. In a second revision in 1911, Binet added some items appropriate for adults as well, creating for the first time a single instrument that purported objectively to rank individuals along the entire spectrum of mental ability.

Binet termed his new scale a test of intelligence. It is interesting to note that the primary connotation of the French term *l'intelligence* in Binet's time was what we might call "school brightness," and Binet himself claimed no function for his scales beyond that of measuring academic aptitude.[11] Unlike many of his contemporaries, he did not believe that heredity was the primary determinant of test performance. Comparing the test scores of two individuals, Binet asserted, was meaningful only if they had been provided equal educational opportunities and environmental stimulation. Nor did he believe that intelligence was necessarily fixed. Because all abilities were influenced by both natural endowment and experience, Binet was convinced that they could be strengthened by appropriate training, or "mental orthopedics."[12]

Binet died shortly after completing the 1911 revision of his scales. Interestingly, his work was largely ignored in his native country. Its reception in America, however, was an entirely different story. Henry H. Goddard, chief psychologist at the Vineland Training School (a highly regarded institution for feebleminded individuals in New Jersey), heard of Binet's test on a trip to Europe in 1908 and brought home the original version to try with his students. In 1909, he received Binet's 1908 revision and translated it into English. Goddard was astounded at how accurately this new measure seemed to describe the functioning levels of his mentally retarded charges. Full of excitement, he began sharing the new test with his colleagues and reporting the results of his studies in professional publications. American psychology would never again be the same.[13]

THE BINET AND SPEARMAN'S *g*

Had Binet lived a few more years, he would undoubtedly have been gratified by the enthusiasm with which his new measure was greeted in the United States. But I suspect he would have been less pleased with the meaning that most Americans chose to attribute to intelligence test scores. Binet designed his scales to assess a group of complex mental abilities that appeared to predict school performance. He believed that these abilities were influenced by both environment and heredity and were thus, with appropriate training, eminently subject to improvement. But as early as 1914, English and American psychologists had appropriated Binet's work for their own—and often very different—purposes. Before proceeding to the fascinating story of the Binet's reception in America, it would be helpful to understand how this appropriation occurred. And this leads us to British psychologist Charles Spearman and his concept of *g*, or general intelligence. As we have seen, the Galton–Cattell version of mental testing did not survive into the twentieth century. But even as the American mental testers were absorbing the discouraging evidence that their measures did not appear reliably to predict any real-world educational or vocational outcomes, and a year before the publication of Binet's seminal work, Spearman had begun taking a fresh look at similar data and coming to some rather different conclusions.

Spearman himself did not directly develop or administer mental tests; his interest was in the theoretical relationships between measures already in use. Of course, Spearman was not the first researcher to pursue such investigations; Clark Wissler, as we have seen, had used the statistical techniques developed by Galton and his protégé Karl Pearson to explore the relationships between individual tests and the outcomes they were presumed to predict. Applying these correlational techniques, he could determine, for example, whether subjects who earned the highest scores on tests of sensory discrimination also achieved the best grades in their psychology classes. The answer in general was a disappointing no. But Spearman took a different approach. Rather than focusing on the individual correlations between specific tests and outcomes, Spearman decided to analyze the pattern of these relationships as a whole, inventing in the process a powerful statistical technique now known as factor analysis. A technical explanation of factor analysis is beyond the scope of this book. Briefly, however, it is a method for looking simultaneously at the relationships between many different variables and determining mathematically whether there is any common factor (or group of factors) underlying them.

And so Spearman combined scores on tests of basic mental functions, school grades, and teacher and peer ratings of mental sharpness into a single matrix that related each variable to every other variable. By analyzing the pattern of correlations between all of these scores, he reported that he could identify one large factor common to all. This factor he termed *g,* or general intelligence. Whenever a sufficient number of mental test items are pooled, he asserted, *g* will inevitably show up. Spearman was convinced that his *g* was more than a simple mathematical description of a theoretical relationship between tests. He believed that this statistical construct reflected an actual, physical, neurological substrate in the brain (what he termed the "free energy of the whole cerebral cortex") and that this brain structure explained most of the important variations in human behavior.[14]

Spearman had first described his findings in a seminal article in the *American Journal of Psychology* in 1904. In this article he stated boldly that *"there really exists a something that we may provisionally term . . . a 'General Intelligence.' "*[15] At the time this article appeared, Binet had not yet published his new test, and Spearman had no candidate for a meaningful, concrete measure of *g*. But the appearance of the Binet Scales changed everything. In a 1914 article, Spearman declared that Binet's test provided a reasonably accurate measure of his heretofore abstract and theoretical concept of general intelligence—a unitary, biologically based, and largely heritable trait that underlies all mental activity and along which individuals can be rank-ordered on a continuum. In a single leap, he had married his global concept of intelligence to a test intended by its developer only as a practical measure of school brightness.[16]

Unlike Binet, Spearman was convinced that scores on intelligence tests reflected something biologically *real,* residing in the brain, determined largely by heredity, and underlying all cognitive functions. The debate between Binet's and Spearman's perspectives continues to this day. Proponents of *g* assert that IQ scores describe, with a fair degree of accuracy, one of the most fundamental aspects of human biology. Arthur Jensen is perhaps the most eminent and influential of the modern supporters of this theory. "I have come to view *g* as one of the most central phenomena in all of behavioral science," he wrote in 1998. "The *g* factor is actually a biologically based variable, which . . . is necessarily a product of the evolutionary process. The human condition in all its aspects cannot be adequately described or understood in a scientific sense without taking into account the powerful explanatory role of the *g* factor."[17] He could hardly have stated the argument for *g* more clearly, or more strongly.

Unsurprisingly, a number of scientists have vigorously contested the far-reaching claims of advocates like Spearman and Jensen. The concept of *g* is merely a statistical artifact, they assert, one of many possible ways to interpret the pattern of relationships among mental test data. "Factors, by themselves," wrote Stephen Jay Gould in his influential

1981 book *The Mismeasure of Man,* "are neither things nor causes; they are mathematical abstractions."[18] Spearman made the mistake, Gould claimed, of turning this mathematical abstraction into a concrete entity and then using it to make causal interpretations. But, as Gould pointed out, other psychologists have found alternative and equally valid ways to interpret this same pattern of relationships.[19] Spearman did not simply *discover g* lurking in his data. Instead, he chose one particular interpretation of these relationships to demonstrate something in which he already believed—unitary, biologically based intelligence.

But back in 1914, few scientists raised any questions about Spearman's claims. His concept of general intelligence fit too perfectly with the evolutionary and hereditarian ideas then dominant in American psychology—indeed, in American intellectual culture in general. And thus it was Spearman's concept of intelligence rather than Binet's that became attached to the Binet Scales upon their introduction into the United States. As we shall see in future chapters, the consequences of this shift in meaning, almost completely unacknowledged and undebated either then or later, remain with us to this day.

THE PROFESSIONAL RECEPTION
OF THE BINET IN AMERICA

Writing in the *Journal of Educational Psychology* in 1912, psychologist J. Carleton Bell observed, "Perhaps no device pertaining to education has ever risen to such sudden prominence in public interest throughout the world as the Binet–Simon measuring scale of intelligence."[20] And indeed, within a few years of Binet's death, his new test had taken American social science by storm. Psychologist Henry H. Goddard had introduced Binet's original 1905 scale to American professionals in a November 1908 article in the *Training School Bulletin.* He followed in 1909 with a translation of Binet's 1908 revision and in 1910 with a famous paper describing his initial research with the Binet at the Vineland Training School. (This was, by the way, the same paper in which Goddard coined the term "moron" to describe individuals with mild intellectual disabilities.)[21]

Goddard's work immediately caught the attention of his professional colleagues. Amazingly, the 1901 *Dictionary of Philosophy and Psychology* had not even contained a separate entry for the word "intelligence"; it simply listed the term as a synonym for "intellect," defining it as "the faculty or capacity of knowing."[22] But during 1910 and 1911, a flurry of papers about the Binet began to appear in psychology and education journals, and several other psychologists, including Frederick

Kuhlmann, Guy Whipple, and Clara Town, published their own trans-
lations and revisions of the Binet Scales. By 1913, a bibliography of research on the Binet cited more than 250 international publications, and
the Fourth International Conference on School Hygiene had devoted a
special session to the test. During the next four years, the Binet bibliography expanded by more than 450 citations.[23]

These various versions of the Binet spread like wildfire throughout
the professional community. Their impact is perhaps best described in
Goddard's own words. He wrote in 1916,

It will seem an exaggeration to some to say that the world is talking of the
Binet–Simon Scale, but consider that the Vineland Laboratory alone, has without effort or advertisement distributed to date 22,000 copies of the pamphlet
describing the tests, and 88,000 record blanks. This in spite of the fact that the
same matter has been freely published in numerous other places. The Scale is
used in Canada, England, Australia, New Zealand, South Africa, Germany.[24]

By the time of America's entry into World War I, more than 70,000 copies of the Binet had been distributed in at least 10 countries.[25]

Inevitably, some professionals had reservations about the new instrument. Several critics homed in on a fundamental issue: the Binet purported to measure intelligence, but there was no agreement as to what
this term actually meant. Some observers cautioned that scores could
not be interpreted without considering the impact of environmental and
educational experiences. Other criticisms were more technical: that the
test was too heavily weighed with verbal items, for example, or that the
items were in the wrong order. But virtually no one questioned the basic
premise behind the Binet Scales. Throughout the community of professional educators and psychologists, there was broad consensus that this
fascinating new test did in fact measure intelligence (however this term
might be defined) and that intelligence thus measured was fundamental
to educational and vocational success.

Many, if not all, of the critics' original objections were resolved in
1916, when Lewis Terman published the first major revision of the Binet
Scales. Terman was a promising young psychologist whose interest in
intelligence and its measurement had been piqued by Goddard's original
reports. When he arrived at Stanford in 1910 to accept a faculty position, he immediately began work on his own revision of the original test.
By 1916, Terman had completed a second, much more rigorous revision
of the Binet Scales. This new test, known as the Stanford–Binet, quickly
displaced earlier, less formal revisions of Binet's measure. Within a few
years, the Stanford–Binet had become the gold standard of American IQ
testing—a distinction it was to hold for decades.[26]

The new Stanford–Binet incorporated two significant innovations. First, during its development, Terman had administered his test to large numbers of American schoolchildren. This allowed him to use these students (rather than Binet's original French subjects) as his norm, or comparison, group, providing a more relevant standard against which to judge individual test performance. Second, and most consequentially, the Stanford–Binet introduced into America the concept of the intelligence quotient, or IQ. Terman defined the IQ as the subject's MA divided by his or her CA. A ten-year-old child who earned an MA score of 10 on the Stanford–Binet would thus have an IQ score of 100, or average. Bright children whose MA exceeded their CA would have higher IQs, while those whose MA was lower than their CA would have lower IQs. (Current IQs are computed somewhat differently, but the basic concept of 100 as the average score remains the same.)

It is no accident that American psychologists embraced the Binet and its successor, the Stanford–Binet, with such unbridled enthusiasm. As we have seen, social scientists had been searching for several decades for just such an instrument. These new measures fit neatly into the framework of evolutionary biology, where newly minted scientists most naturally found their explanations for human behavior. Anthropologists and psychologists interpreted the theory of evolution as demonstrating that the individuals, groups, and races at the bottom of the social hierarchy were in some sense evolutionary throwbacks. By conceptualizing intelligence in terms of mental age, the Binet could be interpreted as offering objective support for this idea, providing a supposedly scientific method for arraying the entire human race along a single scale of evolutionary development. (In later years, this scale was even extended to some of our primate cousins; for example, Koko the gorilla was given the Stanford–Binet and reportedly earned an MA of about three years.)[27] The fact that upper- and middle-class individuals of Anglo-Saxon heritage generally performed well on the Binet, while social misfits, the poor, eastern European immigrants, and the "lower races" earned lower scores, seemed to most scientists to confirm at the same time evolutionary theory, the accuracy of the Binet, and the existing social order.

The technology of the Binet also supported the Progressive era's passion for numbers. True to their Baconian roots, most American scientists viewed measurement as one of the defining characteristics of their discipline, and they were eager to demonstrate the utility of the powerful new statistical tools that they had recently developed. What could be more exciting than an instrument that purported to measure the capacities of the human mind itself? So great was their faith in numbers and statistical techniques that few psychologists viewed their continuing inability to define the exact nature of intelligence as a particular barrier to trying to measure it. Advocates of IQ testing often drew an analogy to electricity. Scientists in the early twentieth century readily admitted that they understood little about the nature of electricity. Their ignorance of its basic nature, however, did not prevent them from measuring electricity or harnessing its power to their uses. An editorial in the *New York Times* in 1916 offered this ringing endorsement of the measurement of human intelligence. "As a matter of demonstrated fact," the writer proclaimed, "the Binet–Simon tests intelligently applied . . . are as trustworthy as the multiplication table. Minds can be standardized, just as electricity is every day and long has been."[28]

Finally, to the community of psychologists struggling to establish a position for their new profession, the Binet Scales must have seemed a godsend. From its earliest days, the discipline of psychology had focused on applied problems in fields such as education, criminology, industry, and advertising. Psychology's interest in producing work of acknowledged practical value was intimately related to the increasing professionalization of the field—part of a broader, Progressive-era trend toward the professionalization of expert knowledge of all types. The Binet provided the young discipline with the perfect vehicle for asserting its expert status and consolidating its professional power.

Within a few years after its introduction into the United States, the Binet had in fact replaced traditional physician diagnosis in institutions for the feebleminded, and psychologists soon extended their diagnostic control to schools, courts, and the welfare system as well. Professional psychologists were understandably quick to lay claims to exclusive use of the new test. In 1916, the American Psychological Association voted to restrict the use of the Binet Scales to qualified psychologists (a restriction, by the way, that is still in effect).[29] With the nearly magical power of their new scientific instruments, psychologists now declared themselves capable of addressing some of society's most intractable problems. Whether the issue was educational policy, the restriction of immigration, or "the menace of the feebleminded," psychologists waded eagerly into the fray, armed with their newfound expertise in measuring intelligence. As we shall see in the next chapter, this association of intelligence tests with these hot button social issues has haunted their use to this day.

Chapter 7

IQ Testing, Social Control, and Merit

As we saw in Chapter 4, the United States at the dawn of the twentieth century was a world far different from Jefferson's idealized agrarian democracy. So dramatic were the changes that had occurred during the course of the 1800s that many Americans feared the imminent collapse of their familiar system of government. Immigrants had begun pouring through the nation's ports at an unprecedented pace. Almost all of these newcomers were poor, and most brought with them alien religions, strange customs, and darker-toned skins. These new arrivals crowded into squalid tenements in the teeming cities, where overburdened public schools struggled to educate masses of children speaking a bewildering variety of languages. The gap between the rich and the poor had never been greater. Capitalists with incredible wealth at their disposal maintained firm control of the levers of power. But they did not wield this power without opposition. Newly formed labor unions, some of them espousing alien ideologies imported from Europe, began calling strikes. The response of the industrialists was often violent and bloody. To some, the nation appeared on the brink of open class warfare. Surely the revered founding fathers had never contemplated this kind of democracy!

The members of America's privileged classes understandably felt their positions threatened by this social upheaval. Some responded by giving up on democracy entirely. Those not fit by heredity or education to exercise power responsibly, they asserted, must be excluded from the country or, if already here, kept under tight control. Others, more optimistic about human nature, believed that ameliorating the worst of existing social ills might restore a comforting order to society—an order achieved under the firm guidance, of course, of experts such as themselves. Interestingly, both the pessimists and the optimists among these groups generally identified themselves as Progressives. Almost all framed their reforms in the language of merit. And increasingly, they appropriated the new technology of IQ testing to advance their causes.

In his inaugural address as president of Colgate University in 1922, George B. Cutten starkly articulated the pessimistic version of social control. "The popular idea of democracy is a delusion," he proclaimed. "Except among a small, selected group, government by the people is an impossibility."[1] Cutten and his colleagues were convinced that, in order to safeguard the stability of the country's treasured institutions, it was necessary to exclude, control, or even eliminate the groups who threatened its well-being. Power belonged to those who had demonstrated the merit to exercise it responsibly. And being good Social Darwinists, most of these thinkers equated merit with adaptive fitness—in other words, the inherited, immutable, biologically determined trait of intelligence. IQ testing provided the perfect mechanism for identifying feebleminded individuals in need of segregation and control. The results of these new tests could also be interpreted as justifying the exclusion of low-scoring, biologically unfit immigrants from southern and eastern Europe.

Another group of Progressive experts advanced a more optimistic version of social control. Their primary causes were education and civil service reform. These reformers maintained their faith in the promise of democracy, but they believed that people must be guided to exercise power responsibly. Like their more conservative compatriots, these Progressives generally agreed that intelligence was both inherited and immutable. In contrast to most Social Darwinists, however, they followed Jefferson in insisting that meritorious diamonds in the rough could be found in all social classes. It was therefore their stated goal to identify merit wherever it might be found, using scientific principles efficiently to guide individuals into the social roles most compatible with their unique pattern of abilities. These reformers very quickly recognized the potential utility of IQ tests in advancing their goals. These tests provided an encouragingly scientific and objective tool for selecting the most qualified individuals for coveted positions. In principle, this practice appeared respectably egalitarian. But unacknowledged was the fact that, if intelligence was in fact largely inherited, and if these experts had (as they assumed) earned their positions of power and influence on the basis of their own personal merit, then a system of selection based on testing would undoubtedly end up favoring their own genetically advantaged sons and daughters.

And so, whether their focus was on exclusion or on selection, advocates of social control found it easy to unite around the ideal of merit. Indeed, the Progressives gave to their signature achievement, civil service reform, the label of the merit system. In appropriating this term, the reformers were of course harkening back to a sacred tenet of American political ideology. But as we have seen, during the course of the eighteenth century the original ideal of merit had shifted dramatically. No longer did this concept center on talents, virtues, and a willingness to use these abilities for the good of society. Merit was now a code word for adaptive fitness. High test scores entitled their possessors to positions of privilege; low scores, on the other hand, justified their exclusion. Either way, access to opportunity in twentieth-century America was increasingly controlled by scores on formal tests of intelligence.

TESTING FOR EXCLUSION

The Progressive reformers who focused their energy on the exclusion of "undesirables" had two primary targets: the darker-skinned immigrants flooding into the country from abroad and the mentally deficient individuals who were already here. Even in the middle of our current furor about illegal aliens, it is hard for most of us today to appreciate the panic that the massive immigration of the late nineteenth and early twentieth centuries elicited in the many Americans. Labor unions worried about reduced wages and competition for their members' jobs. Political conservatives were convinced that the supposedly Bolshevist and anarchist beliefs espoused by some immigrants presaged the imminent destruction of sacred political institutions. To many fearful citizens, the influx of newcomers from southern and eastern Europe seemed to threaten their very way of life. It was within this context, and amidst the furor of the famous Sacco-Vanzetti case of the early 1920s, that a virtually unanimous Congress in 1924 passed the Immigration Act, a landmark reform that upended America's traditionally open immigration policy. This legislation, which remained in effect until 1965, drastically restricted the number of newcomers admitted to the United States from southern and eastern Europe, while completely excluding most Asians. America's vaunted open door policy was at an end.[2]

The various economic and political fears that led to the passage of this legislation seemed to coalesce around a perceived threat to racial purity. In his influential 1916 *The Passing of a Great Race,* Madison Grant (chairman of the New York Zoological Society and trustee of the American Museum of Natural History) closed with the following words:

We Americans must realize that the altruistic ideals which have controlled our social development during the past century and the maudlin sentimentalism that has made America "an asylum for the oppressed," are sweeping the nation toward a racial abyss. If the Melting Pot is allowed to boil without control and we continue to follow our national motto and deliberately blind ourselves to all "distinctions of race, creed or color" the type of native American of Colonial descent will become as extinct as the Athenian of the age of Pericles, and the Viking of the days of Rollo.[3]

Grant's words may seem inflammatory to at least the more liberal among us today, but his sentiments were widely shared among Progressive reformers. Theories of Anglo-Saxon racial superiority appeared to find firm support in nineteenth-century understanding of evolutionary biology. And the newly introduced Binet Scales provided an ideal technology to validate the widespread belief that the Nordic type stood at the peak of the ladder of evolution. As early as 1910, H. H. Goddard had begun using some of the nonverbal items from these scales to identify feebleminded immigrants attempting to enter the country at Ellis Island.[4] A 1917 report of this testing program, found in the popular magazine *Survey,* included a picture captioned with the words "Two Immigrants out of Five Feeble-Minded" (although the editors later admitted that the headline had been misleading).[5] In a 1914 *Popular Science* article, writer Josiah Moore described a study in which researchers had administered the Binet to groups of white and colored schoolchildren in South Carolina. Moore reported that this study demonstrated conclusively that members of different racial groups differed from one another in intelligence, just as they did in physical appearance. Virtually all of these researchers predictably attributed these racial, ethnic, and class disparities to hereditary factors.[6]

This flurry of articles describing supposed racial and ethnic differences on Binet test performance received considerable public attention. Even more powerful, however, was the veritable storm of righteous indignation precipitated by psychologist Carl C. Brigham's *A Study of American Intelligence,* published in 1923. Brigham's book was based on his analysis of scores on the Army Alpha, a group-administered test of intelligence that had been given to nearly two million military recruits during World War I. (The development of the Army Alpha will be described in more detail in a later section of this chapter.) These scores, representing the performance of a virtual cross section of young American males, provided a treasure trove of data for psychologists. In his book, Brigham compared the test scores of various ethnic groups and concluded—to no one's surprise, given the social tenor of the time—that there were large and immutable differences between the races. White men of northern European heritage of course performed the best. Most immigrants, by contrast, were found to be "morons," suggesting that the general intelligence of the country's Anglo-Saxon population was being dangerously degraded by the influx of low-scoring newcomers from southern and eastern Europe. Brigham offered his conclusions without equivocation. "In a very definite way," he wrote, "the results which we obtain by interpreting the army data by means of the race hypothesis support . . . the superiority of the Nordic type."[7]

Of course, not all psychologists supported these racist views. However, virtually all of the most prominent advocates of intelligence testing were firmly convinced that their instruments provided scientific proof of the superiority of the Nordic race, and they did not hesitate to inject their opinions into the public debate about immigration. Most of the scientific publications comparing IQ scores of various ethnic groups included remarks about their implications for immigration policy. Many eminent psychologists spoke out in the popular press as well. For example, in a 1923 article in the *Atlantic Monthly,* Robert Yerkes warned his readers that "a country which encourages, or even permits, the immigration of simple-minded, uneducated, defective, diseased, or criminalistic persons, because it needs cheap labor, seeks trouble in the shape of public expense."[8]

Somewhat surprisingly, there is little evidence that these psychologists' very active and public stance against unrestricted immigration actually had much impact on the passage of the 1924 legislation. There are almost no references to IQ tests in the congressional debates or testimony about the law, probably because the public pressure for immigration restriction was already so strong that the contributions of the psychologists were rather superfluous.[9] Interestingly, the furor over supposed IQ differences among the different European ethnic groups quieted dramatically after the adoption of the 1924 law. As historian Franz Samelson has noted, "the 'scientific' question was by no means settled, but the practical one was."[10] And in fact, by the end of the 1920s, changing social mores and a more sophisticated understanding of the interpretation of IQ test data had caused most psychologists (including Brigham) to recant their most extreme racist views. However, the fact that so many prominent psychologists had, at least for a period, used IQ test data to support theories of Anglo-Saxon superiority solidified a connection between these tests and racist ideology that, rightly or wrongly, has haunted their use to this day.

Closely related to the national furor over unchecked immigration were the experts' shrill warnings about the growing "menace of the

feebleminded." Alfred Binet had originally developed his scales to identify schoolchildren with retarded intellectual development so that they
could receive specialized treatment. For more than a decade after its
introduction into the United States, identification of the mentally subnormal remained the primary function of the Binet test. Today the diagnosis of intellectual disabilities is of concern primarily to affected
individuals, their families, and their teachers. During the early twentieth
century, however, the identification and control of people with subnormal intelligence constituted an issue of major social concern. Americans
of the period were preoccupied with deviants of all types, and nowhere
was this obsession more evident than in the era's panicked reaction
to the "menace of the feebleminded" (a term coined by psychologist
Lewis Terman).[11] Many Progressive-era reformers believed that most
social ills, including crime, poverty, drunkenness, and sexual promiscu-
ity, were due to the high number of individuals with low intelligence at
large in society. Identifying these "defectives" and somehow controlling
their behavior thus became a matter of the highest national priority. It
is certainly no coincidence that this focus on the dangers of rampant
feeblemindedness helped to support the existing social order by blaming
personal deficits rather than an unfair economic structure for the blatant
inequality that characterized the period.[12]

In 1910, in a groundbreaking move, the American Association for the
Study of the Feeble-Minded recommended that mental age scores derived from the Binet be adopted as the basis for the official classification
of mental retardation. State legislatures soon followed, beginning with
New Jersey in 1911. By 1917, the state of Minnesota required that the
Binet be administered to all persons coming before its courts on charges
of delinquency, illegitimacy, child neglect, or poor schoolwork. If the
IQ was determined to be low, the individual could then be committed
to the court as feebleminded. By the end of World War I, IQ tests were
being widely used for the diagnosis of mental retardation in courts, public health agencies, social services agencies, and institutions in progressive states such as New York, Ohio, Indiana, and Minnesota. Although
there were scattered concerns about the accuracy of these tests, public
opinion was generally supportive of their use.[13]

The Binet Scales made it possible for the first time to identify low-
functioning individuals who appeared normal and could thus pass
virtually unnoticed in society.[14] Paradoxically, because of their near-
normality, morons were regarded as even more dangerous to society
than their more severely disabled brethren, who generally remained
under the care and control of their families. The Binet Scales provided
a new scientific tool with which officials could conduct mass screenings

to detect these supposedly dangerous individuals. The primary goal of these screenings was to protect society from their allegedly antisocial and inappropriate behaviors (although of course reformers also expressed at least pro forma concern about the well-being of the afflicted persons). Once identified, these unfortunate individuals were to receive special treatment, preferably in segregated settings far removed from the mainstream of society. Allowing them to remain at large, it was believed, would result in unacceptable levels of crime, poverty, drunkenness, and sexual immorality.

In addition to espousing segregated treatment, many reformers were strong advocates of the practice of eugenics: preventing the reproduction of defective individuals by segregation or, when necessary, by sterilization. Today, of course, this idea represents the very height of political incorrectness. In its day, however, the eugenics movement was an integral component of Progressive reform, and the practice of eugenic sterilization was supported by a number of recently established philanthropic foundations. Many of the IQ testing pioneers, including Edward Thorndike, G. Stanley Hall, Carl Brigham, Lewis Terman, and Robert Yerkes, were active in eugenics societies during the 1920s. By the 1930s, the experience of the Great Depression (which affected the elites as well as the underclass) and a more sophisticated understanding of genetics had caused most prominent psychologists, with the notable exception of Thorndike, to withdraw or modify their support of eugenics. But though it had lost its scientific respectability, eugenic sterilization had by now taken on a life of its own. Involuntary sterilizations of mentally retarded individuals continued in many states until the 1950s and 1960s; in North Carolina, one such sterilization was recorded as recently as 1980. As did its use to support theories of Anglo-Saxon racial superiority, its association with eugenic sterilization has left an ugly blot on the history of intelligence testing.[15]

TESTING FOR SELECTION: THE CIVIL SERVICE AND THE MILITARY

Most Americans today profess to find eugenic sterilization and theories of Nordic racial superiority repugnant. Psychologists view the historical association of IQ tests with these outdated ideologies as something of an embarrassment to their profession. No one today, they hasten to assure us, would even dream of using these measures for such sinister purposes. But few of us have any such qualms about the second—and ultimately far more influential—role that IQ tests began to assume during the 1920s: selecting among applicants for valued positions. By the end of the decade, tests of general intelligence (or their equivalents) were being used to track students in public schools; to control admission to elite colleges, universities, and professional schools; and to guide selection and placement in the military, the civil service, and industry.

Test-driven selection was carried out in the name of the durable American ideal of merit. By identifying those who were most intelligent (as measured by these supposedly objective tests), proponents claimed, they were channeling society's rewards to the individuals most deserving of advancement. But like those who promoted the use of intelligence tests for avowedly racist purposes, advocates of testing for selection assumed that IQ was in large part inherited and basically immutable. Tests, then, could be trusted to identify for future advancement young people very much like those already in charge. Basing selection on intelligence test scores almost magically allowed established groups to maintain their virtual monopoly on privileged positions while at the same time paying lip service to cherished democratic ideals.

It was during the civil service reform movement of the 1870s and 1880s that the word "merit" first became identified with scores on formal tests. Reacting to the abuses of what they termed the "spoils system," Progressive reformers insisted that government employment should be based on merit rather than patronage. These reformers were following in the footsteps of their British counterparts, who had instituted a test-based reform of the Indian Civil Service in 1853. In Britain, the new civil service examination was based entirely on the university curriculum, effectively limiting admission to the service to members of the upper class. But if selection were to be based only on test performance, some critics asked, what happened to the importance of character? Not to worry, responded the committee charged with developing the British examinations. "We . . . think that the intellectual test about to be established will be found in practice to be also the best moral test that can be devised." Prime Minister Gladstone concurred. "Experience at the universities and public schools of this country," he stated confidently, "has shown that in a large majority of cases the test of open examination is also an effectual test of character."[16] The most intelligent candidates, these proponents blithely assumed, would naturally be the most virtuous as well.

American civil service reformers were strongly influenced by their British compatriots, and in many ways the Pendleton Act of 1883, which established the U.S. Civil Service, was modeled on the British system.[17] There was one major difference, however. Bowing to democratic sensibilities, Congress insisted that the new civil service tests be practical in nature, in general requiring no more than an eighth-grade education. Rather than focusing on academic credentials, the Pendleton Act specified, the emphasis of the tests should be on job-related skills and knowledge. Many American reformers, themselves scions of patrician New England families, would have preferred an elitist system similar to that employed in Britain. Political reality, however, required that they accede to a more egalitarian process.[18]

The newly established Civil Service Commission took great pains to emphasize the open and democratic nature of its tests. In its description of the new examinations in its First Annual Report, the commission noted that "in none of these branches do the questions go further than is covered by the ordinary instruction in the common schools of the country." The report went on to assert that "the political opinions, the social standing, the occupations, the sympathies and theories of those who enter the classified service will be as varied as the character, the pursuits, and the feelings of that vast citizenship from which applicants now spontaneously seek the examinations and win their way to office."[19] Specific tests were developed to address the particular skills required for each occupation. For example, applicants for clerical positions were examined in penmanship, composition, grammar, arithmetic, and American history and geography, while simpler tests were devised for letter carriers and technical exams for more specialized positions.

And so, despite the elitist proclivities of many of the Progressive reformers, positions in the U.S. Civil Service were intended to be accessible to ordinary citizens, and the exams focused on acquired skills and knowledge rather than the vaguely defined, class-related, and supposedly innate quality of intelligence. But the Civil Service Commission was not immune to the IQ testing craze that swept the country after World War I. Both during and after the war, the Commission had consulted with prominent psychologists about how these new intelligence tests might further its mission, and in 1922 it established a special research section under the leadership of psychologist Beardsley Ruml. This research organization immediately set out to develop a new test of intelligence, intended to replace the requirement for a high school diploma for many clerical positions. This new exam included such familiar IQ-test items as vocabulary, general information, verbal relations, number relations, and opposites. Despite the clear contrary directive of the original civil service legislation, the commission had now decided, in the words of L. L. Thurstone, that it was more important "to employ people who have the right kind of mind and personality" than to worry about their specific skills and knowledge.[20]

The Civil Service Commission continued to develop skills-oriented specialty tests; indeed, by 1954, it offered more than 100 individual exams. Increasingly, however, applicants were required to pass a test of general intelligence as well as an exam assessing more specific job-related skills. In 1954, the commission introduced the Federal Service Entrance Exam, which had a format very similar to that of the SAT. This test was administered to applicants for jobs that generally required a college education. It was replaced in 1974 by the Professional and Administrative Career Exam, or PACE. In the 1980s, the Supreme Court ruled that employment tests with a disparate racial impact must be demonstrably relevant to actual job duties. IQ-type tests of general aptitude such as the PACE were unable to meet this standard and therefore had to be discarded by the commission. For nearly 60 years, however, demonstrating one's merit by earning a satisfactory score on a test of general intelligence had been a hurdle that applicants for most federal and state civil service positions were required to surmount.

The nineteenth-century advocates of civil service reform had introduced the American public to the idea that merit was most reliably assessed by means of formal tests. But, as we have seen, the original civil service exams had measured job-related skills, not innate cognitive ability. It was actually psychologists working for the U.S. military who developed the first adult intelligence test designed for mass administration. For all its popularity, the individually administered Binet simply required too much time and professional expertise to be practical for mass use; wider application required a test that could easily be given to much larger groups. And during World War I, a group of prominent psychologists produced just such an instrument.

In 1917, shortly after America's entry into the war, a number of the country's most eminent psychologists (among them Henry H. Goddard, Lewis Terman, Robert Yerkes, and Guy M. Whipple) gathered at Vineland Training School to discuss how their profession might best contribute to the war effort. Their original intention was to develop a practical, group-administered test of intelligence that the army could use to screen out feebleminded recruits. However, their goals soon expanded: why not also use the measure to identify potential officer talent and help assign soldiers to the duties for which they were best suited?[21] Working as quickly as they could, the group created an entirely new test of intelligence, which they called the Army Alpha. (Another version of the measure, the Army Beta, was intended for use with recruits who were illiterate.) The new test was designed to be quickly administered to large groups of men by relatively untrained examiners, and its scoring was fast, simple, and objective; in fact, it was in the Army Alpha that the now-ubiquitous multiple-choice question made its debut. The content of the test was appropriate for adults, and its questions were sufficiently difficult to discriminate ability at both the high and the low ends of the intelligence spectrum. The military was enthusiastic about this new measure, and by 1919 it had administered the Army Alpha to more than 1,700,000 men.[22]

Contrary to the hopes of its developers, the military rarely used performance on the Army Alpha to assign recruits to particular jobs or to identify those who had the potential to become officers. (For this latter function, the army seemed to prefer the ratings of personality and character traits developed by psychologist Walter Dill Scott.) However, several army officials did testify that scores on the new test appeared accurately to reflect the abilities of the examinees, and for the first time comments about officers' perceived intelligence began to make their way into personnel ratings. The measure received extensive and generally admiring coverage in the popular press.[23] And, as we saw in a previous section, after the war, psychologist Carl Brigham's analysis of the Army Alpha scores of various ethnic groups was widely interpreted as providing solid scientific support for the theories of Anglo-Saxon racial superiority that permeated the culture at that time.

The psychologists who developed the Army Alpha had achieved only minimal success in their efforts to persuade the military to use their new test for occupational classification and the identification of talent. Where they had failed in World War I, however, they succeeded dramatically in World War II. As they had during the earlier war, psychologists flocked into government service after Pearl Harbor. One of their first assignments was to develop a test of mental ability that could be used to sort military recruits into more than 2,000 occupational and training categories. By the time the war was over, more than 15 percent of the men in the United States had been given these Army and Navy General Classification Tests (GCTs). Although the measures were not officially labeled tests of intelligence, GCT scores in fact correlated very highly with educational status and other markers of mental ability.[24] In the military, as in the civil service, by the end of World War II intelligence testing had come to play a central role in job selection and classification.

TESTING FOR SELECTION: SCHOOLS AND UNIVERSITIES

America's public schools faced daunting challenges as the nineteenth century drew to a close. As late as 1880, only 15 states had required all children to attend school; by 1918, less than 40 years later, every state in the country had enacted compulsory education laws. These overburdened public schools struggled to find ways to educate an increasingly diverse student body. African American laborers from the south, many of whom had never had an opportunity to attend school themselves, began streaming into northern cities, seeking jobs for themselves and education for their children. But their numbers paled in comparison with the flood of European immigrants pouring into America's urban areas. In a 1908 survey of 37 large and small cities, fully 58 percent of students reportedly came from immigrant families, one-third of whom spoke no English all. And in addition to racial and ethnic minority children, public schools were increasingly expected to serve students with mental and physical handicaps, leading to the establishment of the first special education programs.

In good Progressive fashion, schools responded to these challenges by trying to make their practices more scientific. A new breed of educators, anxious to join the ranks of experts, introduced such now-familiar practices as age grading, standardized curricula, and written examinations. These scientifically minded educational administrators believed they could use their limited resources most efficiently by tracking students into specialized programs, be they vocational and commercial curricula, special education classes, or college preparatory tracks. Such tracking required some objective mechanism for sorting students into what were believed to be the most appropriate programs—and the newly introduced Binet Scales were ideally positioned to fill this need. As early as 1910, H. H. Goddard had received permission to administer the new test to 2,000 public school students in New Jersey, and before long teachers from around the country were learning about the Binet at summer programs offered at the Vineland Training Center.[25]

Before World War I, most schools that adopted the Binet Scales used them as their creator had intended: to identify the relatively small number of students with learning problems who would benefit from placement in special education classes. Large-scale screening would have to await the development of a more practical, group-administered test that could be easily scored and interpreted by teachers. A few psychologists had begun working on such a measure during the mid-1910s, but it was not until after World War I that this enterprise really took off. Encouraged by the apparent success of the Army Alpha, a number of foundations (most notably Rockefeller and Carnegie) began supporting the development of group-administered tests of intelligence (or aptitude, as the concept increasingly came to be labeled), designed to assist in educational placement and vocational guidance. The success of their efforts was almost breathtaking. By 1925, fully 64 percent of urban elementary schools were using these tests (the best known of which was the National Intelligence Test, developed by a group headed by Lewis Terman and Robert Yerkes) to sort children by ability level. In the later years of the 1920s, it is estimated that publishing companies sold an astonishing 40 million such tests each year. Intelligence testing had become a fixture in American schools.

Of course, most educators insisted that their tracking practices were intended to promote the well-being of their students—in the words of testing advocate Marion R. Trabue, "discover[ing] the differences in pupils' special gifts, and train[ing] each pupil to be happy and effective in making his particular contribution to human happiness."[26] But it is no accident that school tracking also served the needs of an increasingly powerful corporate America. By using scientifically derived test scores, schools could channel young people into the slots where they could most efficiently serve the needs of a modern industrial economy. Educator Ellwood P. Cubberley, writing in 1916 in the journal *Public School Administration*, felt no need to offer any apologies about this practice. "Our schools," he asserted, "are, in a sense, factories in which the raw products (children) are to be shaped and fashioned into products to meet the various demands of life."[27] The technology of IQ testing helped support the existing power structure by reserving access to privileged positions to those deemed most deserving while at the same time ensuring a steady stream of lower-class workers to fuel the country's industrial machine.

Those students who were selected for college preparatory tracks in high school had yet one more hurdle to surmount: the vaunted SAT. Arguably, no test has had a greater impact on the life of the average young American. This test first appeared in the 1920s. Intrigued by what they were learning about the Army Alpha, many selective Eastern colleges had begun incorporating IQ-type exams into their admission criteria. Hoping to regularize this rather ad hoc process, the College Board (an organization of select Eastern colleges) hired Carl Brigham, one of the creators of the Army Alpha, to develop a new college admission test for its members. The resulting Scholastic Aptitude Test, also based on the Army tests, was administered for the first time in 1926.[28]

Harvard president James B. Conant gave the newly developed SAT an enormous boost in 1934, when he and his protégé Henry Chauncey (later chairman of the American College Board) selected the test as the basis for awarding the new merit-based scholarships being instituted at Harvard. Conant, who came from a rather modest background himself, was a fervent believer in meritocracy. In the words of Nicholas Lemann, his goal was "to depose the existing, undemocratic American elite" and replace it with a new one "chosen democratically on the basis of its scholastic brilliance, as revealed by scores on mental tests."[29] In selecting the students to receive his new scholarships, Conant rejected the traditional achievement tests. Because they were based primarily on the New England prep school curriculum, he believed that these tests discriminated against bright boys from poorer schools. (No girls, of course, need apply.) The SAT, which supposedly measured ability rather than achievement, seemed to him a much more equitable measure. Conant and Chauncey embraced the SAT with almost religious fervor. Indeed, Chauncey reflected in his personal notebook that "what I hope to see established is the moral equivalent of religion but based on reason and science rather than on sentiments and tradition."[30]

Spurred by Conant's prestige and Chauncey's position as president of the American College Board, by the middle of the 1950s most elite Eastern universities were requiring the SAT for admission. In the ensuing decades, most other selective colleges followed suit, and by the end of the century, confronting the SAT had become a rite of passage for most college-bound American high school students. The Educational Testing Service (ETS), publisher of the test, claimed for many years that, because the SAT supposedly measured pure, innate ability, scores could not be affected by practice or coaching. Despite these statements, those students who could afford to do so pored over test preparation workbooks, spent countless Saturdays (and substantial amounts of money) on cram classes, and took and retook the exam repeatedly in efforts to improve their scores. And after many years of denial, the ETS finally conceded that test scores could in fact be improved by coaching—a fact that obviously gave an advantage to affluent young people whose families could afford elaborate test preparation programs.

One of Conant's original justifications for advocating a test that purported to assess ability rather than achievement was that it would open up opportunities for disadvantaged minority and low-income students, and the ETS claimed for years that the test promoted "a substantial increase in opportunities for educational advancement of low-income students."[31] In reality, however, there has always been a substantial gap between the test scores of wealthy, white students and those from low-income, ethnic minority groups. The SAT correlates with parental income about as well as it does with college grades. In fact, it is an ugly truth that colleges could achieve equivalent predictive power by eliminating the test altogether and replacing it with measures of family income and parental education.[32] It is true that the gates of opportunity do swing wide for those exceptional disadvantaged individuals who score well on the SAT. For the most part, however, the students who earn top scores on the SAT are the same privileged, white youth who have always dominated our elite educational institutions. The SAT has thus become both the quintessential marker for merit in American society and a primary mechanism through which privilege is passed from one generation to the next.

Chapter 8

Democratic Ideology and IQ Testing

Historians critical of intelligence testing have generally focused their ire on the well-documented abuses of these measures by racists, xenophobes, and eugenicists. Their somewhat less dramatic but arguably more consequential function as tools of corporate power has received significant scholarly attention as well. But there is another side to the story. For, in fact, it was not only the educated elites who were caught up in the national enthusiasm for intelligence testing; like phrenology in the previous century, IQ tests also attracted the attention of a general public bent on self-improvement. Nineteenth-century self-improvement ideology had been grounded in Protestant religion. Twentieth-century Americans, by contrast, seized on the new discipline of psychology as an up-to-the-minute tool for helping them make the most of their abilities. From Sigmund Freud, whose ideas about the unconscious promised to reveal the innermost mysteries of one's psyche, to John Watson, whose behaviorist theories helped countless parents raise their children according to the latest scientific methods, ordinary Americans had become avid consumers of psychological wisdom. And no topic attracted more popular interest than the seemingly miraculous technology of IQ testing. Yes, the tests may have served as a powerful mechanism for social control, but they also appealed to America's view of itself as a democratic and egalitarian society.

THE POPULAR RECEPTION OF IQ TESTING

Even before the introduction of Binet Scales in 1905, members of the general public were starting to become interested in these newfangled mental tests. In England, for example, more than 9,000 ordinary citizens stood in line for hours at the 1884 London International Health Exhibition, awaiting Sir Francis Galton and the magic tests that he promised would provide them with a scientific assessment of their own mental functioning. They even paid him threepence each for the privilege. After Galton moved his laboratory to his own South Kensington address, the rush continued; no less a personage than Prime Minister William Gladstone sought out Galton for consultation.[1] As had the phrenologists before him, Galton purported to provide members of the public with objective, scientific data about their own abilities, information that they could then use for self-improvement, personal decision making, and social advancement. Indeed, Galton envisioned a time when "we [shall] have anthropometric laboratories" all around the country, allowing people to have their various faculties tested "by the best methods known to modern science."[2]

It did not take long for this popular interest in mental testing to make its way across the Atlantic. Americans in the late nineteenth and early twentieth centuries were inveterate consumers of popular science, and psychology appeared to hold a particular fascination for them. Books, magazines, newspapers, lectures, and traveling expositions catered to these interests. By the late 1800s, lively discussions about techniques for measuring intelligence were beginning to appear in the popular press. For example, the *New York Times* published several articles discussing the relationship of brain weight to intelligence, and other publications enthused about promising assessment strategies like proverbs and word association tests. More far-fetched techniques also received attention. For example, the *Literary Digest* described a brain meter invented by a Russian physician, while both *Scientific American* and *Harper's Weekly* reported on an apparatus developed by English anthropologist John Gray to measure intelligence by means of responses to a series of colored lights.[3]

As we saw in Chapter 6, the most prominent of the early American popularizers of mental testing was probably James McKeen Cattell. Cattell had imported some of Galton's techniques into the United States to use with college students. But true to the pragmatic spirit of American psychology, he was also anxious to expand his work beyond the confines of academia. As a part of this effort, he offered a selected subset of 10 of his measures to members of the general public, an opportunity to which many interested citizens responded enthusiastically. Cattell stated confidently that people would find his mental tests to be both interesting and "useful in regard to training, mode of life or indication of disease."[4]

Cattell was not the only psychologist anxious to demonstrate his wares before the larger public. Under the sponsorship of the infant American Psychological Association, Joseph Jastrow and Hugo Munsterberg set up a mental testing exhibition at the 1893 World's Columbian Exposition in Chicago. There, for a small fee, they administered a variety of tests of sensory capacities and mental powers (similar to those used by Galton and Cattell) to thousands of fascinated volunteers. (Unfortunately, the results of this work were never published because of a conflict between Jastrow and the exhibition officials.) The 1904 International Congress of Arts and Sciences (part of the Louisiana Purchase Exposition) featured a similar display, offering attendees an opportunity to have their mental and physical capabilities assessed.

Given their lively interest in the possibility of actually measuring qualities of the human mind, it is not surprising that Americans greeted news of the Binet Scales with an outpouring of enthusiasm. Within a few years of its introduction, references to the new test had already begun to appear in the popular press. In fact, as early as 1912 psychologist Clara Harrison Town was lamenting to her professional peers that "unfortunately the American public . . . is threatening . . . a wholesale use of the Scale in an unscientific manner."[5] By 1913 and 1914, newspaper writers could assume that their readers were familiar with Binet and his work. A 1913 *Cosmopolitan* article, for example, captioned a picture of the Binet with the following words: "Dr. Alfred Binet, the French psychologist whose experiments in determining mental development have been compared to the work of Darwin and Mendel."[6] And in the years right after World War I, more articles appeared on IQ testing than on any other topic in pure or applied science. But Americans wanted to do more than read about the new test; they wanted to experience it for themselves. In 1913, researchers from Cornell showed off the Binet Scales to thousands of daily visitors at the Washington Hygiene and Demography Conference, and presenters at the Fourth International Conference on School Hygiene conducted public demonstrations throughout their weeklong meeting.[7] Several traveling exhibits also made their way around the country, reaching as far as distant Washington State.

Unsurprisingly, newly minted experts on child-rearing soon got into the act. In a 1913 article, Stoddard Goodhue advised parents that "if your child fails to get on well at school, or manifests any peculiar traits that cause you solicitude, it will be well for you to have the Binet–Simon tests applied by a competent examiner." He then went on to recommend that "the time is probably not distant when every wise parent will apply [the Binet] to his own children" and use the results to direct their educational and vocational choices.[8] Experts urged parents to keep a regular record of their children's IQ test scores and often provided do-it-yourself test questions for their convenience. In 1915, for example, the Chicago *Daily Tribune* printed a copy of the items from the Binet along with the following advice to parents. "Here's a page full of information which will enable TRIBUNE readers to keep track, year by year, of the mental development of their children. Cut out the page—save it."[9] By the 1920s, the concept of intelligence testing was no longer a mere scientific curiosity; it had become an integral part of American culture.

THE DEMOCRATIC APPEAL OF IQ TESTING

What are we to make of this outpouring of popular interest in IQ testing? Given the many dubious ways in which these tests were used by elite groups anxious to maintain their accustomed control of power, why in the world were all of these ordinary people flocking to take mental tests and avidly consuming articles describing this new technology? Were they simply stupid, misguided, and masochistic? Or was there a true democratic appeal to be found in the enterprise of intelligence testing? I would suggest that the latter was the case. For those who advocated a more egalitarian conception of merit, these tests held the promise of opening up new opportunities for talented individuals from less privileged backgrounds.

We have seen how the test-driven conception of merit adopted by most of the early (and, indeed, many of the current) promoters of intelligence testing served to institutionalize privilege. If, as these advocates firmly believed, test performance was determined primarily by biology, the scope for social mobility was clearly limited. Those most adaptively fit had probably already risen naturally to positions of power; the new tests simply provided a more objective way to document their innate superiority. And the laws of genetics suggested that the offspring of these superior persons were also likely to perform well on IQ tests, thus perpetuating privilege in the name of merit.

But even in the early days of IQ testing, the belief that biology determined destiny was not universally accepted. Although they agreed that heredity was important, politically liberal professionals were convinced that environment also played a significant role in cognitive development. In general, these liberals supported the ideal of merit just as avidly as did their more conservative peers, and few of them questioned the basic validity of intelligence tests. Unlike their more conservative brethren, however, the liberals tended to define merit primarily in terms of equity, not efficiency. Rather than serving to maintain social control in the hands of the fittest, they argued, IQ testing should be used as a tool for empowering ordinary, upward-striving Americans. After all, if IQ test performance was *influenced* by environmental experiences, then it could in principle be *improved* by appropriate training and education, thereby promoting the democratic goal of increased social mobility.

As we saw in the last chapter, once group-administered intelligence tests became widely available in the early 1920s, the main function of IQ testing in the public schools shifted from identifying children in need of special education to tracking students on the basis of cognitive ability. This practice clearly served the needs of America's industrial machine by efficiently channeling students into the track most appropriate for their social class. But contrary forces were also at work. Influential philosopher and educator John Dewey was probably the foremost advocate of a radically more democratic perspective on public education. Through his teaching, his scholarly books and articles, and his contributions to the popular press, Dewey argued forcefully that the primary mission of America's schools was *not* to serve the needs of industry; it was to nurture democracy. Public schools were charged with developing to the fullest the unique abilities of each child, regardless of social background. Appropriate, individualized instruction, Dewey believed, would promote democracy by enabling *all* students to contribute their own special gifts for the common good. Although not a particular advocate of intelligence testing, Dewey did suggest that IQ tests might provide information helpful for individualizing instruction. His views found a wide and appreciative audience during the 1920s and 1930s; indeed, to this day most educational theorists acknowledge a profound debt to Dewey's ideas.[10]

Hereditarian psychologists like Terman, Yerkes, and Thorndike were much less optimistic than Dewey about the possibility of enhancing a child's natural abilities through education. Accepting the rosy belief that opportunities for advancement were equally available to all Americans, they were convinced that most people had already found their proper role in the social and economic order. However, even these more conservative psychologists liked to trumpet the potential of their IQ tests to identify the occasional diamond in the rough. Bright boys, they argued, could sometimes be found in the humblest of environments, and IQ tests could help to uncover their previously hidden talents. In a 1920 article, for example, Thorndike asserted that "the psychological test . . . favors gifted boys with poor advantages; the [achievement-based] conventional examination favors rich boys with gifted tutors." A year later,

the New York commissioner of education added that IQ tests can "find
and develop . . . great minds, which live and die in obscurity for want of
appreciation and development."[11] If, as these advocates firmly believed,
IQ tests provided an objective measure of innate ability, free of the influence of class and educational opportunities, then their use could be seen
as supportive of democratic ideals.

As the roaring twenties gave way to the dramatically changed social
circumstances of the depression years, the democratic rationale for testing in the schools became even more salient. Harvard president James
Conant, for example, heralded the equalizing potential of the newly developed Scholastic Aptitude Test. Having grown up in a poor family
himself, Conant was committed to ending the dominance of private-
school educated, northeastern WASPs (a group that Nicholas Lemann
has dubbed "the Episcopacy") in the elite private universities. The SAT,
Conant believed, would advance this goal by identifying talented boys
in every corner of the country and from every social class, regardless of
previous educational opportunities.[12] (The fact that the SAT ended up
favoring the same privileged groups who had always had a monopoly
on power does not dim the luster of Conant's deeply felt if somewhat
naive dream.)

Almost as pervasive as the belief that intelligence tests could identify previously unsuspected talent in the schools was the claim that
they could help guide young people into the careers best suited to their
unique pattern of abilities. Article after article in both popular and professional journals promoted the use of IQ tests for career counseling in
high schools, colleges, vocational guidance bureaus, and industry. Of
course, as with tracking in the public schools, using IQ tests to channel
young people into the most appropriate slots in the industrial machine
served to control access to privilege. Those at the top of the economic
pyramid could reserve the top positions for those deemed most deserving by virtue of high test scores (typically themselves and their children),
while resting assured that the unfortunate individuals relegated to me-
nial, unrewarding, and poorly paid jobs were capable of nothing more
demanding.[13]

But again, this was not the entire story. Reformers, educators, and
businessmen were united in believing that a more rational and efficient
allocation of manpower—fitting the specific abilities of individual employees to the requirements of each job—could help increase the overall size of the economic pie, lessening the burdens of poverty without
threatening the privileged position of those at the top. And the potential benefits of more rational vocational guidance were personal as well
as economic. Middle-class youth no longer assumed that they would

follow their fathers' footsteps; they were now beginning to view vocational choices (the word "vocation" itself means "calling") as a primary source of self-expression and personal satisfaction. In the nineteenth century, individuals seeking vocational guidance had generally turned to phrenology for assistance. IQ testing now promised to provide similar guidance.[14]

As early as 1913, Lewis Terman had suggested that intelligence tests might play a role in the developing field of career counseling. "Mental health," he wrote, "depends intimately upon opportunities for appropriate self-expression in work. To insure this, . . . vocational guidance must be based to no small degree upon measurements of intelligence." Marion Rex Trabue made similar claims in a compilation of intelligence tests published in 1920. "It is certain," he proclaimed, "that a very large share of all human troubles, industrial unrest, discontent, inefficiency and unhappiness is traceable to the lack of proper adjustment between the man and the job. . . . Just as we measure a machine by the most precise gauges and tests available, why not measure the human individual by the most precise means we are able to apply?"[15] Using IQ tests to improve the fit between the person and the job, these experts believed, would inevitably lead to greater happiness for all.

So IQ tests promised to promote a more democratic society and increase individual happiness by providing schools, parents, and industry with a scientific tool for identifying and developing talent, wherever it might be found. But in addition to these tangible benefits, the tests appealed to simple human curiosity. Then, as now, people were infinitely curious about the workings of their own minds, and many were secretly anxious to compare their capabilities with those of others. The author of a 1923 article in *American Magazine* was not alone in admitting that "every time anybody mentions an intelligence test, I want to take it! All of us do."[16] Many of the articles about IQ testing appearing in the popular press printed sample questions or test excerpts that readers could use to test themselves or their children. As the author of an article published in *Survey* in 1922 remarked, "You had only to open your Sunday newspaper to find a new test to try out on the members of your family."[17] (The proliferation of do-it-yourself psychological tests on the Internet today testifies to the continuing power of this natural curiosity.)

In 1918, the *Literary Digest* published a vocabulary test that had been developed by Lewis Terman under the heading, "Of Course You Are a Superior Adult." The article suggested that "within a brief period readers of *The Digest* will doubtless be applying it to their families and friends." A 1919 article in *American Magazine* invited its readers to determine "How High Do You Stand on the Rating Scale?" by responding to a series of items similar to those that had appeared on the Army Alpha test. And in 1920, psychologist Marion Rex Trabue published a book entitled *Measure Your Mind: The Mentimeter and How to Use It,* which he described as "the first comprehensive system of tests . . . to be offered for general use." Although the author intended these tests primarily for industry, business, and education, he added that there was another potential application as well. "This is the use of such tests by the individual upon himself. . . . The man or woman bent on self-improvement or advancement may thus, within certain limits, assess by the application of standardized tests his or her own mental quality and capacity."[18]

The ubiquity of these self-tests is exemplified in a 1922 tongue-in-cheek ad in *The New Republic,* which proclaimed:

Intelligence tests, as any practicing psychologist will tell you, give a sure guide to all sorts of capacity. . . . The five simple tests below have been designed by an eminent, practical (eminently practical) psychologist to test your capacity to be a subscriber to *The New Republic.* . . . If you have indicated your superior intelligence by performing these operations correctly, you will receive *The New Republic* for 13 months.[19]

Certainly this ad appealed to the elitist sensibilities of its readers by assuring them that they were superior to the unlettered masses. But it contained a subtle democratic appeal as well. Whatever your background, your parentage, or your social class, your ability to answer a series of objective questions provided scientific evidence that you, too, were worthy of admission to the exalted ranks of *New Republic* subscribers.

But if this ad captures a bit of the democratic appeal of intelligence testing, it illustrates its limitations as well. Yes, the Binet and its group-administered cousins might provide opportunities to upwardly striving members of the middle and even the working classes—those who yearned to belong in the company of *New Republic* readers. But what of the poor, the foreign-born, those who were intellectually limited? The chances that these tests might work for their benefit were quite dismal. In fact, intelligence tests served primarily to confirm and justify their status on the lowest rungs of society. For those who believed that equality of opportunity was a reality in early twentieth-century America, IQ tests might indeed appear to be agents of democratization. But to the extent that poverty and environmental deprivation affected test scores (as of course inevitably they did), these measures served largely to maintain the status quo.

THE STORY OF LEWIS TERMAN: COMMITTED
SCIENTIST, PROPONENT OF SOCIAL CONTROL,
AND SELF-PROCLAIMED DEMOCRAT

No single figure exemplifies the story of the Binet in America as well as Lewis Terman. Terman was the towering figure in intelligence testing during the first half of the twentieth century. His career epitomizes all of the major themes that characterize our story thus far: the testing movement's foundation in evolutionary science; its appropriation by xenophobes, racists, and elitists; and paradoxically, its proponents' hopes that testing might promote a more open and democratic society. Terman, the 12th of 14 children born to an Indiana farm family, received his public education in a rural one-room school. His aspirations, however, went far beyond his family's rather humble circumstances. He recalled that he first became interested in intelligence from an itinerant phrenologist who predicted a great future for him after examining the bumps on his head. From the beginning, Terman's academic work focused on intelligence and its measurement—first in his master's work at Indiana University, where he explored the relationship between leadership and intelligence, and then at Clark University. His 1906 doctoral dissertation at Clark, supervised by the eminent G. Stanley Hall, compared the mental test scores of "seven bright boys" and "seven dull boys."[20]

Terman was immediately intrigued by H. H. Goddard's initial research reports describing the Binet Scales, and before long he had launched his own investigations using the new test. These efforts culminated in 1916 with his publication of the Stanford-Binet, a completely updated and renamed version of the original measure that quickly became the gold standard of IQ testing—a distinction that it retained for decades. In addition to his work with the Stanford-Binet, Terman participated actively in the development of the Army Alpha tests and several subsequent group-administered tests for school children. He served for two decades as the highly visible chairman of the Psychology Department at Stanford and in 1923 was elected president of the American Psychological Association. A 1959 survey ranked him third on the APA's list of the 10 most outstanding psychologists in American history.[21] For decades, then, the eminent Lewis Terman was the public face of intelligence testing in the United States.

Although never shy about expressing his social and political opinions, Terman considered himself first and foremost to be a scientist. Thoroughly grounded in the evolutionary biology of the day, he was an ardent proponent of the maturational theory espoused by his mentor

G. Stanley Hall. According to Hall, the human mind has evolved in distinct stages, starting with the "lowliest cockroach" and then proceeding through the mammalian brain, the "[non-European] lower races" of mankind, children, and women, finally reaching its pinnacle in the mind of the adult white male. Not surprisingly, given this training, Terman was strongly hereditarian in his beliefs. He was convinced that class boundaries were determined primarily by innate intelligence and that environment played only a minor role in determining personal success.[22]

Terman was a tireless advocate for his profession. He believed strongly that scientific experts should have a major voice in shaping public policy and was particularly proud of the role played in these discussions by psychological tests. Nor did he take kindly to interference from those he considered to be less qualified. His replies to Walter Lippmann in a famous debate on IQ testing conducted in the pages of *The New Republic* in 1922 and 1923 fairly dripped with sarcasm; how dare a mere journalist present himself as competent to contradict the scientific experts! "After Mr. Bryan had confounded the evolutionists, and Volive the astronomers," Terman fumed in one essay, "it was only fitting that some equally fearless knight should stride forth in righteous wrath and annihilate the other group of pseudoscientists known as 'intelligence testers.' Mr. Walter Lippmann, alone and unaided, has performed just this service."[23]

Terman was a quintessential Progressive reformer who placed great value on scientific expertise, efficiency, and a well-ordered society. He railed against admitting into the United States new immigrants from southern and eastern Europe and expressed grave concern about the supposedly large number of feebleminded people at large in society; these groups, he was convinced, were the primary cause of the "enormous amount of crime, pauperism, and industrial inefficiency" then plaguing the nation.[24] As we have seen, it was to describe this supposed danger that he coined the infamous term "menace of the feebleminded."[25] Terman uncritically accepted Carl Brigham's claims that the army testing data demonstrated the inferior intelligence of non-Nordic immigrants, and he used these data to advocate vociferously for the restriction of immigration. His concern about the threat posed by individuals of low intelligence (whether immigrant or native-born) also led Terman to join many of his fellow reformers as an active member of the Human Betterment Foundation, an organization founded to promote eugenic sterilization of the feebleminded. He wrote several popular articles in support of this cause, proudly claiming in one of them that intelligence testing served as "the beacon light of the eugenics movement."[26]

Although Terman put considerable energy into warning America about "the menace of the feebleminded," he is actually better known for his work at the other end of the spectrum of intelligence. From his earliest years as a psychologist, Terman evinced a particular interest in gifted individuals. He believed, in fact, that "the future welfare of the country hinges, in no small degree, upon the right education of these superior children."[27] At the beginning of the twentieth century, when Terman began his work in the field, many people believed that intellectually precocious children were generally maladjusted, physically weak, and sure to burn out young. Terman set out to prove the opposite. In 1911, as a part of his original work with the Binet Scales, he began collecting data on gifted children, and in 1921 he received a foundation grant that allowed him to begin his famous longitudinal study of children identified as geniuses. In one of the best-known studies in the history of psychology, Terman and his colleagues followed this group of children (popularly dubbed "Termites") throughout their lives, in the process demonstrating that in general they were healthier, happier, and better adjusted than their less intelligent peers.[28]

From all of these instances, it would be easy to brand Terman as an elitist. However, he actually considered himself to be a proud, liberal Democrat, strongly committed to the goal of a just society. Historian Russell Marks has described Terman's political views as follows: "He was a liberal in the best sense of the term: he was pragmatic and humanitarian; he held a burning faith in human perfectibility and technological progress; and he maintained an unshakable commitment to equality of opportunity and social melioration."[29] Although Terman believed that inequality of endowment was an inescapable, if unfortunate, fact, he felt that everyone should have the opportunity to make the most of whatever abilities he or she had been given. He was convinced that a society in which individuals were objectively and efficiently sorted into positions on the basis of innate endowment, regardless of class, would promote human progress and provide the highest level of justice for all. In his mind, this was the essence of a democratic society.

Of course, Terman's vision of democracy was based on the rosy assumption that significant class and racial barriers to social advancement no longer existed in the United States. During the heady years of the 1920s, it might have been possible for insulated members of the elite to hold these views; it became much more difficult, however, as the Great Depression ravaged all social classes and the Nazis illustrated the extremes to which the racist and eugenicist theories of respectable liberals could be taken. And indeed, by the 1930s and 1940s, Terman (like many of his fellow Progressives) had recanted the most extreme of his hereditarian views. In his later years, he even became an active crusader for social justice; during the 1930s and 1940s he was a vocal opponent of Nazi policies, and in the 1950s he strongly supported his academic peers who refused to sign loyalty oaths. Terman's career and his shifting views about the nature of intelligence are a striking illustration of the influence of changing social mores on the supposedly hard and objective findings of science. Ironically, America's most prominent advocate of IQ testing provides a perfect example of the degree to which the supposedly scientific concept of intelligence is in fact a product of its particular time and place.

Chapter 9

A Century of IQ Testing: The More Things Change, the More They Stay the Same

It has been more than 100 years since H. H. Goddard introduced the Binet Scales to an eager American public. Over the course of the subsequent century, the concept of intelligence has worked itself deep into the national psyche. Scores on IQ tests have become the primary yardstick by which we measure ourselves against one another. Educators use these scores (or their close equivalents) to track public school students into different programs or levels of instruction. The fabled SAT controls access to elite colleges, universities, and professional schools—and by extension to lucrative employment opportunities. At the other end of the spectrum, low IQ scores can entitle individuals to disability benefits and services. And since the 2002 Supreme Court decision in *Atkins v. Virginia,* which found the execution of people with mental retardation to be unconstitutional, such scores can literally determine whether a defendant convicted of a capital crime lives or dies.[1]

Given our ongoing fascination with the notion of intelligence—and considering the amount of ink that has been expended on research studies, scholarly reviews, and popular books and articles on the subject—one would assume that over the years methods for measuring IQ have become much more sophisticated and basic questions about its nature generally resolved. But one would be wrong. For, in fact, current IQ tests bear an almost startling resemblance to those first developed 100 years ago. And scientific arguments about the nature of intelligence, its hereditability, and its susceptibility to improvement are little closer to resolution than they were in 1920.

ONE HUNDRED YEARS OF INTELLIGENCE TESTS

Over the years, test developers have put considerable energy into refining and improving both individually administered and group-administered IQ tests. They are continually updating test content (and, incidentally, making it significantly more difficult). They carefully scrutinize items for cultural bias. Technical issues such as reliability and the representativeness of norm groups have received considerable attention. Indeed, and with some justification, many psychologists view modern IQ tests as the pride and joy of their profession. But in reality these many revisions and improvements have taken place only around the edges of these measures, leaving their fundamental nature and rationale remarkably unchanged.

Alfred Binet himself would have undoubtedly felt right at home had he been able to take a peek at a modern individually administered IQ test. In fact, the venerable Stanford-Binet, now in its fifth edition, still contains many items similar to Binet's own. Like students in 1905, modern Binet test-takers are asked, for example, to define words, copy geometric designs, remember strings of numbers, and answer questions requiring commonsense judgment. But though the Stanford-Binet is still a respected measure and is used at least occasionally by many psychologists, in recent decades it has been largely supplanted in clinical practice by the various Wechsler Scales.[2]

Psychologist David Wechsler first developed this new individually administered test of intelligence in 1939, while he was working at Bellevue Hospital in New York. The Wechsler-Bellevue, as the measure was known, differed from the Stanford-Binet in some significant respects. Most notably, Wechsler separated items into two conceptually distinct scales, one consisting of verbal questions and the other of visual or hands-on items. This allowed for the calculation of separate Verbal and Performance IQs, in addition to the Full Scale IQ. Wechsler's new format also made it possible meaningfully to interpret scores on individual subtests, permitting an assessment of individual patterns of cognitive strengths and weaknesses. But though technically quite innovative, Wechsler's new test had a very familiar feel. Its content was virtually all recycled from the Stanford-Binet, the Army Alpha tests, and other psychological puzzles in wide use during the 1920s. Included in the verbal subscales were such tried-and-true tasks as defining words, remembering digits, responding to common sense questions, and explaining similarities between two words. The performance subtests required subjects to copy designs with colored blocks, assemble puzzles, find the missing part in a series of pictures, rapidly pair digits with symbols, and put a series of mixed-up pictures in the proper order—all test items that would have been instantly recognizable to a psychologist from the 1910s or 1920s.[3]

The Wechsler Scales have gone through many revisions in the past 70 years, and developers have added two new tests designed specifically for children. The most recent versions include the Wechsler Intelligence Scale for Children–Fourth Edition or WISC–IV (2003), the Wechsler Adult Intelligence Scale–Fourth Edition or WAIS–IV (2008), and the Wechsler Preschool and Primary Scale of Intelligence–Third Edition or WPPSI–III (2002). These various revisions have introduced many technical improvements and some new types of questions into the tests. The continuities between the different versions, however, are much more striking than the differences. (I can speak to this fact with some degree of authority, since over the 30-year course of my professional career I have had to learn to administer the WAIS–R, WAIS–III, WAIS–IV, WISC–R, WISC–III, and WISC–IV. I recently had occasion to examine a 1949 version of the WAIS. The experience was almost eerie. Not only were all of the item *types* totally familiar to me, but some of the actual *questions* were identical to those included in the current version of the test.)

In the same way that almost all individually administered IQ tests follow in the footsteps of the Binet Scales, group-administered tests of intelligence still adhere to the basic format established by the Army Alpha. From Carl Brigham's 1926 Scholastic Aptitude Test (an upward revision of the Army tests) and Lewis Terman's 1921 National Intelligence Test (a downward revision of the same test intended for school children) to the modern SAT and the innumerable tests of cognitive abilities familiar to most elementary school students, the debt to the Army tests is unmistakable. Much of the content of these modern tests is strikingly similar to that of the original; even more significant, however, is the commonality of their formats. For it was the Army Alpha that introduced the now-ubiquitous multiple-choice test to a mass audience. The lure of the easy administration and rapid and objective scoring made possible by this test format was—and remains—irresistible. In their understandable enthusiasm for economy and convenience, however, test developers have paid regrettably little attention to what they are giving up. Anyone who has ever puzzled over the limited and sometimes arbitrary choices offered by these tests (and that includes almost all of us) is painfully aware that ease of scoring has been purchased at the cost of creativity and thoughtfulness. It is worth considering how profoundly this ubiquitous testing format has restricted our understanding of the fundamental nature of intelligence.

During the course of the past century, intelligence tests have undoubtedly become more sophisticated in their construction, less biased in their content, and significantly more difficult. The importance of these technical improvements should not be underestimated. But comparing the Stanford-Binet of 1916, the Army Alpha tests of 1918, or the Wechsler-Bellevue Scales of 1939 to the newest versions of the WAIS, the WISC, or the SAT illustrates starkly how minimally our basic ideas about intelligence have evolved over the years. Were innovators like Binet, Terman, and Wechsler so brilliant, sophisticated, and farsighted that their tests should be viewed as the last word on intelligence? Well, perhaps—but I, for one, am skeptical. I suspect that we have come so completely to equate our treasured notion of intelligence with scores on these now-familiar tests that questioning their basic nature seems almost sacrilegious. So here we are, well into the twenty-first century, still defining intelligence in terms of scores on tests whose basic content and format were laid down during the era of the Model T Ford.

THE ORIGINS OF THE IQ WARS

As we have seen in the previous chapters, early-twentieth-century Americans were very quick to embrace the infant technology of IQ testing. It soon became evident, however, that these new tests would produce losers as well as winners. And so inevitably, the unbridled enthusiasm of the early years gave way to controversy. Indeed, almost from the day that H. H. Goddard introduced the Binet Scales to the American public, advocates on both sides of the issue have used popular and professional journals to conduct an intense—and often acrimonious—debate about the meaning and use of IQ test scores. Their main arguments, clearly articulated by the mid-1920s, have changed remarkably little over the years. This ongoing debate has focused on the following major questions:

1. What do IQ tests actually measure, and how well do they predict real-world educational, vocational, and social success?
2. To what extent does heredity determine IQ scores? Conversely, how much can education and environmental enrichment improve test performance?
3. How might we best use IQ tests in schools, the workplace, and society at large?

Debaters on both sides have framed their arguments in the objective language of science. In reality, however, the opposing viewpoints have generally been associated with liberal versus conservative political ideologies.

Indeed, one can generally predict the positions of both lay and professional combatants in the IQ Wars more accurately from their social and political philosophies than from any so-called scientific evidence.[4]

The war over IQ was well underway by the early 1920s. Most famously, psychologist Lewis Terman and journalist Walter Lippmann staked out conservative and liberal positions respectively in a heated debate conducted in the pages of *The New Republic* in 1922 and 1923.[5] Here, and in countless other articles in both scholarly journals and the popular press, pundits and professionals alike argued about the nature of intelligence, the respective roles of heredity and environment in its development, and the use and misuse of IQ tests.

Given the time and energy devoted to the controversy, one would think that participants could have at least agreed about what IQ tests measured. But even on this fundamental issue, common ground was lacking. In 1921, a symposium of psychologists assembled by Edward Thorndike offered as many definitions of intelligence as there were contributors to the discussion. These experienced testing experts lacked a shared understanding of even their most basic terms. (Interestingly, in 1986 a similar panel convened by eminent psychologist Robert Sternberg achieved little greater agreement.)[6] Conservatives generally framed their arguments in terms of *g,* or general intelligence—real, biologically based, and eminently measurable. Robert Yerkes summarized the conservative position in a 1923 article in *Atlantic Monthly.* "Theoretically," he proclaimed, "man is just as measurable as a bar of steel or a humanly contrived machine." And the IQ test, of course, was the measuring device of choice. Liberals, by contrast, viewed intelligence as much more complex and multidimensional. Yes, they admitted, IQ tests might be useful for certain purposes. The tests, however, could sample only a narrow segment of the many personal qualities crucial to real-life intelligent behavior. As Walter Lippmann asked rhetorically, how could one possibly determine a child's basic worth on the basis of "an hour's monkeying with a set of puzzles"?[7]

If they differed in their definitions of intelligence, conservatives and liberals disagreed even more vehemently about the relative contributions of heredity and environment. The conservative, or hereditarian, position was clearly dominant during the 1920s. Lewis Terman's views were typical of this perspective. "From Galton on down to Thorndike and Davenport," he wrote, scientists have produced considerable evidence to demonstrate that intellectual abilities "are . . . largely determined by native endowment."[8] Conservative testing advocates argued vigorously in the popular press that racial, ethnic, and class disparities in IQ test scores were due almost entirely to the genetic inferiority of the lower-scoring groups. And because these differences were genetically determined, they continued, misguided attempts to ameliorate such disparities through training or education were a soft-headed waste of scarce national resources.

Environmentally based explanations for IQ score differences, although less common, were not entirely absent during these early years. Alfred Binet himself, as we have seen, had been convinced that an active program of mental orthopedics could improve the intelligence of children identified by his measure as needing special educational services. Binet's environmental perspective was shared by a number of prominent social scientists (although, admittedly, few among them were psychologists). For several decades, for example, anthropologist Franz Boas and sociologist Lester Frank Ward had worked to make the case that culture, not heredity, determined much of human behavior. Behaviorist John B. Watson (generally ignored by his psychological colleagues but highly influential among a generation of American parents) argued vigorously that the newborn infant was utterly malleable, just waiting to be molded by his environment. Liberal social commentators such as Walter Lippmann and Walter Bagley repeatedly reminded their readers that IQ scores could not be interpreted without reference to social conditions.[9]

Believing as they did that intelligence—in their view the primary determinant of adaptive functioning—was innate, immutable, and accurately measured by IQ tests, it is not surprising that social conservatives enthusiastically promoted the widest possible use of these measures. Indeed, from their perspective, what was not to like? Tests could efficiently channel individuals into educational and vocational slots. They could improve the genetic stock of the country by excluding biologically inferior foreigners and preventing feebleminded individuals from reproducing. If the effect of such test-centered selection and exclusion practices was to confirm the existing social order, well, this must be nature's plan. Liberals, more concerned about issues of equality and justice, were naturally more cautious. Yes, they admitted, intelligence tests might help advance democracy by identifying previously unsuspected talent among underprivileged groups. But they warned that the tests might also simply confirm the privileges of those already in power and help keep the lower orders in their places. It was therefore incumbent on socially conscious test users to remain vigilant about the possible consequences of their enterprise.

By the end of the 1920s, the battle lines in the IQ Wars had been clearly drawn. Liberals and conservatives had staked out opposing positions about the nature of intelligence, the relative roles of heredity and the environment, and the use and misuse of IQ tests. If their arguments sound familiar to modern readers, it is because their positions have changed so little. True, at some times over the years conservatives have been in the ascendancy, while during others the liberals have had more influence. However, as we shall see in subsequent sections, arguments on both sides have been affected less by advances in scientific knowledge than by social, economic, and political events—and by the unthinking way in which our society equates intelligence with personal worth.

DECADES OF CONTROVERSY

As the exuberant 1920s gave way to the ravages of the Great Depression and the horrors of Nazi Germany, the strictly genetic explanations for intellectual differences so beloved by a generation of psychologists lost much of their appeal. No longer were economic struggles confined to dark-haired immigrants and shiftless members of the lower class; the specter of financial ruin suddenly reached deep into the solidly respectable middle class. Economic uncertainty cut so close to home that even some ardent hereditarians were willing to concede that life experiences might indeed affect class and racial differences in intelligence.

Evidence of this dramatic shift in perspective can be seen as early as 1934. In a study conducted that year, only 4 percent of the 100 eminent psychologists, sociologists, and educators surveyed were willing to state categorically that genetically based racial disparities in innate intelligence had been experimentally proven (although 46% cautioned that such differences remained a reasonable possibility).[10] During the course of the 1930s, several prominent professional organizations, including the American Psychological Association's Society for the Psychological Study of Social Issues (in 1938) and the American Anthropological Association (in 1939), issued statements supporting environmental explanations for racial differences in psychological characteristics.[11] By 1941, writing in the *Encyclopaedia of Educational Research*, Otto Klineberg felt confident in concluding that "the available data offer no support for the view that racial or national origins set different limits to the potentialities of a child."[12] Quite a turnaround from the conventional wisdom of the 1920s!

Environmental explanations for IQ differences resurrected the hopeful possibility (first suggested by Binet himself) that appropriate educational intervention might actually increase a child's intelligence. Hereditarian conservatives had viewed such attempts as a naive and even unconscionable waste of precious national resources. But in the late 1930s a group of researchers at the University of Iowa produced evidence claiming to demonstrate that the conservatives were wrong.

In a series of articles published in professional journals and popular magazines, the researchers reported that groups of young children who attended their special preschool programs were achieving significantly higher scores on IQ tests than those who had not been offered such an opportunity. A 1938 article in *Time* magazine provides one example of the public excitement that these findings generated. According to this article, "One of the few fixed stars in the creed of orthodox psychologists is a belief that people are born with a certain degree of intelligence and are doomed to go through life with the same I.Q." But now, the author reported, "a little group of psychologists . . . in Iowa City" had "laid astounding proofs . . . that an individual's I.Q. can be changed."[13] Optimistic reports such as this offered a welcome tonic to a society struggling with economic insecurity and the looming specter of war.

Testing professionals themselves argued vigorously (and sometimes highly personally) about whether the Iowa results could possibly be valid. Hopeful parents, however, had few such reservations. Within months, popular magazines were filled with articles describing how mothers (fathers seemed strangely absent from the discussion) could nurture their children's intellectual development. Writing in the *Reader's Digest,* for example, Maya Pines challenged mothers with a "heady responsibility: *raising their children's intelligence in the crucial early years when it is most malleable.*"[14] No longer must parents passively accept the luck of the genetic draw; they could now intervene actively to create a better future for their sons and daughters.

The rigors of World War II brought about yet another significant shift in the American psyche. As the country pulled together to confront a common enemy, its citizens of necessity began to focus less on personal advancement and more on the welfare of the nation as a whole. This sense of national purpose remained strong during the early postwar years, as the country entered into a new battle against Godless Communism. The frantic Cold War competition with the Soviet Union and widespread fears that the United States was on the losing end of a so-called science gap were ignited to near frenzy by the launching of Sputnik in 1957. Americans were suddenly desperate to catch up. No longer could the country afford to view the abilities of its youth as a purely personal matter; intelligence had become a precious national resource, and the crucial challenge for the United States was to identify the best and the brightest—those who could help lead the nation to scientific and political victory over the relentless Soviet machine.

IQ tests were, not surprisingly, the tool of choice for identifying this intellectual elite. Public schools, anxious to improve their quality and increase their rigor, began to rely more heavily on test-driven ability tracking. In 1954, the Civil Service Commission introduced a new test, very similar in format to the SAT, to examine applicants for higher-level civil service jobs. And the SAT itself, until now used primarily by elite Eastern universities, was increasingly adopted as an admission requirement by colleges and universities throughout the country, including many major state universities. But most potentially troubling amidst this new flurry of testing activity was the military's decision to use IQ tests to identify and protect the nation's most intellectually talented young men. This important story does not appear to be well known and merits recounting in some detail.

In 1951, shortly after its entry into the Korean War required the country to resume the military draft, the Selective Service System signed a contract with the Educational Testing Service (publisher of the SAT) to develop a College Qualification Test (CQT). The purpose of this test was to determine which college students should qualify for a deferment from the draft; potential draftees scoring above a certain level (in addition to earning satisfactory grades) were automatically deferred, while students with lower scores were required to meet additional criteria. Although deferred students were theoretically subject to being drafted after graduation, it was assumed that most would probably escape the dangers of the battlefield. For political reasons, the ETS and the military were careful to term the SSCQT a test of "scholastic aptitude" rather than intelligence; for all intents and purposes, however, it was a group-administered IQ test.[15]

When the plan for the SSCQT was introduced, it met with predictable charges that the program was elitist and antidemocratic. But the furor soon died down. As one defender of the new tests explained, "In the situation that confronts us, we must take every care not to waste either our barely adequate store of high ability (through inept or sentimental allocation of it) or the time and cost of military training (through giving it to those who will not be able to make use of it.)"[16] National security required special treatment for the intellectual elite, and naive egalitarian notions should not be allowed to interfere with the country's welfare. With the institution of the draft lottery in 1969 and the subsequent abolition of the entire draft a few years later, the SSCQT quietly disappeared from the scene. For more than a decade, however, a young man's score on a test of intelligence could have literally determined whether he lived or died.

The staid, conservative, and nationalistic decade of the 1950s yielded dramatically to the heady years of the 1960s, filled with antiwar protests, civil rights marches, and Great Society programs. As issues of equality and social justice rose to the forefront, environmental explanations for differences in IQ scores suddenly again became fashionable. The work of socially conscious and environmentally oriented psychologists like J. McVickers Hunt and Benjamin Bloom guided policy makers at the highest level of government. A prime example was the rationale for Head Start, one of the crown jewels of the Great Society. In the words of Dr. Robert Cooke, one of the program's founders, Head Start's fundamental theoretical justification was "the concept that intellect is, to a large extent, a product of experience, not inheritance."[17] To even suggest otherwise made one politically suspect.

This renewed emphasis on social justice naturally raised concerns about the possible misuse of intelligence testing. As both popular and professional journals began reporting on IQ-test-related racial disparities in special education placement, college admissions, and hiring decisions, such concerns achieved real political force. In a controversial California decision (*Larry P. v. Riles,* 1979), a state court barred the use of intelligence tests for placing minority children in special education classes. (Similar cases in other states, however, were decided in the opposite direction.) In several other cases (e.g., *Griggs v. Duke Power Co.,* 1971), the U.S. Supreme Court ruled that employers could not use IQ tests for job selection unless they could demonstrate that the content of the test was directly relevant to the job in question. Since such relevance could rarely be proven, tests of aptitude and intelligence were eventually banned from most employment settings.[18]

A backlash against the egalitarian ethos and somewhat naive optimism of the 1960s and early 1970s was probably inevitable. In 1969, as the civil rights movement was veering into a harder-edged black nationalism, psychologist Arthur Jensen ignited a bombshell by publishing an article in the *Harvard Educational Review* that opened with these provocative words: "Compensatory education has been tried and it apparently has failed." He went on to add that "we are left with . . . various pieces of evidence, no one of which is definitive alone, but which, when viewed all together make it a not unreasonable hypothesis that genetic factors are strongly implicated in the average Negro–white intelligence difference."[19] Although Jensen's language was measured, his thesis was incendiary, and the reaction to it was predictably explosive. Liberal academics staged protests against Jensen (and against Richard Herrnstein, who published a similar article two years later), demanding that he be fired from his university position. Typical of the vehemence on the liberal side were reactions like that of journalist Carl Rowan, who wrote angrily, "I say to the Jensens, the Putnams and all the rest, BULLONEY! Do not talk to me about 15 IQ points and black inferiority as long as the deck is so stacked that black people languish in poverty at three times the rate of white people. . . . It is . . . patently obvious . . . that money buys all the things needed, before and after birth, to produce healthy, intelligent human beings."[20] The lines of battle had again been drawn.

The ensuing decades have done little to dampen the intensity of the IQ Wars. Psychologists, educators, and social commentators continue to argue heatedly about the nature of intelligence, the relative roles of environment and genetics, the reasons for the persistent class and racial disparities in IQ scores, and the most appropriate ways of using intelligence tests. The liberal side of the argument has remained the most politically correct. But the resurgence of conservative political ideology during the 1980s and 1990s led to a renewed emphasis on genetic explanations for social inequality. These conservative social views have been fueled on the scientific front by advances in genetics, new knowledge about brain–behavior relationships, and the growing popularity of the field of sociobiology, all of which focus on biological rather than environmental explanations for human behavior.

The conservatives struck a major blow in the mid-1990s, with the publication of Richard Herrnstein and Charles Murray's massive tome *The Bell Curve*. The book's primary argument is that class differences in America are due largely to immutable disparities in innate intelligence. Herrnstein and Murray's social agenda was clear. In their view, liberal social programs were "based on the explicit assumption that ethnic groups do not differ in the abilities that contribute to success in school and the workplace. . . . Much of this book has been given over to the many ways in which that assumption is wrong." They then went on to add that "to think that the available repertoire of social interventions can do the job [of raising IQ] if only the nation spends more money on them is illusory."[21] Predictably, the public reaction to *The Bell Curve* was explosive. For several years after its publication, arguments by liberal and conservative commentators alike flooded opinion pages, magazines, and even scholarly journals, weighing in on Herrnstein and Murray's arguments with energy, passion, and more than a little invective.

With unsettling frequency, in fact, the level of debate about intelligence and its measurement has degenerated from passionate advocacy to blatant personal attack. One particularly egregious example comes from conservative psychologist Helmuth Nyborg, who wrote in a 2003 volume of papers intended as a tribute to Arthur Jensen, "One of the parties [to the IQ controversy] is fairly well characterized by a series of brutal and merciless ad hominem attacks by a group of aggressive and ruthless ideologues, moved more by self-assumed moral authority than truth. . . . The other party [his own, of course] is better characterized as a group of hard-working scientists moved more by empirical arguments than by anything else."[22] At least some liberals gave almost as good as they got. In a 2005 article in the *American Psychologist,* for example, Richard Cooper noted that "for the last four centuries Western science has been obsessed with the need to justify White privilege." He went on to accuse those who "use the rhetoric of science to sell the idea that historical inequity should be embraced as biological inevitability" of insulting all "who value a common humanity."[23] And these words appear in respectable scientific publications! To term the ongoing debate about intelligence and its measurement a "war" is surely no exaggeration.

THE IQ WARS AND SOCIAL VALUES

Given all of the ink and energy expended on the IQ Wars over the past century, it would seem that by now science should have resolved at least some of these controversies. After all, proponents on both sides of the divide generally frame their arguments in terms of hard, cold facts. But the vehemence and emotional intensity of their language suggest that the issues at stake transcend objective science. As Richard Herrnstein, himself one of the primary participants in the fray, has observed, "The issue is intensely emotional. It is almost impossible for people to disagree about the pros and cons of intelligence testing and long avoid the swapping of oaths and anathema."[24] The fact is that the questions raised by IQ testing touch on deeply held social values and fundamental assumptions about human nature.

At the core of many of our battles over IQ testing is the debate about what equality means and how it might best be achieved. Admittedly, a few of the early proponents of testing were avowed elitists who viewed the goal of an egalitarian society as a naive distraction from the more important business of life. But most advocates on both sides of the IQ Wars have supported fundamental democratic ideals. Where they have disagreed has been in their basic understanding of equality. Journalist Mark Snyderman has summarized this issue neatly. "The IQ controversy," he wrote in 1988, "represents a clash of values, often within the same person, between a belief in a meritocratic hierarchy (efficiency) and the desire to see everyone succeed (equality)."[25]

Of paramount importance to the side that we generally label conservative is the ideal of meritocracy. Most conservatives argue that an individual's social and economic position should be determined entirely by his or her own level of commitment, personal talents, and willingness to work; extraneous factors such as financial status, ethnicity, or family background should be irrelevant to advancement. Intelligence tests, they believe, promote meritocracy by objectively identifying talented individuals from all walks of life. But equality of *opportunity,* in their view, is not the same as equality of *condition.* Social conservatives are generally convinced that American society provides roughly equal opportunities to all of its members. Those on top of the economic hierarchy have earned their positions through talent and hard work; those stuck on the lower rungs of the ladder unfortunately lack the personal qualities required for success. Inequality of condition based on personal behavior and individual talents, although perhaps regrettable, is inevitable. The conservative authors of *The Bell Curve* made no apologies for this hardheaded position. A meritocratic society (with merit defined in large part by test scores), they admitted, must tolerate a certain degree of inequality. "[But] never mind," wrote Herrnstein and Murray. "Gifted youngsters are important not because they are more virtuous or deserving but because our society's future depends on them."[26]

Liberals take a decidedly different approach to the matter. True, many support the general principle of meritocracy. But unlike conservatives, most liberals believe that American society still falls lamentably short of offering true equality of opportunity to its citizens. As long as basic social and economic conditions remain unchanged, they argue, IQ tests discriminate unfairly against the poor and members of racial and ethnic minorities. Conservatives may see tests as engines of opportunity, but liberals are more likely to view them as tools of social control, helping maintain an inequitable economic system while providing the privileged with a socially acceptable justification for their unearned advantages. Columnist E. J. Dionne has expressed this liberal perspective quite sharply. "Surely," he observed in a 1995 essay, "it does not require great courage to make arguments that will reassure the well-educated and well-off that they hold their high positions because they are on the whole smarter than everybody else," arguments that conveniently free them from the obligation to "trouble themselves" over their less fortunate countrymen.[27]

These warring ideas about the nature of equality are generally overt and clearly articulated. But other assumptions, although equally powerful, are less openly acknowledged. Foremost among these is the proclivity of liberals and conservatives alike to conflate intelligence with human worth—in the words of historian Lorraine Dashton, to "moralize the intellect."[28] Throughout Western history, we humans have used our possession of the supposedly God-given quality of reason, or intellect, to set ourselves apart from other living creatures. But the modern concept of intelligence has done something more; it has given us a convenient excuse for asserting that some people are innately more valuable than others. If evolutionary theory is correct in assuming that high intelligence is a mark of biological superiority, then brighter individuals, because they supposedly help advance the race as a whole, can easily be viewed as possessing greater moral worth. Dr. John Erskine of Columbia University even entitled a 1916 essay "The Moral Obligation to Be Intelligent."[29]

This conceptual link between intelligence and virtue is illustrated most dramatically by our starkly different cultural attitudes toward individuals at the two extremes of the cognitive continuum. A belief that people with limited intellectual abilities are by definition morally deficient goes back to at least the seventeenth century. John Locke, that seminal theorist of the human mind, believed that rationality was the defining mark of true personhood; in his view, "idiots" did not even qualify as members of the human species. Frenchman Benedict Morel, influential proponent of degeneration theory, also gave intelligence a moral twist, proclaiming that idiocy was the natural and inevitable result of immoral behavior in oneself or one's ancestors. By the 1880s, under the influence of Darwinian ideas, the explanatory focus of mental subnormality had shifted from violation of natural law to evolution. Prominent Italian theorist Cesare Lombroso, for example, viewed individuals who violated normative physical, mental, or behavioral expectations as throwbacks to an earlier period of evolutionary history. These social deviants, being closer to our animal ancestry, would naturally display a less-developed sense of morality.[30]

Following the developmental logic of the Binet Scales, most American psychologists of the early 1900s believed that the cognitive development of the mentally subnormal was arrested at an intellectual level appropriate to that of a younger child. Moral development, they often assumed, was equivalently delayed. For this reason, individuals with low intelligence posed a serious risk to society, threatening stability and good order through their promiscuous, antisocial, or delinquent behaviors. As we have seen, during the 1920s Lewis Terman famously warned the nation about the "menace of the feebleminded," labeling these unfortunate individuals as "democracy's ballast, not always useless but always a potential liability." Psychologist Joseph Peterson went even further. Each "passed away . . . in his turn," he wrote, "little lamented, no doubt, by those on whom they have been burdens, and soon forgotten by the world."[31]

One would like to think that these harsh sentiments are nothing more than an unfortunate relic from an unenlightened past. And indeed, these days no one with any pretensions to social respectability would dare to speak unsympathetically of those formally diagnosed with intellectual disabilities. But though we may now use milder language, this presumed association between low intelligence and immorality remains an underlying current in our social and political discourse. Describing the (admittedly miniscule) correlations between low IQ scores and various measures of social maladjustment, for example, the authors of *The Bell Curve* suggested that "perhaps the ethical principles for not committing crimes are less accessible (or less persuasive) to people of low intelligence." Psychologist Richard Lynn agreed. Writing in 1995, he described the "sociopathic lifestyle" of people with intellectual limitations and lamented their supposed propensity to have large numbers of children.[32]

The effects of this widespread cultural assumption that people with limited intelligence are lacking in morality—indeed, are not quite human—are anything but benign. In 1908, the Reverend Karl Schwartz (a minister, no less!) proclaimed without a shred of apology that "it may be shown that a correct answer to the question as to how and by what process the human race may be empowered to advance would be by the utility of death—the death of the unfit."[33] But no one could think this way today, you might object. Think again! In a 1962 survey of 1800 Mensa members in Great Britain, 47 percent approved the legalized killing of sufficiently subnormal infants.[34] Prominent modern ethicist Joseph Fletcher has stated outright that "any individual of the species Homo sapiens who falls below an I.Q. grade of 40 in a standard Stanford-Binet test . . . is questionably a person; below the mark of 20, not a person."[35] Ethicist Richard McCormick agreed, asserting that individuals with severe mental retardation "probably lack personal status, with a consequent lack of claim upon rights. . . . [W]e need not save it from death's approach."[36]

Clearly, we do not need to dig very deep beneath our supposedly compassionate attitudes toward people with limited intelligence to unearth our unspoken cultural assumption that they lack intrinsic human worth. But what about individuals at the other end of the cognitive continuum? Given our modern obsession with IQ, it may surprise some readers to learn that Western societies have historically been somewhat ambivalent about people who are too smart. On the one hand, the Greek philosophers believed that men of exceptional wisdom and intellect must be touched by a spark of the divine. But this awe has often been mixed with some degree of fear and disdain. The ancients suggested that there might be an association between genius and insanity (a belief that has gained some modern support from the now-well-documented finding that a disproportionate number of highly creative artists, writers, and composers have suffered from manic-depressive illness). Even if not actually mad, intellectually gifted individuals were often viewed as physically weak and socially inept.[37]

There is of course still a strong streak of anti-intellectualism in American popular culture—as any observer of the current political scene can readily attest. But, at least among members of the middle and upper classes, the belief that people who are too smart are likely to be maladjusted has largely dissipated. As we have seen, Lewis Terman's well-publicized genius studies purported to demonstrate that intellectually gifted children generally display superior physical health, social skills, and qualities of character as well. A number of other researchers have reported similar findings.[38] Among the most vociferous of these was psychologist Edward Thorndike, one of the pioneers in the field of educational testing. In his 1913 vice presidential address to the American Association for the Advancement of Science, Thorndike proclaimed, "History records no career, war or revolution that can compare in significance with the fact that the correlation between intellect and morality is approximately .3, a fact to which perhaps a fourth of the world's progress is due."[39] (In other publications, Thorndike placed this correlation at .4 or .5, but nowhere did he cite a single shred of evidence to support these supposedly scientific claims.)

Not many modern pundits equate high intelligence and sound character quite as bluntly as did Thorndike. But though their language may have become somewhat more temperate, many opinion makers continue to express similar sentiments. The authors of *The Bell Curve,* for example, interpreted their research as demonstrating that "intelligence . . . is . . . a force for maintaining a civil society." Eminent historian Richard Hofstadter has claimed that "intellectuals are properly more responsive to . . . values [such as reason and justice] than others." Analyzing our propensity to imbue highly intelligent individuals with an entire panoply of positive qualities, Leslie Margolin has defined the cultural understanding of the gifted child in modern American society as "goodness personified."[40] These starkly opposed images of the "menace of the feebleminded" versus the "personification of goodness" remain powerful symbols of the link that we in Western society have made between intelligence and virtue. Although it may generally operate beneath the level of our consciousness, I have little doubt that this assumption has contributed significantly to the virulence and emotional intensity of the IQ Wars.

Chapter 10

Toward a Broader Conception of Intelligence

The past nine chapters have covered a lot of territory. But after roaming across several centuries, meeting an interesting variety of social critics and scientific theorists, and touching on topics ranging from Puritan theology to phrenology to eugenics, we have consistently come back to the same two fundamental concepts. The first relates to the nature of intelligence and the second to the meaning of merit. So far we have focused mainly on the historical development of these ideas. I would now like to shift gears, offering my own personal assessment of the interrelated issues that have fueled our century-long IQ Wars. In this chapter, I suggest some broader and potentially more productive ways of viewing the concept of intelligence. In the next chapter, I will tackle the contentious question of heredity and IQ, weighing in on the extent to which genes determine intelligence, the meaning of persistent racial differences in IQ scores, and the potential malleability of IQ. Finally, in Chapter 12, I will discuss the appropriate (and inappropriate) use of IQ tests and offer what I consider to be a more equitable and less test-centered view of merit.

Most Westerners assume that intelligence is a universal human trait—brain-based, reliably measurable, and critical to life success. But in reality, as we have seen, this traditional assumption is both relatively recent and markedly culturally specific. In the preceding chapters, we have traced our current ideas about intelligence back to nineteenth-century advances in evolutionary biology and dramatic shifts in the structure of society. As this narrative has demonstrated, the resulting concept of intelligence is actually as much a *social* as a scientific construct. A single, objectively validated definition of intelligence does not—indeed, probably cannot—exist; the predictable result has been a century of theoretical controversy, definitional confusion, and downright nasty personal attacks. However, out of this conceptual morass, two broad approaches to intelligence do emerge. One is relatively narrow, test based, and specific to Western culture, while the other is broad, multifaceted, and culturally relative. Neither, of course, can be classified as right or wrong. An indiscriminate and unacknowledged mixing of the two approaches, however, has led to much unnecessary conflict. A clearer understanding of the meaning, uses, and limitations of what I have termed the psychometric and the adaptive approaches to intelligence illustrates the perils of reflexively using the first as a measure of the second.

PSYCHOMETRIC INTELLIGENCE

"Let us define intelligence as that ability which is measured in common by the various so-called 'intelligence tests,'" wrote psychologist Arthur Otis in 1927. "Presto! Intelligence has now been defined and therefore can be measured!"[1] Otis's words may seem flippant, but his intent was serious. Indeed, this oft-quoted remark epitomizes what we now term the psychometric approach to intelligence. Followers in the psychometric tradition generally equate intelligence with Charles Spearman's *g*: the unitary, biologically based trait that he was convinced was the foundation of all cognitive functioning. And these advocates agree with Spearman that formal tests of intelligence adequately reflect this hypothesized quality. Linda Gottfredson is typical of the many modern psychologists who approach intelligence primarily from a psychometric perspective. "Intelligence," she wrote in a recent *Wall Street Journal* article, is "a very general mental capability that, among other things, involves the ability to reason, plan, solve problems, think abstractly, comprehend complex ideas, learn quickly and learn from experience. . . . Intelligence, so defined, can be measured, and intelligence tests measure it well."[2]

Most Americans see little reason to question Gottfredson's statement. We uncritically accept the notion that through some mysterious process known only to psychologists, IQ tests can plumb the depths of the human brain to reveal how smart we *really* are. An examination of the tests themselves, however, suggests a decidedly more modest function.[3] Alfred Binet developed the first modern test of intelligence specifically to predict success in the standard school curriculum. Over the years, although the meaning attached to IQ scores has expanded significantly, there has been remarkably little change in the tests themselves. In fact, as we saw in the last chapter, most of these measures are still based on item types developed nearly a century ago by Binet and by the developers of the Army Alpha tests. And so not surprisingly, IQ test content is still strongly school related. Even Alan Kaufman, one of the most eminent modern testing gurus, readily concedes this point. Intelligence tests, he wrote in 1994, are "really a kind of achievement test . . . a measure of past accomplishments that is predictive of success in traditional school subjects."[4]

Anyone who questions this conclusion needs only to take a look at the actual content of the Wechsler Adult Intelligence Scale (WAIS), the current gold standard of IQ testing. (Because of copyright and test security issues, I cannot reproduce exact questions from the WAIS–III here. These made-up examples, however, are representative of the actual test items.) One section of the WAIS–III, for example, consists of arithmetic problems that the respondent must solve in his or her head. Others require test-takers to define a series of vocabulary words (many of which would be familiar only to skilled readers), to answer school-related factual questions (e.g., "Who was the first president of the United States?" or "Who wrote the *Canterbury Tales*?"), and to recognize and endorse common cultural norms and values (e.g., "What should you do if a sales clerk accidentally gives you too much change?" or "Why does our Constitution call for division of powers?"). True, respondents are also given a few opportunities to solve novel problems (e.g., copying a series of abstract designs with colored blocks). But even these supposedly culture-fair items require an understanding of social conventions, familiarity with objects specific to American culture, and/or experience working with geometric shapes and symbols.

Intelligence tests also place a premium on two other qualities highly valued in the standard American classroom: abstract thinking and rapid mental processing. A number of the Wechsler subtests, both verbal and nonverbal, assess the respondent's ability to categorize words or pictures and to recognize patterns; generally, the most abstract responses receive the most credit. (For example, if asked "How are a needle and a thread alike?" the subject would receive two points for answering "They are both implements used for sewing," one for "You can sew with them both," and none at all for "You put the thread through the needle.") Almost half of the tasks are timed. On several subtests faster responses earn more points, and on all timed tests a correct answer given even one second too late merits no credit at all. Individuals who approach tasks carefully and methodically and check their work before giving a final answer—qualities that in other settings might be viewed as highly adaptive—are significantly penalized.[5]

Examiners are required to administer and score these tests under very rigid conditions. Although such standardized testing procedures make the instruments highly reliable, they reward conformity and conventional thinking at the expense of creativity and out-of-the-box problem-solving. In many cases, credit is allowed only for responses specifically listed in the administration manual. For example, in one subtest the subject is asked to sort a series of scrambled cartoon pictures into the correct order. Creative arrangements not foreseen by the test developers are counted as incorrect, even if they are logical and consistent with the stimulus pictures. Test instructions, some of them fairly complex, are presented orally, and no deviations, elaborations, or explanations are allowed. Test-takers with poor language skills may fail items simply because they do not understand the directions. And a respondent who misperceives one of the orally presented stimulus numbers on an arithmetic problem, but then goes on to solve the item correctly as he or she hears it, receives no more credit than an individual who offers no response at all.

As these examples clearly illustrate, standard tests of intelligence sample only one sliver of the full richness of human cognition. But they are far from being a pure measure of even this limited spectrum of abilities. Subjects bring with them into the testing session a wide range of social, emotional, and personality characteristics, all of which affect the way they respond to test items. For example, there is clear evidence that anxiety and depression can markedly decrease scores on certain subtests, and traits like curiosity, independence, impulsivity, and distractibility also play a significant role in a subject's performance. Level of motivation is crucial. Test-takers must be willing to cooperate with the examiner; furthermore, they are likely to work harder and perform better if they believe that their scores will have consequences that are personally relevant to them.[6] Yes, it is true that IQ tests provide a reasonably reliable measure of certain qualities required for success in the modern American classroom—conventional verbal skills, rapid mental processing, memory, and a cooperative and generally nonquestioning attitude toward authority. But to assert that even the most carefully constructed test is somehow a pure measure of a hypothesized quality known as general intelligence flies in the face of both scientific evidence and common sense.

Actually, even the most ardent modern proponents of the psychometric approach to intelligence agree that test scores can be significantly affected by noncognitive variables. But though these advocates admit that available instruments are an imperfect measure of general intelligence, they remain firmly convinced that g constitutes the foundation of all intelligent human behavior. In the words of Arthur Jensen, one of this theory's most passionate proponents, brain-based general intelligence plays a powerful role in accounting for "the human condition in all its aspects."[7] This is a bold claim—but is it valid? Is it true that g, as measured by IQ test scores, is the most important factor in determining a person's overall success in life? Let us take a look at the data.

Advocates on one side of the issue assert that psychometric intelligence is more strongly related to a wide variety of important educational, vocational, and social outcomes than is any other measurable trait. Others, looking at the same data, insist just as adamantly that the correlations between IQ scores and general life adjustment are minimal. Who is correct? Well, it depends on what your definition of strongly related is. There is broad agreement that IQ scores account for about 25 percent of the individual variation in school grades and years of schooling completed—a very respectable correlation in the field of psychology.[8] Indeed, considering their strongly school-related content, it would be surprising if these tests did not predict educational outcomes. But significant though it admittedly is, IQ is far from being the only, or even the most important, determinant of academic performance. For example, recent research suggests that personal traits such as self-discipline, ability to delay gratification, and belief in the utility of one's own efforts are in some cases even more strongly correlated with school grades and academic achievement than is IQ.[9]

And the more distant the relationship between an outcome and educational status, the lower the predictive value of IQ test scores becomes. For example, psychometric intelligence accounts for an average of 16 percent of the observed variation in occupational status (values range from 4 to 60 percent, with the stronger relationships found only for those engaged in highly complex, academically demanding jobs).[10] IQ scores explain no more than 4 to 18 percent of individual differences in income. Recent studies demonstrate that inheritance of IQ accounts for a mere 2 percent of the intergenerational transmission of socioeconomic status; parental wealth, race, and schooling are all of considerably more importance, as are a number of personality and motivational characteristics. The relationship between IQ and other socially valued behaviors is almost miniscule, accounting, for example, for less than 4 percent of differences in delinquency and crime and less than 2 percent in divorce and unemployment. So, do we prefer to focus on the 2 to 25 percent of individual variation in life success that appears to be accounted for by psychometric intelligence or on the 75 to 98 percent due to other factors? Personal, social, and political values rather than hard, cold scientific facts are likely to determine our answers to this question.[11]

INTELLIGENCE AS ADAPTIVE BEHAVIOR

The second approach to intelligence, with its focus on adaptation to the environment, is as broad as the psychometric is narrow. Its roots can be traced back to the theories of that pioneering sociologist and ardent evolutionist, Herbert Spencer. Spencer was convinced that the principles of evolution governed the development of mental as well as physical characteristics. He elaborated on these ideas in the 1880 edition of his seminal *Principles of Psychology,* in which he argued that intelligence evolved as organisms adapted more and more successfully to increasingly complex environments.[12] Spencer had a profound influence on the social and intellectual culture of his time. Responding to Edward Thorndike's 1921 call for definitions of intelligence, for example, S. S. Colvin was merely following in Spencer's footsteps when he wrote that "an individual possesses intelligence in so far as he has learned, or can learn to adjust himself to his environment."[13] The eminent psychologist Robert Sternberg is perhaps the most influential modern proponent of the adaptive approach to intelligence. In words that Spencer himself could have written, Sternberg defines intelligence as "purposive adaptation to . . . real-world environments relevant to one's life."[14] Even David Wechsler (whom one might expect as developer of the Wechsler Scales to view intelligence in exclusively psychometric terms) has paid tribute to the adaptive perspective. In an oft-cited 1975 article, he stated that intelligence has to do with the "appropriateness, effectiveness, and worthwhileness of what human beings do or want to do."[15] Appropriateness, effectiveness, worthwhileness—not words we would necessarily expect to hear coming from the dean of modern IQ testing.

The adaptive view of intelligence differs from the psychometric in several important respects. First, unlike the more focused psychometric approach, the adaptive perspective on intelligence is multifaceted, incorporating a broad variety of cognitively based skills and abilities relevant to everyday life. These include, among others, verbal and non-verbal reasoning abilities, social competence, creativity, and practical problem-solving skills. Interestingly—and in sharp contrast to the psychometric assertion that *g* underlies all cognitive functioning—recent research indicates that these various aspects of intelligence are in fact relatively independent of one another. In other words, people high in social competence or creativity are not necessarily those who earn the best scores on conventional IQ tests. Second, adaptive intelligence is not some abstract quality existing within the mind; it is an aspect of *behavior.* And, as David Wechsler has reminded us, in order for behavior to be viewed as intelligent, it must be appropriate, effective, and worthwhile. These terms make it clear that judgments of adaptive intelligence cannot be strictly value-free or objective; they are in fact culturally relative. Because different societies have different values and face different environmental challenges, the behaviors defined as intelligent will naturally vary from one culture to another.

Even proponents of the adaptive approach to intelligence agree that conventional IQ tests do a relatively good job of assessing what they call analytic intelligence—qualities such as verbal facility, abstract problem-solving, processing speed, and memory (at least to the extent that these abilities can be meaningfully measured in the artificial testing environment). And virtually no one denies that analytical abilities are important to success in modern American life. But, argue the advocates of this broader approach to intelligence, analytic abilities alone are not enough. While quite useful in predicting school performance, IQ test scores provide little information about the many other cognitive and personality variables that contribute to a life well-lived. As many of us have no doubt observed, high IQ scores are no guarantee of appropriate, effective, and worthwhile behavior in the real world.

In the past few decades, several best-selling books have introduced the American public to this broader perspective on intelligence. In his 1983 *Frames of Mind,* for example, Howard Gardner outlined his theory of multiple intelligences: seven (later expanded to eight) talents and special skills that he considered to be separate, biologically based forms of intelligence. In addition to the linguistic and logico-mathematical skills tapped by conventional IQ tests, Gardner included in his model musical, kinesthetic, spatial, interpersonal, and intrapersonal abilities. Many academic psychologists complain that Gardner's work lacks a solid scientific foundation, but impressive numbers of regular people (especially in the educational community) have found it both relevant and inspiring.[16]

More recently, psychologist Daniel Goleman has focused attention specifically on the interpersonal aspects of adaptive behavior, concepts that he has popularized in two books, *Emotional Intelligence* (1995) and *Social Intelligence* (2006). Goleman argued that skills like understanding oneself and others, reading social cues, forming relationships, and controlling one's impulses (qualities to which he attached the label "emotional intelligence," or "EQ") are at least as important to life success as are analytical abilities. In fact, he reported, there is some research suggesting that EQ is even more strongly related than conventional IQ scores to various measures of vocational and personal achievement. Many of our grandmothers warned us that book smarts are not of much use if you cannot get along with other people. The research cited by Goleman suggests that Grandma was right.[17]

While Goleman focused on social and emotional skills, Robert Stern-berg and his colleagues have devoted their considerable research ener-gies to two other aspects of intelligent behavior: practical intelligence and creativity. Sternberg describes practical intelligence as the ability to use problem-solving skills, reasoning, and how-to knowledge to solve personally relevant everyday problems. Like social/emotional compe-tence, practical intelligence is relatively independent of conventional IQ scores, and like interpersonal skills, it is quite predictive of successful job performance. Sternberg's second area of interest—creativity—calls on a rather different set of abilities. His research suggests that the cre-ative individual is typically unconventional, imaginative, inquisitive, aesthetically sensitive, and able to hold to contrary opinions in the face of opposition. Needless to say, IQ tests are not designed to measure abilities like these; to the contrary, their highly structured format and rigid scoring criteria actually penalize creative thinking.[18]

Recently, Sternberg reported the findings of an innovative research project that demonstrates the advantages of taking a broader perspec-tive on intelligence. He and his colleagues developed new (although admittedly rather crude) tests of practical intelligence and creativity. They then administered these tests, along with the SAT (a measure of analytic abilities), to almost 800 students at 13 colleges and universi-ties around the country. The results were fascinating. The researchers found that by adding measures of practical intelligence and creativity to SAT results, they could almost double their power to predict college grades. (SAT scores alone accounted for 8.4% of the variation in grades, while the three tests combined accounted for 16.3%.) Clearly, practical intelligence and creativity make their own independent contributions to academic success, over and above that of psychometric IQ. Signifi-cantly, the racial and ethnic score differences typically found on conven-tional IQ tests were also markedly reduced in these broader measures on intelligence. This research suggests that expanding our conception of intelligence might help alleviate troubling racial disparities in college admissions while at the same time improving our ability to identify the students most likely to succeed.[19]

Our discussion so far has focused primarily on the cognitive aspects of intelligence. But a broader conception of intelligence leads us back to the venerable concept of wisdom. As David Wechsler asserted, intelligent behavior should be worthwhile. Our single-minded focus on psycho-metric intelligence has obscured the ancient human understanding—expounded by Biblical sages, Greek philosophers, and early Christian theologians alike—that wisdom, not mere cleverness, is the key to a meaningful and productive life. In recent years, a few psychologists (most notably Mihaly Csikszentmihalyi and his colleagues) have developed an interest in exploring this time-honored concept in more depth. What, they have asked, is the relationship between wisdom and IQ? Interestingly, their research suggests that judgments of an individual's level of wisdom are only minimally related to his or her IQ scores. Adequate knowledge is of course a prerequisite for wisdom. But in addition, the truly wise person must possess qualities that go far beyond analytical intelligence, characteristics such as self-knowledge, self-control, social understanding, and social concern. Understood in this broadest sense, adaptive intelligence—behavior that is appropriate, effective, and worthwhile—is not just a cognitive construct; it is also an ethical one.[20]

CROSS-CULTURAL CONCEPTIONS OF INTELLIGENCE

If one accepts the argument that general intelligence, or *g*, is a biologically based property of the human brain, it then follows that its basic nature should not change significantly from one culture to another. Early researchers interested in cross-cultural comparisons of psychometric intelligence therefore felt quite comfortable in simply administering standard American IQ tests (translated more or less carefully into the appropriate language) to individuals of various cultures and ethnicities. They then confidently attributed any obtained disparities in test scores to different levels of innate intelligence. The limitations of this approach, however, should be clear. *All* tests (whether we label them measures of intelligence, aptitude, or achievement) of necessity reflect learning—and the nature of learning experiences is highly culturally specific. Children in a remote African village, for example, may be deficient in book smarts, but they are probably very knowledgeable about the local plants and animals that provide their daily food. Are we to conclude, solely on the basis of conventional IQ scores, that these young villagers are somehow less intelligent than American school children?

Most modern researchers would agree that the answer to this question is no. For this reason, many of them have put considerable energy into developing tests that they claim are culture fair—that is, measures (many of them nonverbal) whose content does not require familiarity with the dominant Western culture. But even if the daunting theoretical and practical difficulties inherent in such an enterprise could be overcome, a more fundamental problem remains. As we have seen, different cultures of necessity define intelligent behavior in different ways, their perspectives deeply rooted in the values, thinking styles, and environmental challenges unique to each society. Behavior that members of one cultural group view as intelligent might well be perceived by members of another as foolish, misguided, or even antisocial. And so, as testing expert Alexander Wesman pointed out as early as 1968, the "ingenious mining methods" that cross-cultural investigators have used in their attempts to discover "the 'native intelligence' [that] lies buried in pure form deep in the individual" are in fact "not ingenious, but ingenuous."[21]

A closer examination of cultural perspectives on intelligent behavior illustrates Wesman's point very nicely. Take, for example, the commonly acknowledged distinction between Eastern and Western styles of thinking.[22] Psychologist Richard Nisbett has explored this divide in some detail in his fascinating book *The Geography of Thought*. According to Nisbett, American (and more generally Western) modes of thinking and reasoning harken back to the ancient Greeks. Greek philosophers venerated abstract thought, and they developed a system of logic based on the fundamental assumption that only one of two contradictory statements can be correct. Indeed, this assumption is so basic to our understanding of the world that most of us would consider it to be self-evident. Following in the Greek tradition, Westerners view abstraction and analysis as the highest forms of reasoning, and we typically consider objects and ideas in isolation, relatively independent of context. Like the ancient Greeks, most Westerners admire independence, self-confidence, and personal achievement, and we tend to value reason over emotion and speed over reflection. Formal tests of intelligence—individually administered, rigidly timed, analytical, context-free, and objectively scored—reflect quite naturally this Western approach to cognition.[23]

The Eastern style of thinking is no less venerable than the Western, and it is equally sophisticated. Its fundamental assumptions, however, are quite different. Unlike either/or Western logic, in which only one of two apparently contradictory statements can be true at the same time, Eastern thinkers leave open the possibility of both/and. As the ancient symbol of the yin and the yang illustrates, all ideas potentially contain their opposites, and apparent contradictions often reveal a larger truth. Eastern thinking is also highly contextual. Objects and ideas are understood primarily in relationship to one another, and individuals are perceived as part of a larger whole. Eastern-influenced cultures typically value depth of processing over sheer speed and prudence over risk-taking, and they emphasize group rather than personal achievement. For this reason, members of such cultures are likely to view humility as more seemly than brash confidence. In fact, the individual who excels may be frowned on—witness the Japanese saying that "the nail that stands out gets hammered down." In the context of Eastern thought, the idea of using a Western-style standardized test as a measure of culturally meaningful intelligence verges on the ludicrous.[24]

One very minor example of how these different styles of thinking can affect IQ scores can be seen in a section of the WAIS–III in which the respondent is asked to explain how two words are alike. For full credit, the subject is expected to determine the abstract category to which both objects belong. For the hypothetical stimulus words "pitcher" and "glass," for example, the correct answer would be that they are both dishes. No credit at all would be allowed for "you use a pitcher to pour water into a glass," even though from a relational perspective this response would in fact be much more appropriate.

A developing body of research illustrates how these different thinking styles and social values affect Western versus non-Western definitions of intelligence. Members of most cultures, East and West alike, agree that an ideally intelligent person should have a high level of knowledge and well-developed problem-solving skills. But when surveyed about their concept of intelligence, Chinese respondents, for example, also included in their definition more typically Eastern values, including carefulness, perseverance, and effort. Members of the Chewa tribe of Africa identified as intelligent traits such as common sense, obedience, responsibility, and cooperation.[25] Significantly, and consistent with the contextual nature of Eastern thinking, many of these qualities central to non-Western definitions of intelligence fall into the category of social competence. Practical intelligence is also highly valued in many of these cultures. For example, Sternberg and his colleagues tested a group of Kenyan children to determine both their practical knowledge (in this case, information about natural herbal medicines) and their school-related skills. Interestingly, they actually found a negative correlation between these two forms of intelligence.[26] In a less-developed society, where academic pursuits contribute little to daily survival, psychometric IQ might well be totally unrelated to adaptive intelligence.

It is not difficult to understand why different cultures define intelligence in different ways. In a society dependent on hunting for its food supply, for example, the most intelligent members are likely to demonstrate a keen attention to visual detail, rapid processing speed, excellent spatial relations, and highly developed eye–hand coordination. Groups forced to live cheek-to-jowl in very crowded conditions will probably value most highly individuals who have a calm temperament, good social skills, and heightened interpersonal sensitivity. Societies confronted with rapid environmental change will naturally look to leaders who are flexible and creative. Conventional IQ tests would completely fail to identify the most adaptively intelligent members of any of these groups.

Even in American culture, various groups within our polyglot society have developed their own unique perspectives on intelligence. One of the most illuminating demonstrations of how different subcultures develop different ideas about intelligent behavior comes from a fascinating ethnographic study conducted by Shirley Brice Heath in 1983. Heath spent an extended period of time in two working-class communities in a small North Carolina town, making detailed observations of their child-rearing practices. One of these communities (which she dubbed "Roadville") was composed of white families who had emigrated from Appalachia, while the other (labeled "Trackton") consisted of African Americans from rural farming backgrounds.

From an early age, Roadville children learned that there were clear boundaries between private and public domains, and they were taught, either explicitly or implicitly, that it was sometimes necessary to behave in different ways with different people. Parents often engaged their preschool children in activities aimed directly at developing their language and academic skills. Daily activities were generally oriented around clock time. The children of Trackton, on the other hand, were allowed to wander quite freely through their community, which assumed a high level of corporate responsibility for their welfare. Their experience of time was much less structured and segmented than that of the Roadville children, and the language with which they were surrounded was more narrative and metaphorical. Trackton children received little formal instruction from their parents; instead, they learned language and behavioral expectations by watching, listening, and experimenting with their new skills.

Both Roadville and Trackton parents endeavored to raise children who would grow up to be happy, intelligent, and successful adults. However, the two groups had very different conceptions about what constituted intelligent behavior—differences that became immediately apparent when their children started school. For the children of Roadville, the demands of their new classroom were simply a logical extension of a style of thinking, learning, and behaving with which they were already familiar. For the Trackton children, however, school represented a sudden discontinuity from all they had known and experienced to date. It is not difficult to guess which group went on to experience a higher level of academic success—or which students were perceived by their teachers as being more intelligent.[27]

TOWARD RESOLUTION

This chapter has described two significantly different ways of looking at intelligence. The psychometric approach focuses primarily on the verbal and analytic abilities most directly relevant to academic success in modern Western cultures. Our measures of this type of intelligence are carefully constructed, reliable, and reasonably predictive of school performance. But IQ tests sample only one sliver of cognition, virtually ignoring such abilities as social perception, practical intelligence, and creativity, to say nothing of important virtues like honesty, judgment, and wisdom. I do not believe it is necessary to discard the concept of psychometric IQ; as I will argue in the final chapter, intelligence tests can be very useful for certain purposes. The problem comes when we try to use IQ scores as an operational definition for adaptive intelligence, thus making claims for the relevance and importance of these scores that go far beyond the data.[28]

In contrast to the psychometric approach, the adaptive perspective on intelligence is broad, multifaceted, and culturally relative. It defines intelligence not as a measurable *thing* that exists in the brain but as an aspect of *behavior*. This type of intelligence is a complex characteristic that arises from an interaction between the biological structures of the brain, other qualities of the individual (such as personality, values, and motivation), and the environment. By definition, when broadly conceived as the effectiveness, appropriateness, and worthwhileness of behavior, adaptive intelligence is central to life success. But this concept is so inclusive that it eludes any practical attempts to measure it, making it of limited use for purposes of prediction, selection, and intervention.

The adaptive approach to intelligence is also subjective and relative; judgments of what behavior is appropriate and effective naturally vary according to particular cultural needs and values. And despite our current reluctance to use such terms, the worthwhileness of behavior inevitably has a moral component as well. This notion is perhaps best captured in the connotations of the word "wisdom." In a 1990 book chapter, psychologists Mihaly Csikszentmihalyi and Kevin Rathunde very cogently described the difference between psychometric intelligence and wisdom. It is extremely dangerous, they said, "for mankind to assume that because we are so smart, we know what is good for us and for the rest of the universe."[29] Our high IQs have enabled us to construct weapons of unbelievable power and to make massive and irreversible changes in the environment of our planet. The events of recent years, however, suggest that we have not yet developed the wisdom to use these abilities appropriately.

Our modern propensity to worship at the altar of IQ reminds me of Biblical warnings against idols, whose worshippers sacrificed to small gods whose powers they hoped to harness to meet their own needs. But their eagerness to propitiate these little gods, the prophets warned,

prevented these worshippers from developing a more comprehensive vision of the Divine. Our frantic attempts to increase test scores seem
to me a similarly outsized effort directed toward a paltry goal. How
much more productive it would be for us to focus our energies toward
developing intelligence in all of its potential richness, honoring multiple
abilities and carefully weighing the effects of our actions on the broader
society. Providing our children with the skills and knowledge they need
to behave in ways that are effective, appropriate, and worthwhile—that
would indeed be a goal worthy of our most diligent pursuit.

Chapter 11

Toward a More Balanced
Perspective on Heredity and IQ

Probably the most contentious of the issues fueling the IQ Wars is the extent to which heredity determines psychometric intelligence.[1] The emotion with which even supposedly hardheaded scientists approach this question suggests that its social and political implications are far more potent than its actual scientific importance. If IQ scores are largely fixed by genetics, and if psychometric intelligence is basic to life success, then class- and race-based disparities in educational and vocational achievement are, though perhaps unfortunate, probably both inevitable and intractable. If, on the other hand, test performance is significantly affected by environmental experiences, it should be possible to boost the scores of underprivileged groups through appropriate enrichment. These opposing stances reflect deep and long-standing divides in American political life, and even objective scientists are not immune to their impact. But what are the actual data that the two sides cite to fuel their arguments? Let us take a closer look at the evidence.

HEREDITY AND GROUP DIFFERENCES

Over the decades, researchers have used a number of creative techniques to try to tease out the relative roles of genetics and environment in determining psychometric intelligence. One such strategy involves twins: investigators either study identical twins reared apart (identical genetics but different environments) or compare fraternal versus identical twins raised in their birth families (the same environment but different degrees of genetic relatedness). Other researchers have looked at the similarities between adopted children and their biological parents (the genetic component) versus the degree of similarity between these same children and their adoptive parents (the environmental component). Some genetically inclined researchers interpret studies of this type as demonstrating that hereditary factors account for as much as 80 percent of the individual variation in IQ test scores. When data from all of the relevant studies are averaged, however, the genetic contribution appears closer to 50 percent, and in fact more recent, methodologically sound research has placed the hereditability rate of psychometric intelligence at only 30 to 40 percent.[2]

But what do these seemingly precise numbers actually mean? Despite the certainty with which they are usually bandied about, hereditability rates are *not* fixed, objective values; their magnitude is strongly dependent on the degree of environmental variability within the subject population.[3] Let me provide an illustration. Assume that we have a bag of seeds that vary in their genetic quality. Suppose we plant all of these seeds in the same field, where they receive identical exposure to sun, water, and nutrients. Given the complete lack of variability in their growing conditions, any differences among the plants grown from these seeds must be genetic, and the hereditability of their growth rate is of necessity 100 percent. On the other hand, what if we sow half of our seeds in a field that provides ideal conditions for growth and the other half in a field that receives barely enough nourishment to sustain life? Most of the seeds in the first group will flourish while those in the second will be stunted. Although the growth rates of the seeds *within* the two fields will still vary according to their genetic makeup, the environmental differences between the two fields will overwhelm these hereditary factors. The hereditability of growth rate for exactly this same bag of seeds will now appear to be quite low. It is thus clear that hereditability estimates are virtually meaningless in the absence of information about the range of environmental conditions experienced by the population of interest. And without adequate attention to the role of environmental variability (information that few researchers provide, by the way), statistics about genetic contributions to psychometric intelligence are basically uninterpretable—and unworthy of the enormous time, attention, and fervor that they have elicited.

The limitations of the heredity data become even more apparent when we turn to questions about racial differences in psychometric intelligence. Of all of the troubling issues raised by our cultural obsession with IQ test scores, this has been by far the most socially and politically divisive. The facts are fairly clear. Starting in the early 1900s, when such comparisons were first made, African Americans as a group have generally scored about 15 points lower on tests of cognitive ability than have whites (with the performance of Hispanic and Native American groups falling somewhere in between).[4] We cannot simply write off this disparity as an artifact of test bias. IQ scores are equally predictive of academic performance for both blacks and whites, and despite much rhetoric to the contrary, modern tests are carefully designed so that no specific items are biased against any particular group. It does appear that this persistent racial gap might be starting to shrink somewhat. In fact, several recent studies have found only a seven- or eight-point racial discrepancy among groups of younger children, about half of the conventionally cited figure. And it is important to note that there is much greater variability *within* each racial/ethnic group than *between* the groups; some African American individuals have always earned significantly higher scores than most of their white peers. Despite these encouraging trends, however, racial disparities in IQ test performance remain sizable and, given the power of these tests in modern American society, of considerable practical significance.[5]

Whatever the exact magnitude of the black–white IQ gap, there is widespread agreement that it does exist. The real controversy comes when we begin to question the *reasons* for these well-documented racial disparities. Are they primarily due, as most liberals argue, to environmental inequalities? If so, our democratic ideals require that we make every possible effort to eradicate these unjust conditions. But what if, as many conservatives are convinced, American society already offers substantially equal opportunities to all? It would then follow that these stubborn disparities in psychometric intelligence are most likely due at least in part to immutable genetic differences between the races and that misguided efforts at remediation are worse than useless.[6] Since both sides cloak their political arguments in the language of science, it would be instructive to take a look at the data that they cite.

Let us start with the hereditarians. They draw on three main types of evidence to support their position. First, research suggests that heredity accounts for somewhere between 20 and 80 percent of the variation in IQ scores *within* groups, at least within the range of Western cultures that have been studied. (Most hereditarians argue for values at the higher rather than the lower end of this range.) Therefore, they maintain, it is logical to assume that genetic factors account for at least some of the difference *between* racial and ethnic groups as well. Second, there are clearly racial variations in the distribution of some genes— those controlling facial characteristics; hair, skin, and eye color; and degree of susceptibility to certain diseases, for example. It therefore seems unreasonable to deny that there could be any racial differences in the genes responsible for IQ. Finally, hereditarians cite strong evidence that socioeconomic variables account for less than half of the observed 15-point racial gap in IQ scores.[7] What other environmental factors, they ask rhetorically, could possibly be sufficiently potent to explain the remainder of this disparity?

Although it seems compelling at first glance, the hereditarians' first argument is actually based on a logical fallacy. The existence of genetic variation *within* groups in no way proves genetic differences *between* groups. Let us go back to our example of seeds and fields. Assume that we have two fields—or environments—of demonstrably different quality, with one field receiving significantly less sun, water, and nutrients than the other. We find plants of different sizes growing within each of these fields, indicating some genetic variation among the parent seeds. However, on average the plants in the poorer field are significantly smaller and less healthy than those in the richer. The question is: Did the seeds in the two fields come from two different batches, one of them genetically inferior to the other, or did they come from the same lot, with the different characteristics of the two fields accounting for the different patterns of growth? Either answer is logically and scientifically defensible. The only way definitively to determine whether the seeds came from batches of the same or different quality would be to plant seeds from both sets in the same field and compare their progress. Obviously, we have no way to plant members of different racial and ethnic groups into identical physical, economic, social, and cultural environments. And in the absence of this possibility, we have no scientific basis on which to make claims about possible genetic differences between them.

But, argue the hereditarians, we already know that there are genetic differences between the races. After all, members of different racial groups do *look* different, and we agree that physical traits like eye and skin color, hair color and texture, facial features, and body shape are largely under genetic control. These particular characteristics, however, are generally determined by only a few discrete genes. Intelligence, on the other hand, is highly complex and involves many different brain functions; its genetic underpinnings must be multidetermined as well. Regardless of race, human beings have in common about 99.9 percent of their DNA; indeed, many researchers now argue that there is no genetic basis at all for our socially constructed categories of race.[8] Given the overwhelming genetic similarity between the various racial groups and the enormous complexity of intelligence, it is difficult to imagine any genetic mechanism that could account for a 15-point gap in IQ scores.

There are in fact several strands of evidence that argue against the hereditarian position. If genes were responsible for all or even most of the documented racial discrepancy in IQ scores, then individuals of mixed race should logically earn scores intermediate between white and black norms. American history has provided a natural experiment to test just this question. We are all well aware that the ancestry of people socially and culturally defined as black in this country can range from purely African to almost entirely European. Yet studies indicate that very light-skinned African Americans score only marginally better on IQ tests than do their darker-skinned brethren, despite the social and economic advantages that lighter-skinned individuals usually enjoy. Another line of evidence comes from post–World War II Germany, where a number of American GIs fathered children with German women. Some of the fathers were white and some were black. Contrary to the hereditarian prediction, when IQ tests were later administered to the children of these soldiers, the scores of those with black fathers were virtually identical to those with all-white ancestry. In the studies conducted in America, having substantial white heredity did not raise IQ scores. In those conducted in Germany, having substantial black heredity did not lower them. Staunch hereditarians are hard-pressed to account for either result.[9]

Psychologist Claude Steele has approached this issue from a different and very interesting perspective. Around the world, he reports, "caste-like minorities" (for example, the Maoris in New Zealand, Oriental Jews in Israel, the Bakaru in Japan, and the Harijans, or untouchables, of India) score about 15 points lower on IQ tests than do members of the dominant group. (Caste-like minorities are groups whose members are shunted into inferior social positions solely on the basis of group membership, regardless of their own individual talents. In our own country, there is little argument that African Americans have historically been relegated to this status.) In some cases, these minority groups are racially distinct from the majority; in others, however, the disenfranchised minority and the dominant group are racially indistinguishable. In the latter situation, racially based genetic differences cannot possibly account for the observed disparities in IQ scores. And if genetic racial differences between the groups cannot explain the disparities in these cases, it stretches credulity to argue that they account for gaps of an identical size among groups that do differ racially.[10]

In my view, therefore, the evidence *against* genetically based differences in intelligence between racial groups is quite compelling. But if not heredity, then what *is* the explanation for the well-documented 15-point IQ gap? Proponents on both sides of the argument agree that socioeconomic variables account for at least part of this disparity. Despite some recent progress, African Americans as a group remain at a serious economic disadvantage. Recent surveys indicate that their wages average only 80 to 85 percent of those of white Americans, a figure that has remained unchanged since 1975. Even more discouraging, black *family* income is only 67 percent of that of whites, while their average level of family wealth is a miniscule *12 percent* of the average white family wealth.[11] Striking as it is, however, this disparity in socioeconomic status can account for only about half of the racial gap in test scores (although some recent research suggests that adding such factors as grandparents' educational level, household size, and parenting practices to measures of socioeconomic status can increase its explanatory value to up to two-thirds of the observed discrepancy).[12] Even among whites and African Americans of the same educational and income levels, then, we still find significant (although smaller) group differences in test scores.[13]

Hereditarians argue, correctly, that any IQ discrepancies not accounted for by environmental factors must of necessity be due to genetics. But socioeconomic status and educational achievement are not the only environmental variables that potentially affect IQ scores. Consider, for example, the psychological impact of racial discrimination. Many hereditarians seem to view racial discrimination as little more than a worn-out relic of an unenlightened but distant past. After all, they point out, our country has recently elected an African American president. But despite this undeniable progress, there is strong objective evidence that discrimination is still an ever-present reality in the lives of many African Americans. For example, in random tests conducted by fair housing authorities, landlords prove significantly less likely to rent to blacks than to whites with exactly the same income and qualifications. Studies done by the Fair Employment Practices Commission indicate that one out of five African American job applicants experiences some form of racial discrimination; when equally qualified blacks and whites apply for the same job, whites receive more job offers by a small but significant margin. One study even indicated that young white men who admitted to felony convictions were viewed more positively by potential employers than their black peers with clean criminal records. And once on the job, black workers report experiencing more mistreatment in their workplaces than whites.[14] Some fascinating recent work with the Implicit Association Test illustrates the extent to which even liberal, well-meaning whites carry with them unconscious racial stereotypes.[15] (I took an Internet version of this test myself, and my scores proved to be quite sobering.)

Race, then, is a part of the daily experience of African Americans in ways that few whites can truly understand. Individual members of the black community react to their experiences of discrimination in different ways. Some become demoralized and withdraw from the fray, while others use the negative evaluations of others as a spur to even greater achievement. But either way, the psychological impact of coping with discrimination inevitably takes a toll on psychic energy—energy that is not then available for other pursuits. There have been some interesting studies dealing with this topic. In his impeccably researched work on stereotype threat, for example, Claude Steele has demonstrated that when African American college students are told that a test is designed to assess intelligence, they develop performance-interfering anxiety that significantly lowers their test scores as compared with their performance on an identical task *not* described as a test of intelligence. Although Steele is careful not to claim that stereotype threat accounts for the entire black–white discrepancy in IQ, it certainly appears to be at least one significant factor.[16]

Other researchers have focused more broadly on how the experience of discrimination has affected values and self-perceptions within the African American community. Anthropologist John Ogbu, for example, has shown how many members of caste-like minorities lack what he terms "effort optimism." Believing that their efforts are unlikely to be rewarded, they often hold back from even trying to compete in the white world.[17] University professor John McWhorter has further developed this theme in his controversial but thought-provoking book *Losing the Race: Self-Sabotage in Black America*. McWhorter argues that in much of black American culture, intellectual interests and efforts are viewed not just as uncool but as an actual repudiation of one's own racial heritage. Lower performance on IQ tests is an absolutely predictable result. Clearly, the effects of racial discrimination are psychological as well as economic, and their impact on psychometric intelligence is far more subtle and complex than most hereditarians have acknowledged.[18]

There is yet another crucial issue that we must consider. Many commentators, whether conservative and liberal, attribute the black–white IQ gap to supposed deficits within the black community. These advocates differ in their explanatory emphasis, but almost all unthinkingly equate intelligence with IQ scores. Intelligence tests, as we have seen, are narrowly rooted in the dominant American culture, with its strongly held values of independence, individualism, and rationalism. But to survive their centuries of enslavement and exploitation in this country, African Americans have developed a different cultural tradition—one that, as compared with mainstream white culture, focuses on mutual assistance, interdependence, and community support. These particular qualities offer their possessors few advantages on conventional tests of psychometric intelligence. They are highly relevant, however, to intelligence more broadly defined as adaptive functioning. And in fact there is clear evidence that on our rather crude measures of social competence, creativity, and practical intelligence, black and white test-takers earn very similar scores.[19] When it comes to many of the characteristics of intelligent behavior most relevant to real-life success, the much-studied, much-lamented, and much-debated racial gap virtually disappears.

THE MALLEABILITY OF INTELLIGENCE

Directly related to the nature vs. nurture debate is the question of whether IQ scores can be increased through appropriate intervention. If intelligence is largely a product of environmental experience, then it ought to be possible to design programs to improve the test scores of children from at-risk groups. If, on the other hand, intelligence is basically fixed by one's genetic endowment, then such programs are a cruel waste of time and money, offering unrealistic hope to people who would be better served by learning to make the best use of whatever modest talents they have been granted. Not surprisingly, this question has attracted the attention of a number of researchers, and there is now a substantial literature describing the effectiveness of programs intended to raise the IQ scores of children from lower socioeconomic and ethnic minority populations.

Arthur Jensen famously opened his incendiary 1969 article in the *Harvard Educational Review* by stating flatly, "Compensatory education has been tried and it apparently has failed."[20] Any IQ gains attributable to such interventions, he argued, have been both negligible and short-lived. Even Jensen now acknowledges that a few such enrichment programs have enjoyed modest success. The best known of these is probably the Abecedarian Early Intervention Project, an intensive, long-term program designed for young children at risk for intellectual delays. The participants, who were followed for many years after they completed the program, achieved an average long-term gain of five points on standard tests of intelligence. In addition, the treated children completed more years of education and achieved higher levels of skilled employment than untreated controls. Another apparent success story is Rick Heber's Milwaukee Project, an intensive program of enrichment designed for at-risk young children. Heber reported substantial IQ gains among his participants, although the small number of subjects requires us to view these results with caution. Despite these few encouraging reports, however, even advocates of enrichment programs are forced to agree that most of them—especially relatively short-term interventions focused on older children—have failed to demonstrate anything more than small and ephemeral gains in psychometric intelligence. Looking at these data, one might feel compelled to concede that the hereditarians have a point: IQ scores do indeed seem to be highly resistant to change.[21]

Things look somewhat more promising if we broaden our focus beyond narrowly defined IQ scores to look at adaptive functioning in general. Take, for example, the well-known Head Start program. Initial IQ gains achieved by Head Start children have not held up over the years. However, research indicates that the program clearly does lead to other important educational benefits, including fewer placements in special education programs, fewer grade retentions, and a lower high school drop-out rate.[22] Similar findings have been reported for the Perry Preschool Program, a Head-Start-like intervention that resulted in lasting gains in educational achievement, despite the fact that initial IQ score increases washed out over time.[23] These and other studies demonstrate that properly designed programs can succeed in improving such real-life outcomes as frequency of special education placement, high school graduation rates, and likelihood of teen pregnancy, perhaps by affecting important underlying personality and motivational variables. Unlike narrowly defined psychometric intelligence, broader adaptive intelligence does appear to be reasonably malleable.

Well, we now have our answers, it would seem. The bulk of the available research suggests that, although adaptive intelligence is apparently subject to environmental influence, extraordinary efforts are required to achieve any lasting and meaningful gains in IQ test scores themselves. But though the results of these studies seem clear, they actually tell only part of the story. Apparently unknown to many commentators, there is now an entirely separate line of surprising but scientifically impeccable research that leads to exactly the opposite conclusion. Worldwide, since at least 1932, average scores on standard tests of intelligence have in fact been *rising* at the rate of about three points per decade, resulting in a total increase of more than 15 points over this time period. These findings hold true for every one of the more than 20 Western nations studied thus far. Gains have been largest (about five points per decade) on nonvisual and spatial tasks and somewhat more modest (two points per decade) on verbal, school-related tests. Interestingly, some of the most dramatic improvements have been found on the Raven Progressive Matrices, a nonverbal test of abstract reasoning ability that is considered by many hereditarians to be the purest available measure of the supposedly immutable *g*. These IQ score increases have passed unnoticed among the general public because every time the tests are renormed (generally every 10 to 15 years), the developers reset the average score to 100. However, if the original norms were still in use, the IQ of the average American today would be more than 115.[24]

This rising curve phenomenon is very obvious in the clinical practice of assessment. Every time that the Wechsler Scales are renormed, a better performance is required to earn an average score of 100. Thus, for example, the technical manual for the WAIS–III, published in 1997, reports that an individual who earned a score of 100 on its 1981 predecessor, the WAIS–R, would be expected to score only 97 on the revised and renormed test. The upper-level test items have also gotten much more difficult over the years. I recently had an opportunity to look at a 1949 version of the Wechsler-Bellevue Scales. Although the structure of the test and the nature of the items were very familiar (even some of the individual questions were exactly the same), the most difficult items on this older test, especially those on the performance scale, would be only at the upper mid-range of difficulty on the recent WISC–IV. The Wechsler-Bellevue would pose little challenge to many of today's children.[25]

What accounts for this steady and well-documented improvement in IQ test scores? No one really knows. But whatever the reasons, they are clearly environmental in origin; significant genetic change simply cannot take place in human populations over a period of only 50 years. Better nutrition has most likely contributed to the rise in scores, as have increasing levels of education worldwide. And the mass media (movies, television, and now the Internet) have given previously isolated groups a window into the mainstream culture that most intelligence tests reflect. But why is it that the most significant gains have been on the very visual–spatial tasks that hereditarians like to tout as culture-free measures of *g*? Several researchers have raised the intriguing possibility that these improvements might be related to the increasing complexity of our visual environments. The video games to which many young American males appear addicted are an obvious modern example. Or think of the skills involved in safely piloting an automobile through heavy traffic at 70 miles per hour. This task, which most of us perform almost automatically, requires us to react instantaneously to multiple stimuli while traveling at speeds no person on earth had even experienced until a hundred years ago. And the price of a minor error might well be death. It seems reasonable to assume that over time these demands on our visual systems have strengthened previously underutilized areas of the brain and coincidentally improved our performance on conventional tests of intelligence.

Whatever the environmental factors responsible for the rising curve phenomenon, the indisputable fact of its existence creates some real problems for those who argue that intelligence is basically fixed at birth. The defenders of *g* have been strangely silent on this topic, glossing over the data or suggesting that the findings must be due to some technical flaws in the tests themselves. But these are of course the very tests on which they have constructed their entire theory. As psychologist Ulric Neisser, editor of a recent volume on this phenomenon, has pointed out, the pattern of rising IQ test scores

either does or does not reflect real increases in *g*. If it does reflect real increases, *g* clearly is affected by environmental factors because no genetic process could produce such large changes so quickly. Whatever those environmental factors may be, we can at least reject the hypothesis that intelligence is genetically fixed. But if it does not reflect real increases . . . then the tests are evidently flawed, and all arguments based on tests scores become suspect. Either way, things look bad for *g* and the arguments of *The Bell Curve*.[26]

And so there is overwhelming evidence that IQ test scores have been rising steadily and significantly for at least 50 years, and these gains clearly must be environmental in origin. But does this mean that people are actually getting smarter, in any meaningful sense of the word? Few of us would argue that they are. After all, educational critics fret that we are raising a generation of near-illiterate children. Scientists lament the fact that we have to import students from developing countries to fill our vaunted graduate schools of science and mathematics. And it would be difficult to make a case that we have been particularly intelligent in our management of our economy, our environment, or our relationships with other nations. The practical impact of our rising IQ scores has been singularly unimpressive. The concept of psychometric intelligence—grounded in the abilities required for success in the twentieth-century American classroom—appears increasingly irrelevant to adaptive functioning in our complex, interdependent, information-laden, and rapid-changing world.

Chapter 12

Toward a More Equitable Conception of Merit

In 1958, British writer Michael Young published a book entitled *The Rise of the Meritocracy*, a satirical account of a Utopian society in which access to education, social status, and even marital partners is strictly allocated on the basis of IQ scores. In this supposedly idyllic world, "the eminent know that success is just reward for their own capacity. . . . As for the lower classes, . . . they have an inferior status—not as in the past because they were denied opportunity; but because they are inferior."[1] To describe this test-based society, Young coined the word "meritocracy." Not many Americans actually read Young's work, but they quickly seized on his newly minted term, appropriating it uncritically to describe a society in which people are free to rise as far as their own individual talents can take them. The word "meritocracy" has become a synonym for the vaunted American dream.

But, as even a cursory reading makes clear, Young's book was actually a satire. Far from being a paradise, his meritocratic Utopia turns out to be dull, sterile, and ultimately unsustainable; in the end, the "inferior" lower classes rise up violently against their oppressors, seeking to assert their own dignity and worth. And in fact many of the problems that Young foresaw are now clearly evident in our own society. Our test-driven concept of merit is sterile, bland, and lifeless. It elevates the supposed rights of individuals who happen to score well on tests over the good of the larger community. Perhaps most damaging, it provides justification for a social system in which the greatest rewards go to those fortunate enough to have been born into rich and stimulating environments. In the words of David Owen, a meritocratic society such as Young described "convert[s] the tainted advantages of birth and wealth into the neutral currency of 'merit,' enabling the fortunate to believe that they have earned what they have merely been given."[2]

It should be clear by this point in our discussion that IQ scores provide a paltry foundation on which to erect a full-bodied concept of merit: one that incorporates the full range of human abilities, takes into account the values and perspectives of different cultures, and addresses social responsibilities as well as individual rights. In my view, however, the fundamental problem is not with the tests themselves. In fact, as I will demonstrate in the next section, there are many situations in which IQ tests can be very helpful. The problem arises when we elevate these tests to purposes for which they were never intended, equating scores on narrow measures of school-related cognitive abilities with basic human worth.

IQ TESTS IN CLINICAL PRACTICE

Clearly, I have serious reservations about IQ testing. Yet, as I describe in the preface, for more than 30 years these instruments have played a significant role in my professional life. During this period, I have given literally hundreds of intelligence tests, supervised the administration of scores more, and taught graduate courses on IQ testing in several universities. The reader might well wonder how I can justify my own extensive involvement in such a questionable enterprise. My response is that, although IQ tests are all too often used inappropriately, they can also be a very powerful clinical tool. And so, before elaborating on my concerns about the use of these tests for selection and tracking, I would like to take a few pages to describe their more positive potential.

People usually seek psychological assessment for themselves, their children, or their students because they need help in solving a problem of some sort. If the issue of concern relates to learning, an individually administered IQ test can often provide useful guidance. When administered with sensitivity, properly interpreted, and integrated with other information, these tests can help illuminate a person's style of learning, identify areas of difficulty, and provide a basis for effective intervention—information that most clients find very helpful.[3] A few examples from my own practice may help illustrate my point. (Identifying details have been changed to protect privacy.)

1. Her teachers complained that twelve-year-old Susan was lazy and unmotivated. Although she seemed quite capable of learning, she almost never

finished her work; consequently, she was close to failing several subjects and had been moved back into less-challenging classes. Her performance on IQ testing suggested that Susan was blessed with superior verbal skills, excellent reasoning abilities, and a very good memory. However, her mental processing was painfully slow; in fact, her test administration took nearly twice as long as average. After I reviewed these findings with Susan's parents and teachers, we all agreed that she should be transferred into classes that offered her appropriate challenges. To compensate for her very slow processing speed, the school developed a plan that allowed her extra time on tests and reduced the length of some of her assignments. With these modifications in place, Susan was soon performing well in her more advanced classes.

2. Fifteen-year-old Mike was developing a well-deserved reputation as a troublesome kid. He refused to do his schoolwork, was defiant and disrespectful with his teachers, and was beginning to display significant behavior problems both at home and at school. His IQ testing profile indicated that, although his basic reasoning skills were age-appropriate, Mike had severe deficits in verbal expression (a difficulty that was masked by his remarkable fluency in profanity). It was clear that most of his behavior problems stemmed from his extreme frustration in school and his inability to express what he was feeling. Mike was eventually placed in a special school. There he was able to receive the intensive services that he needed, including speech and language therapy, hands-on teaching strategies, and psychotherapy designed to help him learn more appropriate ways of expressing his frustration. Although school remained a challenge for him, Mike's behavior and attitude improved markedly.

3. Ms. Adams was a young single mother sent for evaluation by a local social services agency. She had been accused of neglecting her infant son by failing to respond appropriately to his complex medical needs. Social workers had tried very hard to teach her how to care for her baby, but although Ms. Adams seemed attentive and interested in their advice, her neglectful behaviors persisted. Intelligence testing revealed that, despite her seemingly normal verbal abilities and social skills, she had significant deficits in reasoning and memory. Once her case workers were aware of the extent of her learning problems, they were able to provide instruction that was much more basic, concrete, and repetitive. With appropriate assistance and support, Ms. Adams was able to maintain custody of her child.

4. According to his teachers, nine-year-old Sean was an unusually bright child, and he performed very well in school. But despite his well-developed academic skills, he was shy and socially awkward, afraid to speak up in class, and virtually friendless. As expected, IQ testing indicated that all Sean's school-related cognitive abilities were well above average. What came as a surprise, however, was his truly remarkable level of performance on tests assessing visual–spatial skills. Because such an IQ profile is often associated with artistic talent, his teachers and parents decided to encourage this interest. As other children began to recognize and comment on Sean's newly

developed artistic skills, his self-esteem improved, and he even began to form friendships with a few classmates who shared his interest.

As these four examples demonstrate, IQ tests—when properly administered and interpreted with sensitivity—can be a useful clinical tool. By identifying unsuspected strengths and pinpointing abilities in need of development, testing can point toward new and creative ways of approaching problems. However, IQ is not destiny. Following are a few real-life examples of cases in which other personal qualities more than made up for supposed deficits in psychometric intelligence.

1. Mr. Grant, a highly successful businessman, requested psychological testing because, sensitive about his lack of a college degree, he had decided to take some introductory courses at a local university. He was having terrible difficulty with these courses and wondered whether he had the basic ability required to handle college-level work. He reported that he had always hated school and secretly felt that he was dumb. His IQ test profile indicated that Mr. Grant's scores on most academically loaded subtests were indeed slightly lower than average (although, interestingly, his math skills were excellent). However, it was clear that he possessed other valuable qualities in abundance. His well-developed interpersonal sensitivity, willingness to take risks, and strong work ethic had provided the foundation for substantial success in his chosen field. With my help, Mr. Grant came to understand that his intelligence was of a different but no-less-valuable type.

2. Melissa, a child with some developmental and social delays, had been tested for the first time at the age of five. Her IQ scores at that time were uniformly quite low (although the psychologist who performed this initial evaluation did caution that her performance may have been adversely affected by anxiety). Melissa, however, was blessed with a very supportive family and an excellent school willing to work with her special learning needs. Even more importantly, she herself had a wonderfully cooperative attitude, a cheerful disposition, and an incredible degree of persistence. Her learning was slow but her progress was steady; despite some gaps, she was able to function adequately in regular classes. And by the time her family brought her to me for reevaluation five years later, most of her IQ scores had moved into the average range.

3. Allan was a high school junior who had been diagnosed with significant learning disabilities early in elementary school. Despite the fact that most of his IQ scores were below average, he was managing to maintain an A–B average in a demanding private school. Allan worked exceedingly hard, had developed many successful strategies for coping with his learning disabilities, and was comfortable asking for help when he needed it. In addition, he had excellent social skills and was an extraordinary athlete. Allan came to me for help in college planning, with a specific request that I recommend

appropriate college-level accommodations for his unique style of learning. He was subsequently accepted at the college of his choice, and at last report he was on track to graduate with his class and poised for successful entry into his chosen career.

USING IQ TESTS FOR SELECTION AND TRACKING

As we have seen, when clinicians give IQ tests, it is generally for the benefit of individuals who have come to them for help. The same is not true, however, when schools, agencies, and employers use tests as tools for selection, placement, or tracking. This practice almost inevitably produces both winners and losers. And so it is not surprising that almost all of the controversy related to IQ testing—whether it pertains to affirmative action programs, racial disparities in special education placement, or academic tracking in public schools—occurs when people in authority employ tests of cognitive ability to provide *a priori* predictions of future success in ways that restrict access to valued opportunities or shunt individuals into perceived dead-end tracks.

In most public schools, students referred for special education services are given an individually administered IQ tests like the WISC as a part of the evaluation process. This practice was the subject of several heated court battles in the 1970s and 1980s. Unfortunately, the verdicts in these court cases turned out to be confusing and contradictory. The judge in California's well-known *Larry P. v. Riles,* for example, banned the use of IQ tests for placing minority students in special education programs in his state. In contrast, the Chicago judge in *PASE v. Hannon* listened to basically the same arguments but reached the opposite conclusion.[4] None of these decisions, however, addressed what I believe to be the real issue. The problem is not the specific test used to identify students who have special learning needs; it is the type of help they get after they are identified. All too often, especially in the past, special education students have been labeled and then shunted into low-level, dead-end classes. But this does not have to be the case. When properly designed and flexibly administered, special education programs can actually *increase* options and maximize opportunities by providing students with appropriate supports and creative, individualized instruction. And to the extent that parents regard special services as helpful rather than harmful, they often actually lobby the schools for testing. Much of the dramatic recent increase in the percentage of students classified as learning disabled, for example, is due to middle-class parents seeking more individual attention and special accommodations for their children.

Although most states require individually administered IQ tests for special education evaluation, these tests are far too expensive and time-consuming to be practical for mass screening. Public schools therefore generally employ group-administered intelligence tests (often labeled measures of ability or aptitude) to track students into more or less rigorous academic classes. In 1970, 83 percent of school districts surveyed reported that they used achievement and/or IQ tests as their primary basis for assigning students to classes. In recent years, tracking systems have become somewhat more flexible and less overt. Still, the practice of sorting students by ability level remains all but universal. A nationwide survey conducted in 1995, for example, revealed that only about 15 percent of high school students were enrolled in mixed-ability classes in core subjects such as English, math, and science.[5]

But criticism of academic tracking is beginning to mount. A growing group of educators and psychologists (interestingly, the infamous Arthur Jensen among them) now argue that there is neither a need nor a justification for using IQ tests to limit the opportunities made available to supposedly less able students. The only real purpose of intelligence tests, these critics point out, is to predict (albeit rather imperfectly) academic achievement. But in the school setting, we already have numerous *direct* measures of achievement, and the resources in question (e.g., advanced classes) are scarce only if we choose to make them so. So why not give *all* interested students access to challenging classes? Then, instead of being prejudged by flawed and unnecessary predictors, students willing to take on the challenge can succeed or fail on the basis of their own efforts.

Opponents of this view offer two primary reasons for their objections: that students placed in classes too difficult for them suffer frustration and emotional damage and that the presence of less able students in a classroom retards the progress of their more talented peers. Students are happier and learn more effectively, they argue, when grouped with classmates of similar ability. Recent studies, however, have cast doubt on both of these assertions. For example, citing an extensive body of research, educator Jeannie Oakes has concluded that "tracking seems to retard the academic progress of many students . . . in average and low groups. [It] seems to foster low self-esteem, . . . promote school misbehavior and dropping out, [and] . . . lower the aspirations of students who are not in the top groups."[6] In addition to enhancing equality of opportunity, she argues, allowing freer access to high-level classes significantly increases the achievement of supposedly less able students. Recent experiments with de-tracking in public high schools support Oakes's position. For example, by opening higher level classes to all students, one high school in New York increased its pass rate on the state Regents exam from 78 to 92 percent. Other schools have reported similar experiences.[7] But what of the argument that the presence of less capable students adversely affects the achievement of their higher-IQ classmates? Not true, the research suggests. As long as academic standards are not diluted, there is no consistent evidence to indicate that de-tracking limits the progress of higher-achieving students in any way.[8]

The research is therefore quite consistent in suggesting that there is no harm, and much potential benefit, in encouraging most elementary and high school students to attempt challenging classes, regardless of their scores on intelligence testing. Admittedly, however, the issue becomes a bit more complex when resources are inadequate to offer such opportunities to everyone. For example, elite universities and professional schools cannot simply open their doors to all comers; there is general agreement that their limited space should be reserved for the students best equipped to handle high-level coursework. But how do colleges determine who these students are? Not surprisingly, they generally base their admissions decisions on criteria that purport to select the applicants who will go on to earn the highest college grades. Given the mystique of the fabled SAT, most of us are under the impression that this test is their most valuable predictive tool. But in fact, SAT scores are only modestly related to college success. Previous grades are by far the best predictor of future grades; tests such as the SAT add only a modest 5 percent to the predictive value of an applicant's high school grade point average.[9] In fact, an increasing number of selective colleges, including Bryn Mawr, Bowdoin, Colby, Goucher, Hampshire, and Mt. Holyoke, are no longer even requiring prospective students to take the SAT.[10]

But there is an even more basic issue to consider: by what standards should we judge the ultimate success of the graduates of our colleges and universities? I suspect that most of us are more interested in the professional competence and societal contributions of our college graduates than in their grade point averages. And here the predictive utility of the SAT is even more limited. College grades and eventual vocational success are only weakly related; for example, grades explain a mere 4 to 8 percent of the variation in students' future earnings.[11] The developers of the SAT themselves acknowledge that "high school record and SAT scores [are] only slightly related to income and virtually unrelated to job satisfaction . . . [and] community leadership."[12] In other words, even the Educational Testing Service admits that its premier test is virtually useless for predicting the future professional and social contributions of college and university applicants.

This is not to say that tests play no legitimate role in selecting individuals for admission to competitive college programs. Potential students must have a certain prerequisite body of skills and knowledge if they are to successfully handle challenging coursework. And in combination with high school grades, tests of academic *achievement* can be an effective and efficient way to assess these skills. Colleges can quite easily determine the minimum achievement test scores associated with successful program completion. It is then not only reasonable but entirely appropriate for them to deny admission to applicants who fail to meet these basic standards.[13] After all, accepting individuals who have little chance of success benefits neither the school nor the student. Once these tests have identified a pool of qualified applicants, however, nothing is gained by giving preference to the members of pool who have the highest test scores. It would be far more socially useful to develop criteria that better predict which of these qualified potential students will go on to make the most substantial contributions to their professions and their communities.

It is important here to make a distinction between tests like the SAT that purport to assess learning *potential,* or aptitude, and achievement tests designed to measure acquired skills and knowledge. True, scores on tests labeled as measures of achievement are highly correlated with both IQ and SAT scores. However, the distinction between the two types of instruments is more than just semantic. If a low test score is interpreted to mean lack of aptitude, the natural assumption is that the test-taker is innately and irremediably deficient. The only possible response for this unfortunate individual is to develop more realistic ambitions. Poor performance on an achievement test, on the other hand, only suggests that the student has not yet mastered the required material. The obvious solution is for him or her to work harder and/or receive more effective instruction. Scores interpreted as reflecting low aptitude lead to hopelessness; those indicating inadequate achievement, on the other hand, point to solutions.

It is noteworthy that in 2005 the SAT underwent a significant revision, one that shifted its focus away from the identification of innate aptitude and toward the assessment of concrete educational achievement. This revision was undertaken largely in response to pressure from Richard Atkinson, then president of the massive University of California system. Atkinson argued that the venerable SAT had distorted educational priorities by pressuring schools to divert precious resources away from academic instruction toward the teaching of test-taking strategies. In response to these complaints, the Educational Testing Service eliminated many aptitude sections from the test (including the dreaded analogies) and added more reading comprehension questions, more advanced math items, and an entirely new writing section.[14] It is still too soon to assess the long-term educational impact of this shift in focus. At the very least, however, it appears to have had some significant social implications. Writing in *The Weekly Standard,* for example, critic John Harper asserted that "if under the new exam minority scores continue to lag, it will be obvious that the reason is not that the SAT is a racially biased intelligence test but that the public schools are simply failing to give minority students the skills necessary for success in college."[15] Rather than providing a supposedly scientific excuse for maintaining an unjust and inequitable status quo, racial and ethnic gaps in scores on the new SAT should in theory serve as a spur to greater personal effort and a stronger national commitment to providing equal educational opportunities to all students.

AN ALTERNATIVE PERSPECTIVE ON MERIT

Our long-standing practice of using tests to select individuals for valued opportunities (or, conversely, to track them into dead-end programs) confronts us directly with the central issue of merit. From the days of our founding fathers, we Americans have treasured an image of ourselves as a meritocratic society. Each of us, we believe, should rise or fall solely on the basis of our own personal qualities, accidents of birth, race, or class notwithstanding. It comes as no surprise, therefore, that the language of merit dominates our endless and seemingly intractable arguments over issues such as affirmative action and racial preferences. Opponents of affirmative action frame their position in meritocratic terms, arguing that awarding benefits for any reason other than individual ability flies in the face of our most cherished democratic ideals. This position was made explicit by the Supreme Court in 1982, when Justice Brennan opined in the case of *Plyler v. Doe* that the government should not impose "barriers presenting unreasonable obstacles to advancement on the basis of individual merit."[16]

But few of us even notice the unspoken assumption that ability, or merit, is most reliably judged by a person's score on a test of intelligence or aptitude. Consider, for example, the arguments generally used in court to challenge so-called racial preferences. Most plaintiffs in affirmative action cases base their claims on the assertion that they were denied admission to an educational institution (or passed over for a desirable job) because a less qualified member of a minority group—meaning one with lower test scores—was selected in their place. This practice, they argue, is a fundamental violation of their constitutional rights. The generally unquestioned assumption underlying these assertions is that high test scores give individuals a constitutionally protected right to the means of success in modern America.

It has apparently not occurred to many of us to ask what individual rights based on IQ scores have to do with our cherished national ideal of meritocracy. But interestingly, this very question was in fact recently raised by the publishers of the SAT themselves. In a 2003 amicus curiae brief filed in the Supreme Court, the venerable College Board presented arguments supporting the right of the University of Michigan to use race as one factor in undergraduate admissions (a practice that the Court subsequently ruled unconstitutional in its *Gratz v. Bollinger* decision).[17] In this brief, the Board observed that "the petitioners and their amici assume that a student with higher SAT or other admission test scores is, ipso facto, better qualified." The Board, however, took a contrary position, arguing that its own SAT should never be used as the sole measure of merit. "Some institutions view higher education as an entitlement that should be available to all who are qualified," the authors of the brief noted. "Others see it as a reward for the academically successful, the virtuous, the diligent or the public-spirited. Still others would have their institutions seek and nurture talent, to promote social and economic mobility." Each institution, the College Board argued, has the right to define merit on the basis of its own unique mission—a mission to which test-based admissions may or may not contribute. Although the Board's argument apparently did not prove persuasive to the Supreme Court, it does raise issues worthy of serious consideration.[18]

Anyone familiar with recent American history is aware that our test-centered and rights-oriented view of merit has proven to be politically divisive, racially polarizing, and wasteful of the talents of millions of our citizens. I suspect that few of us would choose simply to jettison our deeply rooted meritocratic ideals. However, I would like to suggest an alternative perspective on the issue. What would happen if, instead of focusing exclusively on individual rights, we were to consider reclaiming the ideas about merit passed on to us by our founding fathers? As we have seen in earlier chapters, the Enlightenment concept of merit was rich and complex. Jefferson, for example, described his natural aristocrats as a group of men (yes, men) possessed of uncommon virtue, industry, and wisdom. He envisioned these worthy individuals as public-spirited and self-sacrificing, accepting the responsibilities of leadership more as an obligation than as a right. This Jeffersonian ideal of a public-spirited, merit-based leadership has not entirely disappeared; its influence can be seen very clearly, for example, in the writings of such mid-twentieth-century opinion makers as James Conant and John Gardner.[19] But such public-spirited language has become increasingly rare. These days, being judged as an individual of extraordinary merit seemingly confers not an obligation to contribute to the broader social good, but rather the right to personal financial gain, generally through access to the elite institutions that serve as gateways to success in contemporary America.[20]

In a fascinating 1985 article, former Harvard admissions director Robert Klitgaard, himself a representative of one of our most prominent bastions of test-focused meritocracy, reflected on this Jeffersonian concept. "In an ideal world of perfect information," he wrote, "students should not be chosen solely on the basis of 'academic merit.'" After all, he continued, "the ancients added 'virtue' to 'wisdom' . . . as criteria for rulers."[21] Ideally, Klitgaard said, he would have been able to consider such qualities of character in his admissions decisions. In the absence of any objective measures of these softer qualities, however, he had been forced to depend on more strictly intellectual criteria. I agree with Klitgaard that there are potential dangers in relying too heavily on subjective assessments of difficult-to-quantify personal qualities. For example, the Tobin Commission, appointed during the 1960s to review admissions decisions at Yale, conceded that "in the past . . . 'character' and 'leadership' have sometimes been rubrics under which favoritism has been shown to candidates of certain family, economic, religious, ethnic, and scholastic backgrounds."[22] More objective admissions criteria have certainly helped to alleviate (although certainly not eliminate) such blatant examples of favoritism.

But we are paying a high price for our test-centered myopia. I have argued throughout this book that our simplistic and unreflective equation of psychometric intelligence with individual merit has had far-reaching (if perhaps unintended) consequences—limiting our recognition of talent, perpetuating economic and racial inequalities, and leading us to lose sight of such time-honored qualities as integrity, interpersonal sensitivity, and social responsibility. But, as the preceding chapters have illustrated, there is nothing magic about IQ. Although moderately useful for certain purposes, our modern, test-focused concept of intelligence, based as it is on a set of circumstances particular to our own time and place, has come to assume an importance completely disproportionate to its actual value. In my view, our founding fathers had it right. There is no particular merit in simply being smart. Rather, true merit consists of the willingness to use one's qualities of mind and character, not just for individual gain, but for the good of the larger society. If we were able to reclaim this rich understanding of meritocracy that is our heritage, our fruitless and interminable arguments about class, race, and IQ could then fade away into the oblivion that they so richly deserve.

Notes

CHAPTER 1: WORSHIPPING AT THE ALTAR OF IQ

1. "Albert Einstein Licenses," http://einstein.biz/licensees (accessed September 23, 2010).

2. Walter Isaacson, "Who Mattered and Why," *Time*, December 31, 1999, 62.

3. Quoted in Jeffrey Crelinsten, "Einstein, Relativity, and the Press: The Myth of Incomprehensibility," *Physics Teacher* 18 (1980): 118.

4. Isaacson, "Who Mattered," 62.

5. Quoted in Peter Coles, "Einstein, Eddington and the 1919 Eclipse," in *Historical Development of Modern Cosmology, ASP Conference Proceedings,* vol. 252, ed. Vincent Martinez, Virginia Trimble, and Maria Jesus Pons-Borderia (San Francisco, CA: Astronomical Society of the Pacific, 2001), 38.

6. Peter Coles, "Einstein, Eddington and the 1919 Eclipse."

7. This popular fascination with Einstein's extraordinary mind has even extended to his physical brain. Several pathologists have dissected portions of it, trying to discover the secret of his genius. In 2000, author Michael Paterniti wrote a best-selling book called *Driving Mr. Albert* in which he describes a bizarre cross-country trip in which he attempted to return Einstein's brain (which had been kept preserved in a jar by the pathologist who performed the autopsy) to his granddaughter in California. She declined to keep it. Michael Paterniti, *Driving Mr. Albert: A Trip across America with Einstein's Brain* (New York, NY: Dial Press, 2000).

8. "About Marilyn," http:/www.marilynvossavant.com/bio.html (accessed November 16, 2006); Marilyn Vos Savant, "Ask Marilyn," *Parade,* January 16, 2005, http://www.parade.com/articles/editions/2005/edition_01-16-2005/ask_marilyn_0?print= ; Marilyn Vos Savant, "Ask Marilyn," *Parade,* January

2, 2005, http://www.parade.com/articles/editions/2005/edition_01–02–2005/ ask_marilyn_0?prnt = 1; Marilyn Vos Savant, "Ask Marilyn," *Parade,* July 31, 2005, http://www.parade.com/articles/editions/2005/edition_07–31–2005/ ask_marilyn_0?prnt = 1.

9. Julie Baumgold, "In the Kingdom of the Brain," *New York Magazine* 22 (1989): 36–42.

10. Quoted in Henry L. Minton, "Lewis M. Terman and Mental Testing: In Search of the Democratic Ideal," in *Psychological Testing and American Society, 1890–1930,* ed. Michael M. Sokal (New Brunswick, NJ: Rutgers University Press, 1987), 95.

11. Nicholas Lemann, *The Big Test: The Secret History of the American Meritocracy* (New York, NY: Farrar, Straus and Giroux, 2000), 273.

12. Jerome Kagan, "The Concept of Intelligence," *The Humanist* 32 (1972): 8.

13. Richard Lynn, "Back to the Future," in *The Bell Curve Debate: History, Documents, Opinions,* ed. Russell Jacoby and Naomi Glauberman (New York, NY: Times Books, 1995), 355; Victor Serebriakoff, *A Guide to Intelligence and Personality Testing: Including Actual Tests and Answers* (Park Ridge, NJ: Parthenon Publishing Group, 1988), 3.

14. Quotations cited in David Owen, *None of the Above: Behind the Myth of Scholastic Aptitude* (Boston, MA: Houghton Mifflin, 1985), xiii.

15. Daniel Seligman, *A Question of Intelligence: The IQ Debate in America* (New York, NY: Birch Lane Press, 1992), 9.

16. Orville G. Brim, David C. Glass, John Neulinger, and Ira J. Firestone, *American Beliefs and Attitudes about Intelligence* (New York, NY: Russell Sage Foundation, 1969).

17. And this young man's perceptions of how the world views him were devastatingly accurate. Children are mercilessly teased for riding the cheese bus (the short yellow school buses that are often used to transport special education students). And the worse insult that one child can hurl at another on the playground is to call him or her a "retard." Advocacy organizations keep changing labels to try to reduce stigma; in the last hundred years, we have progressed from idiots and morons through mental deficiency to mental retardation and now intellectual disability. But changes in language do not change the overriding fact that our society considers people with low intelligence to have little personal worth.

18. Joni Winn, "Boosting Baby's IQ," *Saturday Evening Post* 255 (1983): 46.

19. "The Quest for a Super Kid," *Time* 157 (2001): 50–56.

20. Joni Winn, "Boosting Baby's IQ"; Gaylen Moore, "The Superbaby Myth," *Psychology Today* 18 (1984): 6–7.

21. Paula Span, "Early Learning That Works," *Good Housekeeping* 229 (1999): 70–71; Marco R. della Cava, "The Race to Raise a Brainier Baby," *USA Today,* June 25, 2002, 1D–2D; Alexandra Robbins, *The Overachievers: The Secret Lives of Driven Kids* (New York, NY: Hyperion, 2006).

22. Kay S. Hymowitz, "Survivor: The Manhattan Kindergarten," *City Journal,* Spring 2001, www.city-journal.org/html/11_2_survivor.html; Chuck Shepherd, "News of the Weird: In New York City, Prep Courses for 3-Year-Olds for

Admission to 'Prestigious' Kindergartens!" *Yahoo! News,* newsoftheweird.com/archive/nw091213.html (accessed December 13, 2009).

23. Robert K. Fullinwider and Judith Lichtenberg, *Leveling the Playing Field: Justice, Politics, and College Admissions* (New York, NY: Rowman & Littlefield Publishers, 2004).

24. Lemann, *The Big Test;* Allan Nairn and Associates, *The Reign of ETS: The Corporation That Makes Up Minds* (Washington, DC: Ralph Nader, 1980); Samantha Henig, "How the Other Half Matriculates," *The Washington Post,* December 10, 2001, C10.

25. Kagan, "The Concept of Intelligence."

26. Pamela Paul, "Want a Brainier Baby?" *Time,* January 16, 2006, 102–109; Sandra G. Boodman, "Wishful Thinking," *The Washington Post,* October 9, 2007, F1, F4.

27. Brim et al., *American Beliefs and Attitudes about Intelligence.*

28. Edward Zigler and Mary E. Lang, "The 'Gourmet Baby' and the 'Little Wildflower,' " *Zero to Three Journal* 7, no. 2 (1986): 8.

29. "The Quest for a Super Kid," *Time* 157 (2001): 50.

30. Suzuki Violin School of Columbus-Worthington, "5 Reasons to Play a Musical Instrument," newsletter, October 2006, www.suzukicolumbus.org.

31. Liza Mundy, "High Anxiety," *The Washington Post Magazine,* October 23, 2005, W20.

32. Daniel C. Molden and Carol Sorich Dweck, "Finding 'Meaning' in Psychology," *American Psychologist* 61 (2006): 192–203; Brandon E. Gibb, Lauren B. Alloy, and Lyn Y. Abramson, "Attributional Styles and Academic Achievement in University Students: A Longitudinal Investigation," *Cognitive Therapy and Research* 26 (2002): 309–15; Lisa S. Blackwell, Kali H. Trzesniewski, and Carol Sorich Dweck, "Implicit Theories of Intelligence Predict Achievement across an Adolescent Transition: A Longitudinal Study and an Intervention," *Child Development* 78 (2007): 246–63; Jay Matthew, "Self-Discipline May Beat Smarts as Key to Success," *The Washington Post,* January 17, 2006, A10.

33. Robbins, *Overachievers,* 221.

34. Linda S. Gottfredson, "What Do We Know about Intelligence?" *The American Scholar,* Winter, 1996, 15–30. See also Alissa Quart, *Hothouse Kids: The Dilemma of the Gifted Child* (New York, NY: Penguin Press, 2006).

35. David Halberstam, *The Best and the Brightest* (Greenwich, CT: Fawcett Publications, 1973), 56–57.

36. Margot Pepper, "No Corporation Left Behind: How a Century of Illegitimate Testing Has Been Used to Justify Internal Colonialism," *Monthly Review* 58 (2006), http://www.monthlyreview.org/1106pepper.htm.

37. David Owen, "The S.A.T. and Social Stratification," *Journal of Education* 168 (1986): 81–92; Meredith Phillips, Jeanne Brooks-Gunn, Greg J. Duncan, Pamela Klebanov, and Jonathan Crane, "Family Background, Parenting Practices, and the Black–White Test Score Gap," in *The Black–White Test Score Gap,* ed. Christopher Jencks and Meredith Phillips (Washington, DC: Brookings Institution Press, 1998), 103–146.

38. William A. Galston, "The Affirmative Action Debate," *Report from the Institute for Philosophy and Public Policy* 17, no. 1/2 (1997).

39. Interestingly, amidst all of the hoopla about affirmative action for African Americans, virtually nothing is said about another type of affirmative action—one that benefits males. In recent years, a number of liberal arts colleges have become alarmed by the declining numbers of men in their student bodies. It appears that their female applicants are simply better qualified! And so they purposely tweak their admission standards to give an edge to male applicants. (See, for example, Sarah Karnasiewicz, "The Campus Crusade for Guys," *Salon.com,* February 15, 2006, http://salon.com/mwt/feature/2006/02/15/affirmative_action/; Gadi Dechter, "Towson Angles to Draw Males," *Baltimore Sun,* October 29, 2006, articles.baltimoresun.com/2006-10-29/news/0610290013_1_towson-males-student-body; Jennifer Delahunty Britz, "To All the Girls I've Rejected," *New York Times,* March 23, 2006, http://www.nytimes.com/2006/03/23/opinion/23britz.html.) Apparently, our society believes it is fine to use test scores to keep members of racial minorities in their proper place. But when white males start to suffer, it is time to take action!

40. PollingReport.com, www.pollingreport.com/race.htm (accessed November 16, 2006).

41. Tamar Lewin, "Michigan Rejects Affirmative Action, and Backers Sue," *New York Times,* November 9, 2006.

42. David S. Broder, "Jesse Helms, White Racist," *The Washington Post,* August 29, 2001, A21.

43. James Fallows, "The Best and the Brightest: How Fair Are the College Boards?" *Atlantic Monthly,* February 1980, 48; Brigitte Berger, "Methodological Fetishism," in *The Bell Curve Debate: History, Documents, Opinions,* ed. Russell Jacoby and Naomi Glauberman (New York, NY: Times Books, 1995), 344.

CHAPTER 2: INTELLIGENCE IN HISTORICAL CONTEXT: THE COLONIAL EXPERIENCE

1. Richard J. Herrnstein and Charles Murray, *The Bell Curve: Intelligence and Class Structure in American Life* (New York, NY: Free Press Paperbacks, 1994), 1.

2. Lorraine Dashton, "The Naturalized Female Intellect," *Science in Context 5* (1992): 211.

3. On Greek and early Christian philosophies of reason, see Daniel N. Robinson, *An Intellectual History of Psychology* (New York, NY: Macmillan, 1976); Howard Gardner, *Frames of Mind: The Theory of Multiple Intelligences* (New York, NY: Basic Books, 1983); Margery Sabin, "The Community of Intelligence and the Avant-Garde," *Raritan* 4 (1985): 1–25; C.D.C. Reeve, *Practices of Reason: Aristotle's Nicomachean Ethics* (Oxford: Clarendon Press, 1992); Kurt Danziger, *Naming the Mind: How Psychology Found Its Language* (Thousand Oaks, CA: Sage, 1997).

4. Perry Miller, *The New England Mind: The Seventeenth Century* (New York, NY: Macmillan, 1939); Richard Hofstadter, *Anti-Intellectualism in American Life* (New York, NY: Vintage Books, 1962); Elizabeth Flower and Murray G. Murphey, *A History of Philosophy in America,* vol. 1 (New York, NY: G. P. Putnam's Sons, 1977); Merle Curti, *Human Nature in American Thought: A History* (Madison, WI: University of Wisconsin Press, 1980).

5. Miller, *New England Mind,* 107.

6. Miller, *New England Mind;* Alan Heimert, *Religion and the American Mind from the Great Awakening to the Revolution* (Cambridge, MA: Harvard University Press, 1966); Curti, *Human Nature.*

7. Arthur O. Lovejoy, *The Great Chain of Being: A Study of the History of an Idea* (Cambridge, MA: Harvard University Press, 1961 [1933]); Henry F. May, *The Enlightenment in America* (New York, NY: Oxford University Press, 1976); Daniel N. Robinson, "Wisdom through the Ages," in *Wisdom: Its Nature, Origin, and Development,* ed. Robert J. Sternberg (New York, NY: Cambridge University Press, 1990), 13–24.

8. John Locke, *An Essay Concerning Human Understanding,* ed. Peter H. Nidditch (Oxford: Clarendon Press, 1974); E. J. Lowe, *Locke on Human Understanding* (New York, NY: Routledge, 1995).

9. Carl Bridenbaugh, *Mitre and Sceptre: Transatlantic Faiths, Ideas, Personalities, and Politics, 1689–1775* (New York, NY: Oxford University Press, 1962); Hofstadter, *Anti-Intellectualism;* Jean V. Matthews, *Toward a New Society: American Thought and Culture, 1800–1830* (Boston: Twayne, 1991).

10. Quoted in James Kloppenberg, *Uncertain Victory: Social Democracy and Progressivism in European and American Thought, 1870–1920* (New York, NY: Oxford University Press, 1986), 338.

11. Alexander Pope, *Essay on Man,* ed. Frank Brady (New York, NY: Bobbs–Merrill, 1965), 43, 48.

12. Nicholas Lemann, *The Big Test: The Secret History of the American Meritocracy* (New York, NY: Farrar, Straus and Giroux, 2000); David Layzer, "Science or Superstition," in *The Bell Curve Debate: History, Documents, Opinions,* ed. Russell Jacoby and Naomi Glauberman (New York, NY: Times Books, 1995), 672.

13. Linda K. Kerber, "The Revolutionary Generation: Ideology, Politics, and Culture in the Early Republic," in *The New American History,* rev. ed., ed. Eric Foner (Philadelphia, PA: Temple University Press, 1997), 31–59.

14. Plato, *The Republic,* ed. G.F.R. Ferrari, trans. Tom Griffith (Cambridge: Cambridge University Press, 2000), 415c; "The Federalist No. 57," in *The Federalist,* ed. Edward Earle Meade (New York, NY: Modern Library, 1937), 370; Lester J. Cappon (ed.), *The Adams–Jefferson Letters: The Complete Correspondence between Thomas Jefferson and Abigail and John Adams,* vol. 2 (Chapel Hill, NC: University of North Carolina Press, 1959), 391.

15. Thomas Jefferson, "Notes on the State of Virginia," in *The Portable Thomas Jefferson,* ed. Merrill D. Peterson (New York, NY: Viking, 1975), 198. On revolutionary era political thought, see P.G.A. Pocock, *Virtue, Commerce,*

and History: Essays on Political Thought and History, Chiefly in the Eighteenth Century (Cambridge: Cambridge University Press, 1985); Ann Fairfax Withington, *Toward a More Perfect Union: Virtue and the Formation of American Republics* (New York, NY: Oxford University Press, 1991); Thomas Bender, "Intellectual and Cultural History," in *The New American History,* rev. ed, ed. Eric Foner (Philadelphia: Temple University Press, 1997), 181–202.

16. Daniel Seligman, *A Question of Intelligence: The IQ Debate in America* (New York, NY: Birch Lane Press, 1992), viii–ix.

17. On the Great Awakening, see Merle Curti, "Intellectuals and Other People," *American Historical Review* 60 (1955): 259–82; Alan Heimert, *Religion and the American Mind from the Great Awakening to the Revolution* (Cambridge, MA: Harvard University Press, 1966); May, *Enlightenment in America.* On nonelite revolutionary thought, see Hofstadter, *Anti-Intellectualism;* Robert Wiebe, *The Opening of American Society* (New York, NY: Alfred A. Knopf, 1984); Gordon S. Wood, *The Radicalism of the American Revolution* (New York, NY: Alfred A. Knopf, 1992).

18. Quoted in Hofstadter, *Anti-Intellectualism,* 69.

CHAPTER 3: SCIENCE IN NINETEENTH-CENTURY AMERICA: INTELLECT, INTELLIGENCE, AND THE SCIENCE OF MAN

1. Alexander Pope, "Epitaph, XII, Intended for Sir Isaac Newton, in Westminster Abbey," *The Works of Alexander Pope, Esq.,* vol. 2 (London: Cadell and Davies, 1797), 403.

2. Michel Foucault, *The Order of Things: An Archaeology of the Human Sciences* (New York, NY: Random House, 1970). On science in early America, see George H. Daniels, *American Science in the Age of Jackson* (New York, NY: Columbia University Press, 1968); Daniel N. Robinson, *An Intellectual History of Psychology* (New York, NY: Macmillan Publishing Company, 1976); John Burnham, *How Superstition Won and Science Lost: Popularizing Science and Health in the United States* (New Brunswick, NJ: Rutgers University Press, 1987); Daniel J. Wilson, *Science, Community, and the Transformation of American Philosophy, 1860–1930* (Chicago, IL: University of Chicago Press, 1990).

3. Perry Miller, *The New England Mind: The Seventeenth Century* (New York, NY: Macmillan Company, 1939); Merle Curti, *The Growth of American Thought* (New York, NY: Harper and Brothers, 1943); Alan Heimert, *Religion and the American Mind from the Great Awakening to the Revolution* (Cambridge, MA: Harvard University Press, 1966).

4. Alfred H. Fuchs, "Contributions of American Mental Philosophers to Psychology in the United States," in *Evolving Perspectives on the History of Psychology,* ed. Wade E. Pickren and Donald A. Dewsbury (Washington, DC: American Psychological Association, 2002), 79–99.

5. John M. O'Donnell, *The Origins of Behaviorism: American Psychology, 1870–1920* (New York, NY: New York University Press, 1985), 53–54.

6. Thomas Upham, *Elements of Mental Philosophy* (New York, NY: Harper & Brothers, 1841); Mark Hopkins, *An Outline Study of Man; or, the*

Body and Mind in One System (New York, NY: Charles Scribner's Sons, 1883); Donald Meyer, *The Instructed Conscience: The Shaping of the American National Ethic* (Philadelphia, PA: University of Pennsylvania Press, 1972).

7. Hopkins, *Outline Study of Man.*

8. Foucault, *Order of Things,* 251.

9. Richard Hofstadter, *Social Darwinism in American Thought,* rev. ed. (Boston, MA: Beacon Press, 1955); Kurt Danziger, *Naming the Mind: How Psychology Found Its Language* (Thousand Oaks, CA: Sage, 1997).

10. Robert Chambers, *Vestiges of the Natural History of Creation,* ed. James A. Secord (Chicago, IL: University of Chicago Press, 1994); Daniels, *American Science in the Age of Jackson.*

11. Charles Darwin, *The Descent of Man* (Princeton, NJ: Princeton University Press, 1981); Carl N. Degler, *In Search of Human Nature: The Decline and Revival of Darwinism in American Social Thought* (New York, NY: Oxford University Press, 1991).

12. In view of the eugenic use to which his theories were later put, it is interesting that Darwin was a firm believer in the Lamarckian theory of the inheritance of acquired traits. Proper habit, training, and instruction could improve an individual's mental organization, and these virtuous tendencies could then be passed on to his or her offspring. His views were in fact far less deterministic than those of many of his later followers.

13. Charles Darwin, *Expression of the Emotions in Man and Animals* (London: John Murray, 1872).

14. Hofstadter, *Social Darwinism.* On the reception of theories of evolution in the United States, see also Elizabeth Flower and Murray G. Murphey, *A History of Philosophy in America,* vol. 2 (New York, NY: G. P. Putnam's Sons, 1977); Degler, *In Search of Human Nature.*

15. Other clergymen, less socially liberal, used Darwin to support racist, xenophobic, and anti-immigrant social policies. For example, in a highly influential pamphlet entitled *Our Country: Its Possible Future and Its Present Crisis,* written in 1885, prominent Congregationalist minister Josiah Strong argued, "Mr. Darwin is . . . disposed to see, in the superior vigor of our people, an illustration of his favorite theory of natural selection. . . . There can be no reasonable doubt that North America is to be the great home of the Anglo-Saxon, the principal seat of his power, the center of his life and influence." Josiah Strong, *Our Country: Its Possible Future and Its Present Crisis,* ed. Jurgen Herbst (Cambridge, MA: Harvard University Press, 1963), 206, 210.

16. Robert L. Carneiro, "Editor's Introduction," in *The Evolution of Society: Selections from Herbert Spencer's Principles of Sociology* (Chicago, IL: University of Chicago Press, 1967), ix–lvii; J.D.Y. Peel, *Herbert Spencer: The Evolution of a Sociologist* (Aldershot, Hampshire: Gregg Revivals, 1992).

17. Herbert Spencer, *Principles of Psychology,* 3rd ed. (New York, NY: D. Appleton and Co., 1910), 388–89.

18. Danziger, *Naming the Mind.*

19. John Higham, *From Boundlessness to Consolidation: The Transformation of American Culture 1848–1869* (Ann Arbor, MI: William L. Clements

Library, 1969); Hugh Elliot, *Herbert Spencer* (London: Constable & Company, 1917).

20. Edwin G. Boring, *A History of Experimental Psychology*, 2nd ed. (New York, NY: Appleton-Century-Crofts, Inc., 1957); David de Guistino, *Conquest of Mind: Phrenology and Victorian Social Thought* (London: Croom Helm, 1975).

21. Foucault, *Order of Things;* Edward L. Youmans, "Observations on the Scientific Study of Human Nature" in *The Culture Demanded by Modern Life: A Series of Addresses and Arguments on the Claims of Scientific Education* (New York, NY: D. Appleton, 1867), 375.

22. On scientific racism, see William Stanton, *The Leopard's Spots: Scientific Attitudes toward Race in America, 1815–1859* (Chicago, IL: University of Chicago Press, 1960); Stephen Jay Gould, *The Mismeasure of Man,* rev. ed. (New York, NY: W. W. Norton, 1996).

23. William Graham Sumner, "Sociology," in *Collected Essays in Political and Social Science* (New York, NY: Henry Holt and Company, 1885), 95–96.

24. Although Taine used the word "intelligence" to title his book, his work actually focused on what we would term the "intellect," or the faculty of reason or understanding possessed by all normal people. John Samuel Carson, "Talents, Intelligence, and the Constructions of Human Difference in France and America, 1750–1920" (PhD diss., Princeton University, 1994).

25. On the history of psychology, see O'Donnell, *The Origins of Behaviorism*; Kurt Danziger, *Constructing the Subject: Historical Origins of Psychological Research* (Cambridge: Cambridge University Press, 1990); Fuchs, "Contributions of American Mental Philosophers."

26. David Leary, "Telling Likely Stories: The Rhetoric of the New Psychology, 1880–1920," *Journal of the History of the Behavioral Sciences* 23 (1987): 315–31; JoAnne Brown, *The Definition of a Profession: The Authority of Metaphor in the History of Intelligence Testing, 1890–1930* (Princeton, NJ: Princeton University Press, 1992).

27. Theodore Porter, *The Rise of Statistical Thinking, 1820–1900* (Princeton, NJ: Princeton University Press, 1986).

28. Daniel J. Kevles, *In the Name of Eugenics: Genetics and the Uses of Human Heredity* (New York, NY: Alfred A. Knopf, 1985); Porter, *Rise of Statistical Thinking;* Danziger, *Constructing the Subject.*

29. George Boas, "From Truth to Probability," *Harper's Magazine* 154 (1927): 520.

30. Donald Zochert, "Science and the Common Man in Ante-Bellum America," *Isis* 65 (1974): 448–473; John Burnham, *How Superstition Won and Science Lost: Popularizing Science and Health in the United States* (New Brunswick, NJ: Rutgers University Press, 1987); Barbara Sicherman, "Sense and Sensibility: A Case Study of Women's Reading in Late Victorian America," in *Reading in America: Literature and Social History,* ed. Cathy N. Davidson (Baltimore, MD: Johns Hopkins University Press, 1989), 201–25.

31. Theodore Morrison, *Chautauqua: A Center for Education, Religion and the Arts in America* (Chicago, IL: University of Chicago Press, 1974); Andrea

Stulman Dennett, *Weird and Wonderful: The Dime Museum in America* (New York, NY: New York University Press, 1997).

CHAPTER 4: MERIT AND SOCIAL STATUS IN NINETEENTH-CENTURY AMERICA

1. Quoted in William H. Whyte, Jr., *The Organization Man* (New York, NY: Simon and Schuster, 1956), 16.

2. On social upheaval in the early United States, see Paul Boyer, *Urban Masses and Moral Order in America, 1820–1920* (Cambridge, MA: Harvard University Press, 1978); Robert Wiebe, *The Opening of American Society* (New York, NY: Alfred A. Knopf, 1984); James P. Shenton and Kevin Kenny, "Ethnicity and Immigration," in *The New American History,* rev. ed., ed. Eric Foner (Philadelphia, PA: Temple University Press, 1997), 353–73. On merit, see Russell Marks, "Legitimating Industrial Capitalism: Philanthropy and Individual Difference," in *Philanthropy and Cultural Imperialism: The Foundations at Home and Abroad,* ed. Robert F. Arnove (Boston, MA: G. K. Hall & Co., 1980), 87–122; David Hogan, "Examinations, Merit, and Morals: The Market Revolution and Disciplinary Power in Philadelphia's Public Schools, 1838–1868," *Historical Studies in Education* 4 (1992): 31–78; Nicholas Lemann, *The Big Test: The Secret History of the American Meritocracy* (New York, NY: Farrar, Straus and Giroux, 2000).

3. Quoted in Richard Weiss, *The American Myth of Success: From Horatio Alger to Norman Vincent Peale* (New York, NY: Basic Books, 1969), 33.

4. John M. Murrin, Paul E. Johnson, James M. McPherson, Gary Gerstle, Emily S. Rosenberg, and Norman L. Rosenberg, *Liberty, Equality, Power: A History of the American People, Volume I: to 1877* (New York, NY: Harcourt Brace College Publishers, 1996).

5. Richard Hofstadter, *The American Political Tradition and the Men Who Made It* (New York, NY: Vintage Press, 1948), 60.

6. Edward Pessen, *Jacksonian America: Society, Personality, and Politics,* rev. ed. (Homewood, IL: Dorsey Press, 1978).

7. Daniel Walker Howe, *The Political Culture of the American Whigs* (Chicago, IL: University of Chicago Press, 1979); Sean Wilentz, "Society, Politics, and the Market Revolution, 1815–1848," in *The New American History,* rev. ed., ed. Eric Foner (Philadelphia, PA: Temple University Press, 1997), 61–84.

8. Cecil Frances Alexander, "All Things Bright and Beautiful," in *Oxford Dictionary of Quotations,* 5th ed., ed. Elizabeth Knowles (Oxford: Oxford University Press, 1999), 11.

9. Arthur M. Schlesinger, Jr., *The Age of Jackson* (Boston, MA: Little, Brown, and Company, 1945), 507.

10. Richard L. McCormick, "Public Life in Industrial America, 1877–1917," in *The New American History,* rev. ed., ed. Eric Foner (Philadelphia, PA: Temple University Press, 1997), 107–32; Alexander Keyssar, *The Right to Vote: The Contested History of Democracy in the United States* (New York, NY: Basic Books, 2000).

11. Shenton and Kenny, "Ethnicity and Immigration."

12. John M. Murrin, Paul E. Johnson, James M. McPherson, Gary Gerstle, Emily S. Rosenberg, and Norman L. Rosenberg, *Liberty, Equality, Power: A History of the American People, Volume II: Since 1863,* 2nd ed. (New York, NY: Harcourt Brace, 1999); Richard L. McCormick, "Public Life in Industrial America, 1877–1917."

13. William Graham Sumner, "Sociology," in *Collected Essays in Political and Social Science* (New York, NY: Henry Holt and Company, 1885), 92. See also Merle Curti, *The Growth of American Thought* (New York, NY: Harper and Brothers, 1943); Robert Wiebe, *The Search for Order, 1877–1920* (Westport, CT: Greenwood Press, 1967).

14. Hogan, "Examinations, Merit, and Morals."

15. Josiah Strong, *Our Country: Its Possible Future and Its Present Crisis,* ed. Jurgen Herbst (Cambridge, MA: Harvard University Press, 1963), 140–41. On Social Darwinism in Protestantism, see Merle Curti, *Human Nature in American Thought: A History* (Madison, WI: University of Wisconsin Press, 1980).

16. On Progressivism and social reform, see Daniel Rodgers, "In Search of Progressivism," *Reviews in American History* 10 (1982): 113–32; Henry L. Minton, "Lewis M. Terman and Mental Testing: In Search of the Democratic Ideal," in *Psychological Testing and American Society, 1890–1930,* ed. Michael M. Sokal (New Brunswick, NJ: Rutgers University Press, 1987), 95–112; Carl N. Degler, *In Search of Human Nature: The Decline and Revival of Darwinism in American Social Thought* (New York, NY: Oxford University Press, 1991); Richard L. McCormick, "Public Life in Industrial America, 1877–1917."

17. Nicholas Lemann, *The Big Test: The Secret History of the American Meritocracy* (New York, NY: Farrar, Straus and Giroux, 2000), 18.

18. Jackson J. Benson, *Wallace Stegner: His Life and Work* (New York, NY: Viking, 1996), 137.

19. *Webster's New World Dictionary of the American Language,* 2nd college ed. (New York, NY: Prentice Hall, 1986), s.v. "self."

20. Arthur O. Lovejoy, *The Great Chain of Being: A Study of the History of an Idea* (Cambridge, MA: Harvard University Press, 1961); Curti, *Human Nature in American Thought;* Daniel Walker Howe, *Making the American Self: Jonathan Edwards to Abraham Lincoln* (Cambridge, MA: Harvard University Press, 1997).

21. E. J. Lowe, *Locke on Human Understanding* (New York, NY: Routledge, 1995).

22. Quoted in Daniel Walker Howe, *Making the American Self,* 107.

23. Ralph Waldo Emerson, "The American Scholar," in *Selected Writing of Ralph Waldo Emerson,* ed. Brooks Atkinson (New York, NY: Modern Library, 1950), 62.

24. Walt Whitman, "Song of Myself," in *Leaves of Grass,* ed. Harold W. Blodgett and Sculley Bradley (New York, NY: New York University Press, 1965), 28, 48, 53.

25. George Combe, *The Constitution of Man,* 8th ed. (Edinburgh: MacLachlan, Stewart, & Co., 1847), 8.

26. Benjamin Franklin, *Poor Richard's Almanack,* 1749; Benjamin Franklin, *Poor Richard's Almanack,* 1736.

27. Daniel Walker Howe, *Making the American Self.*

28. William Ellery Channing, *Self-Culture (An Address Introductory to the Franklin Lectures)* (London: John Cleave, 1838), 2, 4, 10.

29. On the concept of the self-made man, see John Cawelti, *Apostles of the Self-Made Man* (Chicago, IL: University of Chicago Press, 1965); Wiebe, *The Opening of American Society.*

30. Benjamin Franklin, *Poor Richard's Almanack,* 1735.

31. Quoted in Weiss, *The American Myth of Success,* 33.

32. Weiss, *American Myth of Success.*

33. Edward Bellamy, *Looking Backward, 2000–1887* (New York, NY: Modern Library, 1931).

CHAPTER 5: PHRENOLOGY: A PRECURSOR TO IQ TESTING

1. On physiognomy, see G. P. Brooks and R. W. Johnson, "Johann Caspar Lavater's Essays on Physiognomy," *Psychological Reports* 46 (1980): 3–20; Michael M. Sokal, "Introduction: Psychological Testing and Historical Scholarship—Questions, Contrasts, and Context," in *Psychological Testing and American Society, 1890–1930,* ed. Michael M. Sokal (New Brunswick, NJ: Rutgers University Press, 1987), 1–20; Alan F. Collins, "The Enduring Appeal of Physiognomy: Physical Appearance as a Sign of Temperament, Character, and Intelligence," *History of Psychology* 2 (1999): 251–76.

2. On Gall and Lavater, see Brooks and Johnson, "Johann Caspar Lavater's Essays on Physiognomy"; Raymond E. Fancher, "Gall, Flourens, and the Phrenological Movement," in *A History of Psychology: Original Sources and Contemporary Research,* ed. Ludy T. Benjamin (New York, NY: McGraw Hill, 1988), 101–108. On phrenology and nineteenth-century science, see Arthur Wrobel, "Orthodoxy and Respectability in Nineteenth-Century Phrenology," *Journal of Popular Culture* 9 (1975): 38–50; David de Guistino, *Conquest of Mind: Phrenology and Victorian Social Thought* (London: Croom Helm, 1975); G. P. Brooks, "The Faculty Psychology of Thomas Reid," *Journal of the History of the Behavioral Sciences* 12 (1976): 65–77; John M. O'Donnell, *The Origins of Behaviorism: American Psychology, 1870–1920* (New York, NY: New York University Press, 1985).

3. On phrenology and nineteenth-century science, see Arthur Wrobel, "Orthodoxy and Respectability in Nineteenth-Century Phrenology"; David de Guistino, *Conquest of Mind;* O'Donnell, *The Origins of Behaviorism.*

4. On the popularization of phrenology, see T. M. Parssinen, "Popular Science and Society: The Phrenology Movement in Early Victorian Britain," *Journal of Social History* 8 (1974): 1–20; Roger Cooter, *The Cultural Meaning of Popular Science: Phrenology and the Organization of Consent in Nineteenth-Century Britain* (New York, NY: Cambridge University Press, 1984).

5. George Combe, *The Constitution of Man,* 8th ed. (Edinburgh: MacLachlan, Stewart, 1847); Cooter, *Cultural Meaning of Popular Science.*

6. T. M. Parssinen, "Popular Science and Society: The Phrenology Movement in Early Victorian Britain," *Journal of Social History* 8 (1974): 1–20; Victor L. Hilts, "Obeying the Laws of Hereditary Descent: Phrenological Views on Inheritance and Eugenics," *Journal of the History of the Behavioral Sciences* 18 (1982): 62–77.

7. Combe, *The Constitution of Man,* 296.

8. David Bakan, "The Influence of Phrenology on American Psychology," *Journal of the History of the Behavioral Sciences* 2 (1966): 200–20; Anthony A. Walsh, "The American Tour of Dr. Spurzheim," *Journal of the History of Medicine and Allied Sciences* 27 (1972): 187–205.

9. J. D. Davies, *Phrenology: Fad and Science: A Nineteenth Century Crusade* (New Haven, CT: Yale University Press, 1955).

10. Madeleine B. Stern, *Heads and Headlines: The Phrenological Fowlers* (Norman, OK: University of Oklahoma Press, 1971). On practical phrenology, see Allan S. Horlick, "Phrenology and the Social Education of Young Men," *History of Education Quarterly* 11 (1971): 23–38; Guenter B. Risse, "Vocational Guidance during the Depression: Phrenology versus Applied Psychology," *Journal of the History of the Behavioral Sciences* 12 (1976): 130–40; Christine McHugh, "Phrenology: Getting Your Head Together in Ante-Bellum America," *Midwest Quarterly* 23 (1981): 65–77; Michael M. Sokal, "Practical Phrenology as Psychological Counseling in the 19th Century United States," in *The Transformation of Psychology,* ed. Christopher D. Green and Marlene Shore (Washington, DC: American Psychological Association, 2001), 21–44.

11. O. S. Fowler and L. N. Fowler, *New Illustrated Self-Instructor in Phrenology and Physiology* (New York, NY: Fowler and Wells, 1859); Nelson Sizer, *Choice of Pursuits, or What to Do and Why* (New York, NY: Fowler and Wells, 1877); Horlick, "Phrenology and the Social Education of Young Men"; Risse, "Vocational Guidance during the Depression."

12. John F. Kasson, *Rudeness and Civility: Manners in Nineteenth-Century Urban America* (New York, NY: Hill and Wang, 1990); Samuel Robert Wells, *How to Behave* (New York, NY: Fowler and Wells, 1857).

13. Quoted in David Bakan, "The Influence of Phrenology on American Psychology," *Journal of the History of the Behavioral Sciences* 2 (1966): 204.

14. Davies, *Phrenology: Fad and Science.*

15. Risse, "Vocational Guidance during the Depression."

16. Cooter, *The Cultural Meaning of Popular Science;* O'Donnell, *The Origins of Behaviorism.*

CHAPTER 6: INTELLIGENCE AND ITS MEASUREMENT

1. Richard J. Herrnstein and Charles Murray, *The Bell Curve: Intelligence and Class Structure in American Life* (New York, NY: Free Press Paperbacks, 1994), 1; Lorraine Dashton, "The Naturalized Female Intellect," *Science in Context* 5 (1992): 211.

2. Alexander Bain, *The Emotions and the Will,* 4th ed. (London: Longmans, Green, and Co., 1899), 24.

3. On the prehistory and early history of mental testing, see Milos Bondy, "Psychiatric Antecedents of Psychological Testing before Binet," *Journal of the History of the Behavioral Sciences* 10 (1974): 180–94; Kurt Danziger, *Constructing the Subject: Historical Origins of Psychological Research* (Cambridge: Cambridge University Press, 1990); David Wright and Anne Digby (eds.), *From Idiocy to Mental Deficiency: Historical Perspectives on People with Learning Disabilities* (New York, NY: Routledge, 1996); Nathan Brody, "History of Theories and Measurements of Intelligence," in *Handbook of Intelligence,* ed. Robert J. Sternberg (Cambridge: Cambridge University Press, 2000), 16–33.

4. For modern principles of testing, see Kevin R. Murphy and Charles O. Davidshofer, *Psychological Testing: Principles and Applications* (Englewood Cliffs, NJ: Prentice Hall, 1988).

5. Francis Galton, "Psychometric Facts," *Popular Science Monthly* 14 (1878): 771–80; Michael M. Sokal, "James McKeen Cattell and the Failure of Anthropometric Testing, 1890–1901," in *The Problematic Science: Psychology in Nineteenth-Century Thought,* ed. William R. Woodward and Mitchell G. Ash (New York, NY: Praeger, 1982), 322–45.

6. James McKeen Cattell, "Mental Tests and Measurements," *Mind* (1890): 373–81; Michael M. Sokal, "James McKeen Cattell and Mental Anthropometry: Nineteenth-Century Science and Reform and the Origins of Psychological Testing," in *Psychological Testing and American Society, 1890–1930,* ed. Michael M. Sokal (New Brunswick, NJ: Rutgers University Press, 1987), 21–45; Sheldon H. White, "Conceptual Foundations of IQ Testing," *Psychology, Public Policy, and Law* 6 (2000): 33–43.

7. Edward Thorndike, *An Introduction to the Theory of Mental and Social Measurements* (New York, NY: Science Press, 1904).

8. Charles Spearman, "The Measurement of Intelligence," *Eugenics Review* 6 (1915): 312.

9. Theta H. Wolf, *Alfred Binet* (Chicago, IL: University of Chicago Press, 1973); Alfred Binet and Theodore Simon, "Upon the Necessity of Establishing a Scientific Diagnosis of Interior States of Intelligence (1905)," in *The History of Mental Retardation: Collected Papers,* vol. 1, ed. Marvin Rosen, Gerald R. Clark, and Marvin Kivitz (Baltimore, MD: University Park Press, 1976), 329–53; John Samuel Carson, "Talents, Intelligence, and the Constructions of Human Difference in France and America, 1750–1920" (PhD diss., Princeton University, 1994).

10. Alfred Binet and Theodore Simon, *The Development of Intelligence in Children (The Binet–Simon Scale),* trans. Elizabeth S. Kite (New York, NY: Arno Press, 1973), 45.

11. Elizabeth Wilson Lindsay, "A History and Criticism of the Use of the Word 'Intelligence' in Psychological Literature" (master's thesis, University of Missouri, 1925).

12. White, "Conceptual Foundations of IQ Testing," 39.

13. Henry H. Goddard, "Four Hundred Feeble-Minded Children Classified by the Binet Method (1910)," in *The History of Mental Retardation: Collected*

Papers, vol. 1, ed. Marvin Rosen, Gerald R. Clark, and Marvin Kivitz (Baltimore, MD: University Park Press, 1976), 355–66; Leila Zenderland, *Measuring Minds: Henry Herbert Goddard and the Origins of American Intelligence Testing* (Cambridge: Cambridge University Press, 1998).

14. Charles Spearman, "The Measurement of Intelligence," *Eugenics Review* 6 (1915): 313. On *g,* see Charles Spearman, "General Intelligence Objectively Determined and Measured," *American Journal of Psychology* 15 (1904): 201–93; Ulric Neisser, "Introduction: Rising Test Scores and What They Mean," in *The Rising Curve: Long-Term Gains in IQ and Related Measures,* ed. Ulric Neisser (Washington, DC: American Psychological Association, 1998), 3–22; Brody, "History of Theories and Measurements of Intelligence."

15. Spearman, "General Intelligence Objectively Determined and Measured," 272. Italics in original.

16. Spearman, "Measurement of Intelligence"; Bernard Norton, "The Meaning of Intelligence," in *The Meritocratic Intellect: Studies in the History of Educational Research,* ed. James V. Smith and David Hamilton (Aberdeen: Aberdeen University Press, 1979), 59–66.

17. Arthur R. Jensen, *The g Factor: The Science of Mental Ability* (Westport, CT: Praeger, 1998), xii.

18. Stephen Jay Gould, *The Mismeasure of Man,* rev. ed. (New York, NY: W. W. Norton, 1996), 285.

19. An explanation of how the results of factor analysis depend on the axis on which one chooses to rotate the factors is well beyond the scope of this book (although Gould does a remarkably clear job of explaining it). Suffice it to say that there is full agreement among statisticians that there are many different mathematically equivalent and equally valid ways in which one can conduct a factor analysis on a given set of data.

20. J. Carleton Bell, "Abstracts and Reviews. Recent Literature on the Binet Test," *Journal of Educational Psychology* 3 (1912): 102.

21. Henry H. Goddard, "The Binet and Simon Tests of Intellectual Capacity," *Training School Bulletin* 5, no. 10 (December 1908): 3–9; Goddard, "A Measuring Scale for Intelligence," *Training School Bulletin* 6, no. 11 (January 1910): 146–55; Goddard, "Four Hundred Feeble-Minded Children"; Carson, "Talents, Intelligence, and the Constructions of Human Difference"; Zenderland, *Measuring Minds.*

22. James M. Baldwin, *Dictionary of Philosophy and Psychology* (New York, NY: Peter Smith, 1940), 558.

23. Lewis M. Terman, "A Report of the Buffalo Conference on the Binet–Simon Tests of Intelligence," *Pedagogical Seminary* 20 (1913): 549–54; Zenderland, *Measuring Minds.*

24. Henry H. Goddard, "Introduction," in *The Development of Intelligence in Children,* ed. Alfred Binet and Theodore Simon, trans. Elizabeth S. Kite (Baltimore, MD: Williams and Wilkins, 1916), 6.

25. JoAnne Brown, *The Definition of a Profession: The Authority of Metaphor in the History of Intelligence Testing, 1890–1930* (Princeton, NJ: Princeton University Press, 1992); Hyman Bronwen, " 'Intelligence' in Early American Psychology: From Common Parlance to Psychological Concept" (PhD diss., University of Manitoba, 1981); Zenderland, *Measuring Minds*. There are many other illustrations of the impact of the Binet Scales. For example, the *Psychological Index,* an index to research literature in psychology first published in 1894, did not even have a category for mental tests until its 1912–1914 edition, when articles on the Binet began to flood the professional journals. The 1910 edition of Guy Whipple's *Manual of Mental and Physical Tests* had included a simple listing for the Binet; in his 1915 revision of the manual, however, Whipple omitted the Binet, saying that it now required a volume of its own. My own survey of the *Readers' Guide to Periodical Literature* reveals no listings under the headings of ability, mental, or intelligence tests in the 1905–1909 edition; in 1910–1914 there were 31 such listings, in 1915–1918 there were 56, and in 1919–1921 there were 121 listings under the category of intelligence tests. And finally, my survey of WorldCat (an index of books published all over the world) shows that in the United States no books about intelligence tests were published in 1905. In 1910, 17 percent of the books found under the keyword "intelligence" were related to such tests, however, and in 1915, a full 53 percent of books about intelligence focused on the topic of IQ tests.

26. Lewis M. Terman, "The Binet–Simon Scale for Measuring Intelligence: Impressions Gained by Its Application upon Four Hundred Non-selected Children," *Psychological Clinic* 5 (1911): 199–206; Alan S. Kaufman, *Assessing Adolescent and Adult Intelligence* (Boston, MA: Allyn and Bacon, 1990). Time does march on, and by the 1960s the Stanford-Binet had been largely replaced by the newer Wechsler Scales. Even now, however, it remains a respected and widely used instrument. In 2003, in fact, almost a full century after Binet's original development of the scale, a brand-new fifth edition of the Stanford-Binet was released.

27. Francine Patterson and Wendy Gordon, "The Case for the Personhood of Gorilla," in *The Great Ape Project,* ed. Paola Cavalieri and Peter Singer (New York, NY: St. Martin's Griffin, 1993), 58–77.

28. "Scorns the Aid of Science," *New York Times,* July 20, 1916, 10. Stephen Jay Gould has perceptively observed that "much of the fascination of statistics lies embedded in our gut feeling—and never trust a gut feeling—that abstract measures summarizing large tables of data must express something more real and fundamental than the data themselves" (*Mismeasure of Man,* 269). Attaching an objective number to an amorphous concept somehow makes the concept more valid in our minds. I recognize this tendency in myself when I am scoring an intelligence test. As I get toward the end of my calculations, I find myself increasingly excited as I come closer to discovering what the subject's "real" IQ score is. Despite my training and my extensive knowledge about the limitations of the tests, I find myself responding as if this summary

statistic somehow represented something more real than the rich masses of data on which it is based.

29. Brown, *Definition of a Profession.*

CHAPTER 7: IQ TESTING, SOCIAL CONTROL, AND MERIT

1. George B. Cutten, "The Reconstruction of Democracy," *School and Society* 16 (1922): 477.

2. John M. Murrin, Paul E. Johnson, James M. McPherson, Gary Gerstle, Emily S. Rosenberg, and Norman L. Rosenberg, *Liberty, Equality, Power: A History of the American People. Volume II: Since 1863,* 2nd ed. (New York, NY: Harcourt Brace, 1999).

3. Madison Grant, *The Passing of a Great Race,* 4th ed. (New York, NY: Charles Scribner's Sons, 1923), 263.

4. Leila Zenderland, *Measuring Minds: Henry Herbert Goddard and the Origins of American Intelligence Testing* (Cambridge: Cambridge University Press, 1998).

5. Helen Winkler and Elinor Sachs, "Testing Immigrants," *Survey* 39 (1917): 152–53.

6. Josiah Moore, "A Comparison of White and Colored Children Measured by the Binet Scale of Intelligence," *Popular Science* 84 (1914): 75–79.

7. Carl C. Brigham, *A Study of American Intelligence* (Princeton, NJ: Princeton University Press, 1923), 182.

8. Robert Yerkes, "Testing the Human Mind," *Atlantic Monthly* 131 (1923): 365.

9. Franz Samelson, "On the Science and Politics of the IQ," *Social Research* 42 (1975): 467–92.

10. Franz Samelson, "From 'Race Psychology' to 'Studies in Prejudice': Some Observations on the Thematic Reversal in Social Psychology," *Journal of the History of the Behavioral Sciences* 14 (1978): 271.

11. Russell Marks, "Lewis M. Terman: Individual Differences and the Construction of Social Reality," *Educational Theory* 24 (1974): 336–55.

12. Steven Gelb, "The Beast in Man: Degenerationism and Mental Retardation, 1900–1920," *Mental Retardation* 33 (1995): 1–9; Zenderland, *Measuring Minds;* Patrick J. Ryan, "Unnatural Selection: Intelligence Testing, Eugenics, and American Political Cultures," *Journal of Social History* 30 (1997): 669–85.

13. For example, Howard A. Knox, "Measuring Human Intelligence," *Scientific American* 112 (1915): 52–53; "The Measurement of Intelligence," *The Dial* 61 (1916): 316; "Testing the Criminal's Mind," *Literary Digest* 52 (1916): 1839–40; Raymond Dodge, "Mental Engineering after the War," *The American Review of Reviews* 60 (1919): 606–10; Molly Ladd-Taylor, "The 'Sociological Advantages' of Sterilization: Fiscal Policies and Feeble-Minded Women in Interwar Minnesota," in *Mental Retardation in America: A Historical Reader,* ed. Steven Noll and James W. Trent (New York, NY: New York University Press, 2004), 281–99.

14. It was to describe this group that H. H. Goddard had coined the term "moron" in a famous 1910 article. Henry H. Goddard, "Four Hundred Feeble-Minded Children Classified by the Binet Method (1910)," in *The History of Mental Retardation: Collected Papers*, vol. 1, ed. Marvin Rosen, Gerald R. Clark, and Marvin Kivitz (Baltimore, MD: University Park Press, 1976), 355–66.

15. On U.S. eugenics and eugenic sterilization, see Daniel J. Kevles, *In the Name of Eugenics: Genetics and the Uses of Human Heredity* (New York, NY: Alfred A. Knopf, 1985); Philip Reilly, *The Surgical Solution: A History of Involuntary Sterilization* (Baltimore, MD: Johns Hopkins University Press, 1991); Katherine Castles, "Quiet Eugenics: Sterilization in North Carolina's Institutions for the Mentally Retarded, 1945–1965," *Journal of Southern History* 68 (2002): 849–78. On advocacy of eugenics among psychologists, see Kurt Danziger, *Constructing the Subject: Historical Origins of Psychological Research* (Cambridge: Cambridge University Press, 1990); JoAnne Brown, *The Definition of a Profession: The Authority of Metaphor in the History of Intelligence Testing, 1890–1930* (Princeton, NJ: Princeton University Press, 1992).

16. Quoted in Richard Emory Titlow, *Americans Import Merit: Origins of the United States Civil Service and the Influence of the British Model* (Lanham, MD: University Press of America, 1979), 57, 71.

17. Although the provisions of this act originally included only about 10 percent of federal employees under the so-called merit system, over the years its reach expanded, and many cities and states instituted their own merit systems as well. Ronald N. Johnson and Gary D. Libecap, "Patronage to Merit and Control of the Federal Government Work Force," *Explorations in Economic History* 31 (1994): 91–119; Patricia Wallace Ingraham, *The Foundation of Merit: Public Service in American Democracy* (Baltimore, MD: Johns Hopkins University Press, 1995).

18. On U.S. civil service testing, see L. L. Thurstone, "Intelligence Tests in the Civil Service," *Public Personnel Studies* 1 (1923): 1–24; Herbert A. Filer and L. J. O'Rourke, "Progress in Civil Service Tests," *Journal of Personnel Research* 1 (1923): 484–520; Samuel Kavruck, "Thirty-Three Years of Test Research: A Short History of Test Development in the U.S. Civil Service Commission," *American Psychologist* 11 (1956): 329–33; Titlow, *Americans Import Merit*; Ingraham, *Foundation of Merit*.

19. United States Civil Service Commission, *First Annual Report* (Washington, DC: Government Printing Office, 1884), 21, 30.

20. L. L. Thurstone, "Intelligence Tests in the Civil Service," *Public Personnel Studies* 1 (1923): 6. See also Filer and O'Rourke, "Progress in Civil Service Tests."

21. Historian Richard T. von Mayrhauser has observed that the tests also had another unspoken purpose—"to avoid Britain' s failure to prevent its talented men from being slaughtered in the trenches." Intelligent young men were a national resource that must be preserved. Richard T. von Mayrhauser, "The Practical Language of the American Intellect," *History of the Human Sciences* 4 (1991): 379.

22. James Reed, "Robert M. Yerkes and the Mental Testing Movement," in *Psychological Testing and American Society, 1890–1930*, ed. Michael M. Sokal (New Brunswick, NJ: Rutgers University Press, 1987), 75–94; Franz Samelson, "Was Early Mental Testing (a) Racist Inspired, (b) Objective Science, (c) A Technology for Democracy, (d) The Origin of Multiple-Choice Exams, (e) None of the Above?" in *Psychological Testing and American Society, 1890–1930*, ed. Michael M. Sokal (New Brunswick, NJ: Rutgers University Press, 1987), 113–27; Danziger, *Constructing the Subject*; John Samuel Carson, "Talents, Intelligence, and the Constructions of Human Difference in France and America, 1750–1920" (PhD diss., Princeton University, 1994); Zenderland, *Measuring Minds*.

23. For example, Bruce Barton, "How High Do You Stand on the Rating Scale?" *American Magazine* 87 (1919): 7–9; "Measuring the Abilities of Men by Psychological Tests," *Literary Digest* 60 (1919): 66–74.

24. Ellen Herman, *The Romance of American Psychology: Political Culture in the Age of Experts* (Berkeley, CA: University of California Press, 1995). Interestingly, given the national outcry that had greeted the publication of results of the Army Alpha tests, advocates for the expansion of higher education argued after World War II that the GCT test results actually demonstrated that *more* Americans should be given the opportunity to attend college—an argument that helped lead to the adoption of the GI Bill. Michael Ackerman, "Mental Testing and the Expansion of Educational Opportunity," *History of Education Quarterly* 35 (1995): 279–300.

25. On the introduction of IQ testing in schools, see Erwin V. Johanningmeier, "American Educational Research: Applications and Misapplications of Psychology to Education," in *The Meritocratic Intellect: Studies in the History of Educational Research*, ed. James V. Smith and David Hamilton (Aberdeen: Aberdeen University Press, 1979), 41–57; Paul Davis Chapman, *Schools as Sorters: Lewis M. Terman, Applied Psychology, and the Intelligence Testing Movement, 1890–1930* (New York, NY: New York University Press, 1988); Zenderland, *Measuring Minds*.

26. Quoted in Brown, *Definition of a Profession*, 135–36.

27. Quoted in Clarence J. Karier, "Testing for Order and Control in the Corporate Liberal State," *Educational Theory* 22 (1972): 158.

28. First called the Scholastic Aptitude Test and then the Scholastic Assessment Test, the exam now goes simply by the politically innocuous label of the SAT. Its story has been very ably told by Nicholas Lemann; my discussion draws heavily on his work. Nicholas Lemann, *The Big Test: The Secret History of the American Meritocracy* (New York, NY: Farrar, Straus and Giroux, 2000). See also Nathan Brody, "History of Theories and Measurements of Intelligence," in *Handbook of Intelligence*, ed. Robert J. Sternberg (Cambridge: Cambridge University Press, 2000), 16–33.

29. Lemann, *Big Test*, 5, 49.

30. Quoted in Lemann, *Big Test*, 69.

31. David Owen, "The S.A.T. and Social Stratification," *Journal of Education* 168 (1986): 81.

32. James Fallows, "The Best and the Brightest: How Fair Are the College Boards?" *Atlantic Monthly,* February 1980, 37–48; Stephen Murdock, *IQ: A Smart History of a Failed Idea* (Hoboken, NJ: John Wiley and Sons, 2007).

CHAPTER 8: DEMOCRATIC IDEOLOGY AND IQ TESTING

1. Kurt Danziger, *Constructing the Subject: Historical Origins of Psychological Research* (Cambridge: Cambridge University Press, 1990).

2. Francis Galton, *Inquiries into Human Faculty and Its Development* (New York, NY: E. P. Dutton, 1907), 28.

3. "White Matter, Not Gray," *New York Times,* December 8, 1907, 10:4; "Brain Weights," *New York Times,* October 11, 1907, 8:3; "To Measure Brain Power," *Literary Digest* 47 (1913): 241; "Measuring Your Intelligence: John Gray's New Instrument for Testing 'Perseveration,'" *Scientific American* 104 (1911): 91–92; "Measuring the Intelligence," *Harper's Weekly* 57 (1913): 21.

4. James McKeen Cattell, "Mental Tests and Measurements," *Mind* 15 (1890): 373. On the popularization of intelligence testing in the United States, see Donald Napoli, *Architects of Adjustment: The History of the Psychological Profession in the U.S.* (Port Washington, NY: Kennikat Press, 1981); Michael M. Sokal, "James McKeen Cattell and Mental Anthropometry: Nineteenth-Century Science and Reform and the Origins of Psychological Testing," in *Psychological Testing and American Society, 1890–1930,* ed. Michael M. Sokal (New Brunswick, NJ: Rutgers University Press, 1987), 21–45; Nathan Brody, "History of Theories and Measurements of Intelligence," in *Handbook of Intelligence,* ed. Robert J. Sternberg (Cambridge: Cambridge University Press, 2000), 16–33.

5. Clara Harrison Town, "The Binet-Simon Scale and the Psychologist," *Psychological Clinic* 5 (1912): 240.

6. Stoddard Goodhue, "Give Your Children a Chance," *Cosmopolitan* 55 (1913): 721.

7. Lewis M. Terman, "A Report of the Buffalo Conference on the Binet-Simon Tests of Intelligence," *Pedagogical Seminary* 20 (1913): 549–54.

8. Goodhue, "Give Your Children a Chance," 469.

9. "Here's Your Chance to Test Your Mental Development according to Famous Binet System," *Chicago Daily Tribune,* April 29, 1915, 5.

10. John Dewey, *Democracy and Education: An Introduction to the Philosophy of Education* (New York, NY: Macmillan, 1924); Paula S. Fass, "The IQ: A Cultural and Historical Framework," *American Journal of Education* 88 (1980): 431–58.

11. Edward L. Thorndike, "New Psychological Tests: Are They a Substitute for Content Examinations?" *Educational Review* 59 (1920): 102; "Intelligence Tests," *School and Society* 14 (1921): 314.

12. Nicholas Lemann, *The Big Test: The Secret History of the American Meritocracy* (New York, NY: Farrar, Straus and Giroux, 2000), 49.

13. Russell Marks, "Legitimating Industrial Capitalism: Philanthropy and Individual Difference" in *Philanthropy and Cultural Imperialism: The*

Foundations at Home and Abroad, ed. Robert F. Arnove (Boston, MA: G. K. Hall, 1980), 87–122.

14. Carl Murchison, "Criminals and College Students," *School and Society* 12 (1920): 24–30; Alexandra K. Wigdor and William Garner (eds.), *Ability Tests: Uses, Consequences, and Controversies,* Part 1 (Washington, DC: National Academy Press, 1982).

15. Terman, "Report of the Buffalo Conference," 554; Marion Rex Trabue and Frank Parker Stockbridge, *Measure Your Mind: The Mentimeter and How to Use It* (Garden City, NY: Doubleday, Page, and Co., 1920), 7.

16. Allan Harding, "Test Yourself and See How You Compare with College Students," *American Magazine* 96 (1923): 50.

17. Horace B. English, "Is America Feeble-Minded?" *Survey* 49 (1922): 79.

18. "Test of Your Intelligence," *Literary Digest* 56 (1918): 19; Bruce Barton, "How High Do You Stand on the Rating Scale?" *American Magazine* 87 (1919): 7; Trabue and Stockbridge, *Measure Your Mind,* vi, 21.

19. [Advertisement], *The New Republic,* vol. 32, 1922, v.

20. Lewis M. Terman, "Genius and Stupidity: A Study of Some of the Intellectual Processes of Seven 'Bright' and Seven 'Stupid' Boys," *Pedagogical Seminary* 13 (1906): 307–73. On Terman generally, see Russell Marks, "Lewis M. Terman: Individual Differences and the Construction of Social Reality," *Educational Theory* 24 (1974): 336–55; Paul Davis Chapman, *Schools as Sorters: Lewis M. Terman, Applied Psychology, and the Intelligence Testing Movement, 1890–1930* (New York, NY: New York University Press, 1988); Jennifer Randall Crosby and Alfred H. Hastorf, "Lewis Terman: Scientist of Mental Measurement and Product of His Time," in *Portraits of Pioneers in Psychology,* vol. IV, ed. Gregory A. Kimble and Michael Wertheimer (Washington, DC: American Psychological Association, 2000), 130–47.

21. Jerome M. Sattler, *Assessment of Children's Intelligence and Special Abilities,* 2nd ed. (Boston, MA: Allyn and Bacon, 1982).

22. Lewis M. Terman, "The Psychological Determinist; or Democracy and the IQ," *Journal of Educational Research* 6 (1922): 57–62; Henry L. Minton, "Lewis M. Terman and Mental Testing: In Search of the Democratic Ideal," in *Psychological Testing and American Society, 1890–1930,* ed. Michael M. Sokal (New Brunswick, NJ: Rutgers University Press, 1987), 95–112.

23. Lewis M. Terman, "The Great Conspiracy, or the Impulse Imperious of Intelligence Testers Psychoanalyzed and Exposed by Mr. Lippmann," in *The IQ Controversy: Critical Readings* (New York, NY: Pantheon, 1967), 30.

24. Lewis M. Terman, "The Measurement of Intelligence (1916)," in *The Bell Curve Debate: History, Documents, Opinions,* ed. Russell Jacoby and Naomi Glauberman (New York, NY: Times Books, 1995), 545.

25. For a history of the phrase, see J. W. Trent, Jr., *Inventing the Feeble Mind: A History of Mental Retardation in the United States* (Berkeley, CA: University of California Press, 1994).

26. Quoted in Franz Samelson, "Putting Psychology on the Map: Ideology and Intelligence Testing," in *Psychology in Social Context,* ed. Allen R. Buss (New York, NY: John Wiley & Sons, 1979), 105–106.

27. Terman, "The Measurement of Intelligence (1916)," 550.

28. Lewis M. Terman, "The Discovery and Encouragement of Exceptional Talent," *American Psychologist* 9 (1954): 221–30; Hamilton Cravens, "A Scientific Project Locked in Time: The Terman Genetic Studies of Genius, 1920s–1950s," *American Psychologist* 47 (1992): 183–89.

29. Marks, "Lewis M. Terman: Individual Differences," 336.

CHAPTER 9: A CENTURY OF IQ TESTING: THE MORE THINGS CHANGE, THE MORE THEY STAY THE SAME

1. *Atkins v. Virginia*, 536 U.S. 304 (2002).

2. There are other well-regarded, individually administered tests of intelligence, including the Woodcock–Johnson Tests of Cognitive Abilities and the Kaufman Assessment Battery for Children. However, these measures are used much less frequently and generally only in school settings.

3. Stephen Murdock, *IQ: A Smart History of a Failed Idea* (Hoboken, NJ: John Wiley and Sons, 2007). On modern IQ testing, see Jerome M. Sattler, *Assessment of Children's Intelligence and Special Abilities*, 2nd ed. (Boston, MA: Allyn and Bacon, 1982); Alan S. Kaufman, *Intelligent Testing with the WISC–III* (New York, NY: John Wiley and Sons, 1994).

4. On controversy over IQ definitions, see David Wechsler, "Intelligence Defined and Undefined: A Relativistic Approach," *American Psychologist* 30 (1975): 135–39; Robert J. Sternberg, "Implicit Theories of Intelligence as Exemplar Stories of Success: Why Intelligence Test Validity Is in the Eye of the Beholder," *Psychology, Public Policy, and Law* 6 (2000): 159–67; Sheldon H. White, "Conceptual Foundations of IQ Testing," *Psychology, Public Policy, and Law* 6 (2000): 33–43.

5. See, for example, Walter Lippmann, "The Mental Age of Americans," *The New Republic* 32 (1922): 213–25; Lewis M. Terman, "The Great Conspiracy or the Impulse Imperious of Intelligence Testers, Psychoanalyzed and Exposed by Mr. Lippmann," *The New Republic* 33 (1922): 116–20.

6. Edward L. Thorndike, "Intelligence and Its Measurement: A Symposium," *Journal of Educational Psychology* 12 (1921): 123–47, 195–216; Robert J. Sternberg and Cynthia A. Berg, "Quantitative Integration: Definitions of Intelligence: A Comparison of the 1921 and 1986 Symposia," in *What Is Intelligence? Contemporary Viewpoints on Its Nature and Definition* (Norwood, NJ: Ablex Publishing, 1986), 155–62.

7. Robert Yerkes, "Testing the Human Mind," *Atlantic Monthly* 131 (1923): 370; Walter Lippmann, "The Abuse of the Tests," in *The IQ Controversy: Critical Readings*, ed. N. J. Bloch and Gerald Dworkin (New York, NY: Pantheon Books, 1976), 19.

8. Lewis M. Terman, "The Psychological Determinist; or Democracy and the IQ," *Journal of Educational Research* 6 (1922): 60.

9. Hamilton Cravens, *The Triumph of Evolution: American Scientists and the Heredity-Environment Controversy, 1900–1940* (Philadelphia, PA: University of Pennsylvania Press, 1978); Carl N. Degler, *In Search of Human Nature:*

The Decline and Revival of Darwinism in American Social Thought (New York, NY: Oxford University Press, 1991).

10. Charles H. Thompson, "The Conclusions of Scientists Relative to Racial Differences," *Journal of Negro Education* 3 (1934): 494–512.

11. "18 Social Scientists Discuss: Does Race Really Make a Difference in Intelligence?" *U.S. News and World Report*, October 26, 1956, 74–76.

12. Otto Klineberg and T. R. Garth, "Racial and National Differences in Mental Traits," in *Encyclopaedia of Educational Research*, rev. ed., ed. Walter S. Monroe (New York, NY: Macmillan, 1952), 953.

13. "I.Q. Control," *Time*, November 7, 1938, 44–46.

14. Maya Pines, "You Can Raise Your Child's IQ," *Reader's Digest*, vol. 93, 1968, 116.

15. George Q. Flynn, *The Draft: 1940–1973* (Lawrence, KS: University Press of Kansas, 1993); Nicholas Lemann, *The Big Test: The Secret History of the American Meritocracy* (New York, NY: Farrar, Straus and Giroux, 2000).

16. M. H. Trytten, *Student Deferment in Selective Service: A Vital Factor in National Security* (Minneapolis, MN: University of Minnesota Press, 1952).

17. Robert E. Cooke, "Introduction," in *Project Head Start: A Legacy of the War on Poverty*, ed. Edward Zigler and Jeanette Valentine (New York, NY: Free Press, 1979), xxiii. See also Edward Zigler and Karen Anderson, "An Idea Whose Time Had Come: The Intellectual and Political Climate for Head Start," in *Project Head Start*, ed. Zigler and Valentine, 3–19.

18. *Larry P. v. Riles*, 495 F. Supp. 926 (N.D. Cal. 1979); *Griggs v. Duke Power Co.*, 401 U.S. 424 (1971).

19. Arthur R. Jensen, "How Much Can We Boost IQ and Scholastic Achievement?" *Harvard Educational Review* 39 (1969): 2, 82.

20. Carl T. Rowan, "How Racists Use 'Science' to Degrade Black People," *Ebony*, May 1970, 31–40.

21. Richard J. Herrnstein and Charles Murray, *The Bell Curve: Intelligence and Class Structure in American Life* (New York, NY: Free Press Paperbacks, 1994), 416, 449.

22. Helmuth Nyborg, "The Sociology of Psychometric and Bio-Behavioral Sciences: A Case Study of Destructive Social Reductionism and Collective Fraud in 20th Century Academia," in *The Scientific Study of General Intelligence: Tribute to Arthur R. Jensen*, ed. Helmuth Nyborg (New York, NY: Pergamon, 2003), 475.

23. Richard S. Cooper, "Race and IQ: Molecular Genetics as Deus ex Machina." *American Psychologist* 60 (2005): 75.

24. Richard Herrnstein, "IQ," in *The Bell Curve Debate: History, Documents, Opinions*, ed. Roger Jacoby and Naomi Glauberman (New York, NY: Times Books, 1995), 600.

25. Mark Snyderman and S. Rothman, *The IQ Controversy: The Media and Public Policy* (New Brunswick, NJ: Transaction Books, 1988), 31.

26. Herrnstein and Murray, *Bell Curve*, 442.

27. E. J. Dionne, "A Long Tradition," in *The Bell Curve Debate: History, Documents, Opinions,* ed. Russell Jacoby and Naomi Glauberman (New York, NY: Times Books, 1995), 236.

28. Lorraine Dashton, "The Naturalized Female Intellect," *Science in Context* 5 (1992): 212.

29. Alexander MacKendrick, "Intelligence as a Moral Obligation," *The Dial* 60 (1916): 117–20.

30. E. J. Lowe, *Locke on Human Understanding* (New York, NY: Routledge, 1995); Steven A. Gelb, " 'Not Simply Bad and Incorrigible': Science, Morality, and Intellectual Deficiency," *History of Education Quarterly* 29 (1989): 359–79; Alan F. Collins, "The Enduring Appeal of Physiognomy: Physical Appearance as a Sign of Temperament, Character, and Intelligence," *History of Psychology* 2 (1999): 251–76.

31. Henry L. Minton, "Lewis M. Terman and Mental Testing: In Search of the Democratic Ideal," in *Psychological Testing and American Society, 1890–1930,* ed. Michael M. Sokal (New Brunswick, NJ: Rutgers University Press, 1987), 95; Joseph Peterson, *Early Conceptions and Tests of Intelligence* (Westport, CT: Greenwood Press, 1926), 23.

32. Herrnstein and Murray, *Bell Curve,* 241; Richard Lynn, "Back to the Future," in *The Bell Curve Debate: History, Documents, Opinions,* ed. Russell Jacoby and Naomi Glauberman (New York, NY: Times Books, 1995), 356–57.

33. Rev. Karl Schwartz, "Nature's Corrective Principle in Social Evolution (1908)," in *The History of Mental Retardation: Collected Papers,* vol. 2 (Baltimore, MD: University Park Press, 1976), 150–51.

34. David J. Smith, "Reflections on Mental Retardation and Eugenics, Old and New: Mensa and the Human Genome Project," *Mental Retardation* 32 (1994): 234–38.

35. Joseph Fletcher, *Humanhood: Essays in Biomedical Ethics* (Buffalo, NY: Prometheus Books, 1979).

36. Joseph L. Fletcher, "Four Indicators of Humanhood—The Inquiry Matures," *The Hastings Center Report* 4 (1974): 5. Many years ago, toward the beginning of my professional career, I led a sex education group for young adults with mild and moderate mental retardation, some of them suffering from Down syndrome. Predictably, the participants were fascinated by the topic of sex and full of questions. One day, a young man floored me with this query: "Why do they sometimes stick in great big needle in a pregnant lady's stomach?" Somewhere, he must have heard about amniocentesis. I was left speechless. How was I to explain to this group of young people, all of them full of life and eager to learn, that the purpose of this procedure was to give parents the option of preventing people like themselves and their friends from ever being born? I have no memory of how I responded to this young man's question. However, it certainly made me think deeply about our cultural assumption that a life with impaired intelligence is not worth living.

37. Robert S. Albert, "Toward a Behavioral Definition of Genius," *American Psychologist* 30 (1975): 140–51; Roblyn Rawlins, "Long Rows of Short

Graves: Sentimentality, Science, and Distinction in the 19th Century Construction of the Intellectually Precocious Child," in *Symbolic Childhood,* ed. Daniel
Thomas Cook (New York, NY: Peter Lang, 2002), 89–108.

38. Erwin V. Johanningmeier, "American Educational Research: Applica-
tions and Misapplications of Psychology to Education," in *The Meritocratic In-
tellect: Studies in the History of Educational Research,* ed. James V. Smith and
David Hamilton (Aberdeen: Aberdeen University Press, 1979), 41–57; Craig A.
Wendorf, "History of American Morality Research, 1894–1932," *History of
Psychology* 4 (2001): 272–88.

39. Edward L. Thorndike, "Educational Diagnosis," *Science* 37 (1913): 142.

40. Herrnstein and Murray, *Bell Curve,* 254; Richard Hofstadter, *Anti-
Intellectualism in American Life* (New York, NY: Vintage Books, 1962), 29;
Leslie Margolin, *Goodness Personified: The Emergence of Gifted Children*
(New York, NY: Aldine de Gruyter, 1994).

CHAPTER 10: TOWARD A BROADER CONCEPTION
OF INTELLIGENCE

1. Arthur S. Otis, "Some Queer Misconceptions Regarding Intelligence
Tests," *American School Board Journal* 75 (1927): 134.

2. Reprinted in Linda R. Gottfredson, "Mainstream Science on Intelligence:
An Editorial with 52 Signatories, History, and Bibliography," *Intelligence* 24
(1997): 13–23.

3. The discussion that follows focuses specifically on individually administered intelligence tests in the tradition of Binet and Wechsler. However, most
of these points are even more relevant to the group-administered tests used for
most school placement and college admission decisions.

4. Alan S. Kaufman, *Intelligent Testing with the WISC–III* (New York, NY:
John Wiley and Sons, 1994), 6.

5. It should also be noted that the most recent revisions of the Wechsler
Intelligence Scale for Children (the WISC–IV) and the Wechsler Adult Intelligence Scale (WAIS–IV) place somewhat less emphasis on speed and on strictly
academic knowledge than do earlier versions of the scale. Testing professionals
are increasingly focusing more on how individuals process information than on
their overall IQ test scores. However, this trend has yet to make its way into the
general culture.

6. On factors affecting IQ results, see David Wechsler, "Intelligence Defined
and Undefined: A Relativistic Approach," *American Psychologist* 30 (1975),
135–39; Kaufman, *Intelligent Testing with the WISC–III;* Brigitte Berger,
"Methodological Fetishism," in *The Bell Curve Debate: History, Documents,
Opinions,* ed. Russell Jacoby and Naomi Glauberman (New York, NY: Times
Books, 1995), 342–45.

7. Arthur R. Jensen, *The g Factor: The Science of Mental Ability* (Westport,
CT: Praeger, 1998), xii.

8. Ulric Neisser, Gwyneth Boodoo, Thomas J. Bourchard, Jr., A. Wade
Boykin, Nathan Brody, Stephen J. Ceci, Diane F. Halpern, John C. Loehlin,

Robert Perloff, Robert J. Sternberg, and Susana Urbina, "Intelligence: Knowns and Unknowns," *American Psychologist* 51 (1996): 77–101.

9. For example, Angela L. Duckworth and Martin E. P. Seligman, "Self-Discipline Outdoes IQ in Predicting Academic Performance of Adolescents," *Psychological Science* 16 (2005): 939–44.

10. As psychologist David McClelland pointed out a number of years ago, the correlations that do exist between intelligence test scores and income are mediated by the fact that in modern American society school serves as a gate-keeper for access to many higher-paying occupations. David C. McClelland, "Testing for Competence Rather Than for 'Intelligence,'" *American Psychologist* 28 (1973): 1–14.

11. There is a large literature on correlations between IQ, personal background, and various life outcomes. See, for example, Linda S. Gottfredson, "What Do We Know about Intelligence?" *The American Scholar* 65 (1996): 15–30; Robert N. Hauser, "Trends in Black–White Test-Score Differentials: I. Uses and Misuses of NAEP/SAT Data," in *The Rising Curve: Long-Term Gains in IQ and Related Measures,* ed. Ulric Neisser (Washington, DC: American Psychological Association, 1998), 219–49; Linda S. Gottfredson, "*g*, Jobs, and Life," in *The Scientific Study of General Intelligence: Tribute to Arthur R. Jensen,* ed. Helmuth Nyborg (New York, NY: Pergamon, 2003), 293–342; Neisser et al., "Intelligence: Knowns and Unknowns."

12. Herbert Spencer, *Principles of Psychology,* 3rd ed. (New York, NY: D. Appleton, 1880).

13. Edward L. Thorndike, "Intelligence and Its Measurement: A Symposium," *Journal of Educational Psychology* 12 (1921): 136.

14. Robert J. Sternberg, *Beyond IQ: A Triarchic Theory of Human Intelligence* (New York, NY: Cambridge University Press, 1985), 45. It is of relevance that the professionally accepted definition of mental retardation, conceived by most of us as the disorder most purely related to intelligence (or lack thereof), includes as one of its key components deficits in adaptive behavior. According to the DSM-IV (the diagnostic manual for mental disorders used by most professionals), "The essential feature of Mental Retardation is significantly subaverage general intellectual functioning . . . that is accompanied by significant limitations in adaptive functioning. . . . Adaptive functioning refers to how effectively individuals cope with common life demands and how well they meet the standards of personal independence expected of someone in their particular age group, sociocultural background, and community setting." American Psychiatric Association, *Diagnostic and Statistical Manual of Mental Disorders,* 4th ed. (Washington, DC: American Psychiatric Association, 1994), 39–40.

15. Wechsler, "Intelligence Defined and Undefined," 135.

16. Howard Gardner, *Frames of Mind: The Theory of Multiple Intelligences* (New York, NY: Basic Books, 1983).

17. Daniel Goleman, *Emotional Intelligence* (New York, NY: Bantam Books, 1995); Daniel Goleman, *Social Intelligence: The New Science of Human Relationships* (New York, NY: Bantam Books, 2006).

18. Robert J. Sternberg, "Implicit Theories of Intelligence as Exemplar Stories of Success: Why Intelligence Test Validity Is in the Eye of the Beholder," *Psychology, Public Policy, and Law* 6 (2000): 159–67; Robert J. Sternberg, "Beyond *g*: The Theory of Successful Intelligence," in *The General Factor of Intelligence: How General Is It?*, ed. Robert J. Sternberg and Elena L. Grigorenko (Mahwah, NJ: Lawrence Erlbaum Associates, 2002), 447–79.

19. R. J. Sternberg, "The Rainbow Project: Enhancing the SAT through Assessment of Analytic, Practical, and Creative Skills," *Intelligence* 34 (2006): 321–50. See also Deborah Smith Bailey, "What's Wrong with College Admissions," *Monitor on Psychology* 34, no. 9 (2003): 54–55.

20. Mihaly Csikszentmihalyi and Kevin Rathunde, "The Psychology of Wisdom: An Evolutionary Interpretation," in *Wisdom: Its Nature, Origin, and Development,* ed. Robert J. Sternberg (New York, NY: Cambridge University Press, 1990), 25–51; Paul B. Baltes and Ursula M. Staudinger, "Wisdom: A Metaheuristic (Pragmatic) to Orchestrate Mind and Virtue Toward Excellence," *American Psychologist* 55 (2000): 122–36.

21. Alexander G. Wesman, "Intelligent Testing," *American Psychologist* 23 (1968): 267–74. On issues in cross-cultural assessment of intelligence, see Patricia M. Greenfield, "You Can't Take It with You: Why Ability Assessments Don't Cross Cultures," *American Psychologist* 52 (1997): 1115–24; Sternberg, "Implicit Theories of Intelligence as Exemplar Stories"; Etienne Benson, "Intelligence across Cultures," *Monitor on Psychology* 34, no. 2 (2003): 56–58.

22. This distinction is of course greatly oversimplified; each culture incorporates at least some elements of both styles of thinking. But the basic difference between these two cognitive styles can easily be identified in societies around the world.

23. Richard E. Nisbett, *The Geography of Thought: How Asians and Westerners Think Differently . . . and Why* (New York, NY: Free Press, 2003).

24. J. W. Berry, "Towards a Universal Psychology of Cognitive Competence," *International Journal of Psychology* 19 (1984): 335–61; Robert J. Sternberg, "The Concept of Intelligence," in *Handbook of Intelligence*, vol. 2, ed. Robert J. Sternberg (Cambridge: Cambridge University Press, 2000), 3–15; Nisbett, *Geography of Thought.*

25. Berry, "Towards a Universal Psychology of Cognitive Competence."

26. Robert J. Sternberg, Catherine Nokes, P. Wenzel Geissler, Ruth Prince, Frederick Okatcha, Donald A. Bundy, and Elena L. Grigorenko, "The Relationship between Academic and Practical Intelligence: A Case Study in Kenya," *Intelligence* 29 (2001): 401–18.

27. Shirley Brice Heath, *Ways with Words: Language, Life, and Work in Communities and Classrooms* (New York, NY: Cambridge University Press, 1983). See also Lynn Okagaki and Robert J. Sternberg, "Parental Beliefs and Children's School Performance," *Child Development* 64 (1993): 36–56.

28. One example of the perils of confusing these two constructs (and one in which the usual liberal and conservative perspectives are reversed) can be seen in the political arena. Many members of the intellectual class condescendingly

regarded Ronald Reagan as an amiable dunce, and, indeed, it is likely that his scores on conventional tests of IQ would not have been particularly impressive. However, in terms of advancing his own agenda, Reagan went on to become one of the most effective presidents in recent U.S. history. In the broader sense of the term, Reagan proved to be much more intelligent than many of his high-IQ opponents.

29. Csikszentmihalyi and Rathunde, "The Psychology of Wisdom," 44.

CHAPTER 11: TOWARD A MORE BALANCED PERSPECTIVE ON HEREDITY AND IQ

1. Because we have yet to develop any reliable measures of more broadly defined adaptive intelligence, this discussion of necessity excludes any exploration of possible genetic effects on its expression. In his famous studies of *Hereditary Genius,* published in 1869, Sir Francis Galton did in fact attempt to demonstrate the hereditary nature of broadly defined intelligence; in the absence of any objective measure of IQ, he used eminence as his mark of genius. Unfortunately, Galton completely ignored any possible contribution of social status or other environmental factors to eminence in Victorian England. Therefore, although fascinating as social history, his study is virtually worthless as science. Sir Francis Galton, *Hereditary Genius: An Inquiry into Its Laws and Consequences* (New York, NY: St. Martin's Press, 1978).

2. On the heritability of IQ, see Steven G. Vandenberg and George P. Vogler, "Genetic Determinants of Intelligence," in *Handbook of Intelligence,* ed. Benjamin B. Wolman (New York, NY: John Wiley and Sons, 1985), 3–57; Alan S. Kaufman, *Assessing Adolescent and Adult Intelligence* (Boston, MA: Allyn and Bacon, 1990); Ulric Neisser, Gwyneth Boodoo, Thomas J. Bourchard, Jr., A. Wade Boykin, Nathan Brody, Stephen J. Ceci, Diane F. Halpern, John C. Loehlin, Robert Perloff, Robert J. Sternberg, and Susana Urbina, "Intelligence: Knowns and Unknowns," *American Psychologist* 51 (1996): 77–101; Jerome M. Sattler, *Assessment of Children: Cognitive Applications,* 4th ed. (San Diego, CA: Jerome M. Sattler, 2001). For a comprehensive review of all the issues discussed in this chapter, see Richard E. Nisbett, Joshua Aronson, Clancy Blair, William Dickens, James Flynn, Diane F. Halpern, and Eric Turkheimer, "Intelligence: New Findings and Theoretical Developments," *American Psychologist* 67 (2012), 130-59.

3. For a cogent discussion of this issue, see Richard E. Nisbett, *Intelligence and How to Get It: Why Schools and Cultures Count* (New York, NY: W. W. Norton, 2009).

4. It is essential to keep in mind that these disparities have been demonstrated only for psychometric intelligence, not for intelligence more broadly defined.

5. On racial IQ disparities, see Robert M. Kaplan, "The Controversy Related to the Use of Psychological Tests," in *Handbook of Intelligence,* ed. Benjamin B. Wolman (New York, NY: John Wiley and Sons, 1985), 465–504; Neisser et al., "Intelligence: Knowns and Unknowns"; Robert J. Sternberg, Elena L.

Grigorenko, and Kenneth K. Kidd, "Intelligence, Race, and Genetics," *American Psychologist* 60 (2005): 46–59; Nisbett, *Intelligence and How to Get It*.

6. Richard J. Herrnstein and Charles Murray, *The Bell Curve: Intelligence and Class Structure in American Life* (New York, NY: Free Press Paperbacks, 1994). Some proponents of genetic explanations have been even less temperate in their language. For example, Nobel Prize–winning scientist William Shockley stated blatantly in a 1972 article that "perhaps nature has color-coded groups of individuals so that we can pragmatically make statistically reliable and profitable predictions of their adaptability to intellectually rewarding and effective lives." William Shockley, "The Apple-of-God's-Eye Obsession," *The Humanist* 32 (1972): 16.

7. Meredith Phillips, Jeanne Brooks-Gunn, Greg J. Duncan, Pamela Klebanov, and Jonathan Crane, "Family Background, Parenting Practices, and the Black–White Test Score Gap," in *The Black–White Test Score Gap,* ed. Christopher Jencks and Meredith Phillips (Washington, DC: Brookings Institution Press, 1998), 103–46.

8. David C. Rowe, "Under the Skin: On the Impartial Treatment of Genetic and Environmental Hypotheses of Racial Differences," *American Psychologist* 60 (2005): 60–70.

9. Nisbett, *Intelligence and How to Get It*.

10. Claude M. Steele, "A Threat in the Air: How Stereotypes Shape the Intellectual Identities and Performance of Women and African Americans," *American Psychologist* 52 (1997): 613–29.

11. Ronald F. Ferguson, "Shifting Challenges: Fifty Years of Economic Change toward Black–White Earnings Equality," in *An American Dilemma Revisited: Race Relations in a Changing World,* ed. Obie Clayton, Jr. (New York, NY: Russell Sage Foundation, 1996), 76–111; David Satcher, George E. Fryer, Jr., Jessica McCann, Adewale Troutman, Steven H. Woolf, and George Rust, "What If We Were Equal? A Comparison of the Black–White Mortality Gap in 1960 and 2000," *Health Affairs* 24 (2005): 459–64; Nisbett, *Intelligence and How to Get It*.

12. Phillips et al., "Family Background, Parenting Practices, and the Black–White Test Score Gap."

13. Larry V. Hedges and Amy Lowell, "Black–White Test Score Convergence since 1965," in *The Black–White Test Score Gap,* ed. Christopher Jencks and Meredith Phillips (Washington, DC: Brookings Institution Press, 1998), 149–81.

14. On employment discrimination, see John Yinger and Michael Fix, "Testing for Discrimination in Housing and Related Markets," in *A National Report Card on Discrimination in America: The Role of Testing,* ed. Michael Fix and Margery Austin Turner (Washington, DC: The Urban Institute, 1998), 31–36; "Illegal Job Discrimination Persists in the U.S. Workplace as Affirmative Action Weakens," *ASA News,* http://www2.asanet.org/media/jobdiscrimin.html (accessed June 18, 2002); Nisbett, *Intelligence and How To Get It;* Elizabeth A. Deitch, Adam Barsky, Rebecca M. Butz, Suzanne Chan, Arthur P. Brief,

and Jill C. Bradley, "Subtle Yet Significant: The Existence and Impact of Everyday Racial Discrimination in the Workplace," *Human Relations* 56 (2003): 1299–1324.

15. Nilanjana Dasgupta, Anthony G. Greenwald, and Mahzarin R. Banaji, "The First Ontological Challenge to the IAT: Attitude or Mere Familiarity?" *Psychological Inquiry* 14 (2003): 238–43.

16. Claude M. Steele, "A Threat in the Air."

17. Cited in Nisbett, *Intelligence and How to Get It*, 104.

18. John H. McWhorter, *Losing the Race: Self-Sabotage in Black America* (New York, NY: Free Press, 2000).

19. Kevin O. Cokley, "Racial(ized) Identity, Ethnic Identity, and Afrocentric Values: Conceptual and Methodological Challenges in Understanding African American Identity," *Journal of Counseling Psychology* 52 (2005): 517–26; Biko Martin Sankofa, Eric A. Hurley, Brenda A. Allen, and A. Wade Boykin, "Cultural Expression and Black Students' Attitudes toward High Achievers," *Journal of Psychology* 139 (2005): 247–59; Robert J. Sternberg, The Rainbow Project Collaborators, and the University of Michigan Business School Project Collaborators, "Theory-Based Admissions Testing for a New Millennium," *Educational Psychologist* 39 (2004): 185–98.

20. Arthur R. Jensen, "How Much Can We Boost IQ and Scholastic Achievement?" *Harvard Educational Review* 39 (1969): 2.

21. Herman H. Spitz, *The Raising of Intelligence: A Selected History of Attempts to Raise Retarded Intelligence* (Hillsdale, NJ: Lawrence Erlbaum Associates, 1986); Neisser et al., "Intelligence: Knowns and Unknowns"; Frances A. Campbell, Craig T. Ramey, Elizabeth Pungello, Joseph Sparling, and Shari Miller-Johnson, "Early Childhood Education: Young Adult Outcomes from the Abecedarian Project," *Applied Developmental Science* 6 (2002): 42–57.

22. It is interesting that the original goal of Head Start was *not* to improve IQ scores; the program's developers were far more interested in such practical outcomes as preschool readiness skills, social and emotional development, and improvements in health and nutritional status. However, they decided that the best way to sell their program to Congress and a test-obsessed American public was to promise measurable improvements in children's intelligence. This is yet another example of our society's unfortunate propensity to view IQ scores as more important than the real-life educational outcomes whose prediction is theoretically their primary function. Edmund W. Gordon, "Evaluation during the Early Years of Head Start," in *Project Head Start: A Legacy of the War on Poverty*, ed. Edward Zigler and Jeanette Valentine (New York, NY: Free Press, 1979), 399–404; Campbell et al., "Early Childhood Education."

23. Nisbett, *Intelligence and How to Get It*.

24. Discussion of rising test scores is primarily based on Ulric Neisser (ed.), *The Rising Curve: Long-Term Gains in IQ and Related Measures* (Washington, DC: American Psychological Association, 1998).

25. The Psychological Corporation, *WAIS–III and WMS–III Technical Manual* (San Antonio, TX: Harcourt Brace, 1997).

26. Ulric Neisser, "Introduction: Rising Test Scores and What They Mean," in *The Rising Curve: Long-Term Gains in IQ and Related Measures,* ed. Ulric Neisser (Washington, DC: American Psychological Association, 1998), 5.

CHAPTER 12: TOWARD A MORE EQUITABLE CONCEPTION OF MERIT

1. Michael Young, *The Rise of the Meritocracy, 1870–2033: The New Elite of Our Social Revolution* (New York, NY: Random House, 1959), 86–87.

2. David Owen, "The S.A.T. and Social Stratification," *Journal of Education* 168 (1986): 91.

3. Even the most ardent critics of intelligence testing generally support using tests in this way. For example, Stephen Jay Gould, in a book otherwise strongly critical of the modern concept of intelligence, gratefully relates how such testing benefited his learning-disabled son. Stephen Jay Gould, *The Mismeasure of Man,* rev. ed. (New York, NY: W. W. Norton, 1996), 185.

4. *Larry P. v. Riles,* 495 F. Supp. 926 (N.D. Cal. 1979); *PASE v. Hannon* 506 F. Supp. 831 (N.D. Ill. 1980); Rogers Elliott, *Litigating Intelligence: IQ Tests, Special Education, and Social Science in the Courtroom* (Dover, MA: Auburn House, 1987).

5. Jeannie Oakes, *Keeping Track: How Schools Structure Inequality,* 2nd ed. (New Haven, CT: Yale University Press, 2005).

6. Oakes, *Keeping Track,* 40.

7. "Tracking Trounces Test Scores," *Education Digest* 69 (2004): 15–17.

8. Inspired by the dramatic success of teacher Jaime Escalante in preparing at-risk, minority students in his East Los Angeles high school to pass the difficult Advanced Placement Calculus exam, school districts around the country have begun rethinking their restrictions on admission to AP classes as well. Enrollment in AP classes has increased 140 percent in the last decade, with one out of three high school graduates having taken at least one test. Many schools are now encouraging all students to take AP classes, reasoning that they will benefit even if they are not able to pass the test. The project was the subject of the popular movie *Stand and Deliver.* George Madrid, Paul Powers, Kevin Galvin, Donald L. Kester, Will Santos, and Steve Yamarone, *Jaime Escalante Mathematics and Science Program. National Science Foundation. Final Project Report* (ERIC, ED 424311, 1997); *Stand and Deliver,* directed by Ramon Menendez (1988; Warner Bros.).

9. Wayne J. Camara and Gary Echternacht, *The SAT 1 and High School Grades: Utility in Predicting Success in College,* College Board Research Notes, RN-10 (New York, NY: College Board, 2000).

10. Oakes, *Keeping Track.*

11. Philip L. Roth and Richard L. Clarke, "Meta-Analyzing the Relation between Grades and Salary," *Journal of Vocational Behavior* 53 (1998): 386–400.

12. Camara and Echternacht, *SAT 1 and High School Grades,* 9.

13. It is interesting that the original purpose of the American College Testing program (used primarily by schools in the Midwest) was to determine just

such minimum scores. This is in marked contrast with the SAT, which from the beginning was designed to identify the best and the brightest. Nicholas Lemann, *The Big Test: The Secret History of the American Meritocracy* (New York, NY: Farrar, Straus and Giroux, 2000).

14. John Cloud, "Inside the New SAT," *Time,* October 27, 2003, 48–56.

15. John W. Harper, "The New, Improved SAT," *The Weekly Standard,* http://www.weeklystandard.com/author/john-w.-harper (accessed August, 26, 2002).

16. *Plyler v. Doe,* 457 U.S. 202 (1982).

17. *Gratz v. Bollinger,* 539 U.S. 244 (2003).

18. Brief of Amici Curiae The College Board, *Gratz v. Bollinger,* 123 S.Ct. 602 (2002), 6.

19. John W. Gardner, *Excellence: Can We Be Equal and Excellent Too?* (New York, NY: Harper Brothers, 1961); James Bryant Conant, *Thomas Jefferson and the Development of American Public Education* (Berkeley, CA: University of California Press, 1962).

20. Richard J. Herrnstein and Charles Murray, *The Bell Curve: Intelligence and Class Structure in American Life* (New York, NY: Free Press Paperbacks, 1994). The public-spirited view of merit may be ailing, but it is not yet completely dead. In the 2003 *Grutter v. Bollinger* Supreme Court case, for example, several leaders of America's military advocated the retention of affirmative action on exactly these grounds. An impressive array of generals and admirals argued that their organizations could not function properly without an equitable distribution of minority members throughout the leadership ranks. Yes, affirmative action might deny a few individuals positions to which they felt entitled. But appropriate attention to racial factors in selection and promotion was necessary to promote the overall good of the larger society. *Grutter v. Bollinger,* 539 U.S. 306 (2003).

21. Robert Klitgaard, *Choosing Elites: Selecting "The Best and the Brightest" at Top Universities and Elsewhere* (New York, NY: Basic Books, 1985), 181.

22. Quoted in Lemann, *Big Test,* 151.

Index

About the Author

ELAINE E. CASTLES is a clinical psychologist who has more than 30 years experience in administering, interpreting, and teaching about IQ tests. She is also the author of *"We're People First": The Social and Emotional Lives of Individuals with Mental Retardation* (Praeger, 1996).